PRAISE FOR *TRANSFORM* *CUSTOMER–BRAND RELATIO.*

"Christina Garnett is a master of customer experience tied to brand loyalty. Her new book is a deeply intelligent and thoughtful breakdown of all the parts that comprise building true brand affinity and loyalty. A must-read for anyone who is building a brand or in charge of a team doing so."
Goldie Chan, Founder and Head of Content and Creative, Warm Robots

"This is the kind of book that won't sit on your shelf; it will live on your desk. Whether you're in marketing, community, customer experience, or anywhere adjacent: this is your playbook. It blends psychological insight with practical application in a way that is both deeply human and strategically sharp. As a senior community professional and former marketer, I felt seen, understood, and inspired. This book doesn't just teach you how to serve customers—it reminds you why it matters."
Nikki Thibodeau, Regional Vice President, Digital Engagement and Community, Calix

"Many marketers feel pressured to chase virality and force connections with their customers. But what if we're approaching customer relationships all wrong? In *Transforming Customer-Brand Relationships* community growth expert Christina Garnett shows us how to shift from chasing metrics to building genuine advocacy. Drawing from behavioral psychology and real-world case studies, she delivers a framework for authentic storytelling and community building that drives long-term loyalty from your customers. Whether you're managing social strategy or leading brand initiatives, this book gives you the tools to create emotional resonance that will outlast any viral moment."
Sonia Baschez, Fractional CMO, Bend Growth Co.

"Provides specific, straightforward, savvy guidance on how brands can establish the kinds of relationships that delight customers and keep them coming back for more. I'm looking forward to using it in my social media courses."
Kara Alaimo, Professor of Communication, Fairleigh Dickinson University

"Christina Garnett nails what every modern brand leader needs to understand: customers don't want transactions, they want connection. This book is like having a passionate, insightful CCO riding shotgun with you, cheering you on as you build real emotional loyalty. It's smart, actionable, and packed with heart. In the modern age, connection is hard. If you care about turning customers into true brand fans who purchase and advocate for your product (and you'd better if you want to build a successful business), then buy and read this book. Actually, buy two copies and give one to your favorite business leader."
Dan Tyre, Founder and CEO, Tyre Angel

"Christina Garnett is the real deal and this book proves it. It's more than a guidebook; it's a wake-up call. Christina flips the script on outdated marketing and shows you how to build a brand that actually cares. From frontline support to social listening to community that connects, she gives you the strategy (and receipts!) to turn casual customers into ride-or-die fans. If you're still chasing clicks instead of conversations, this book will change the way you lead."
Brooke Sellas, CEO, B Squared Media

"A must-read for those looking to navigate the complexity of today's consumer landscape. This book is a smart, actionable guide for marketers who want to build real emotional connections with their customers. It moves beyond old-school tactics and shows how to create meaningful experiences. A fresh take on brand loyalty in the digital age."
Areej AbuAli, Founder, Women in Tech SEO

"A holistic primer in building brandoms. Christina Garnett's depth of experience and connection to experts across fields is on full display. The unique value of this book lies in its comprehensive outline—from social listening to customer service to storytelling and beyond, they all need to work together to create real customer loyalty. In a world where the competition is endless and always deepening, leaders who understand how to build trusted customer relationships across all aspects of the customer experience and leverage those relationships as their competitive advantage are the clear winners."
Liz Richardson, Co-Founder and CCO, Captivate Collective

"Christina Garnett provides a comprehensive analysis of how brands create successful customer experience workflows to develop authentic communities. This book offers a prescriptive guide for organizations to level up their capabilities and build stronger brand loyalty."
Saimah Haque, Digital Marketing Consultant

"Christina Garnett's distinctness lies in how she threads together neuroscience, social listening, and brand strategy into a clear system: a living layer of your brand and profitable force multiplier. I've read every book you could find on the shelf, and this is the one I'd hand to any new community leader. Iron sharpens iron."
Grace Clarke, Head of Community, Shopify

Transforming Customer– Brand Relationships

Use Emotional Connection to Build Loyalty

Christina Garnett

KoganPage

First published in Great Britain and the United States in 2025 by Kogan Page Limited

Kogan Page
Kogan Page Ltd, 2nd Floor, 45 Gee Street, London EC1V 3RS, United Kingdom
Kogan Page Inc, 8 W 38th Street, Suite 902, New York, NY 10018, USA
www.koganpage.com

EU Representative (GPSR)
Authorised Rep Compliance Ltd, Ground Floor, 71 Baggot Street Lower, Dublin D02 P593, Ireland
www.arccompliance.com

Kogan Page books are printed on paper from sustainable forests.

ISBNs
Hardback   978 1 3986 2134 3
Paperback   978 1 3986 2132 9
Ebook   978 1 3986 2133 6

British Library Cataloguing-in-Publication Data
A CIP record for this book is available from the British Library.

Library of Congress Control Number
2025025230

Typeset by Integra Software Services, Pondicherry
Printed and bound by CPI Group (UK) Ltd, Croydon CR0 4YY

To the hubs, my lighthouse and best friend.
To my kids, who keep me curious and hopeful.
To the brilliant women who inspire me: Jenny Li, Chi, Guilda, Goldie,
Nicole, Natalie, Jess, Jiya, Sonia, Krystal, Kalina, Alison, Lee, Abby,
Christina, and so many more.

CONTENTS

ABOUT THE AUTHOR

I'm Christina Garnett, a fractional chief customer officer and advisor with extensive experience across various industries, from Fortune 500 companies to startups. My career has been dedicated to enhancing customer satisfaction and building brand loyalty through community engagement and social listening. Whether it's doing crisis communications and social listening during the pandemic for Fortune 500 brands or launching the HubSpot advocacy program and community with activations like the INBOUND Correspondents program, my work seeks to connect brands with their customers. Throughout this book, I aim to provide you with practical strategies to form meaningful connections with your audience to foster relationships that last.

EXPERT CONTRIBUTORS

For this book, we have consulted a range of thought leaders and subject matter experts to provide a comprehensive view on the power of emotional connections in building brand loyalty. These experts were chosen based on their extensive knowledge and proven track records in various aspects of customer engagement, behavioral science, social media strategy, and storytelling.

Criteria for Selection

- Domain expertise: Experts were selected based on their specialized knowledge and contributions to fields relevant to emotional connections and brand loyalty. This includes professionals in behavioral science, customer psychology, social media trends, and content creation.
- Diverse perspectives: To provide a well-rounded understanding, we included voices from different industries and backgrounds. This diversity ensures that the insights are both wide-ranging and applicable to varied business contexts.
- Proven impact: Many of the interviewed experts have a history of making tangible improvements in how brands interact with their customers, showcasing real-world applications of their theories and strategies.

Interview Process

Our interviews were conducted through a blend of video calls and written correspondence, allowing for flexibility and depth in conversations. Each expert session was designed to go into their specific areas of knowledge while discussing real-case scenarios and forward-thinking strategies. This approach not only highlighted the theoretical aspects but also captured actionable insights directly from those shaping the future of customer–brand relationships.

The insights gathered from these sessions form a crucial component of this book, ensuring that you gain from the experiences and innovations of leaders who have successfully navigated the complexities of creating emotional connections in challenging markets. These shared experiences aim to provide you with both inspiration and practical advice as you work to transform your brand's relationship with its customers.

Experts Included

Interviewed experts include:

Holly Miller Anderson, Marketing and SEO Strategist at UnderArmour (SEO, Ecommerce, CX)

Marjorie Anderson, Director of Community at Exos and Principal Strategist at Community by Association LLC (Community Building)

Clement Bryant, TV and film marketer (Fandom and Social Media)

Kalina Bryant, customer engagement and branding expert and Founder of UnapologeTECH (Customer Engagement and Branding)

Alison Bukowski, VP of Customer Experience at Point of Reference (Customer Marketing, Customer Experience)

Dr. Georgie Carroll, fan culture expert (Brandom, Fandom, and Social Media)

Dr. Windy Dees, Professor and Graduate Program Director for Sports Management at the University of Miami (Fandom and Sports Management)

Danny Gardner, Head of US and North America Social Intelligence at Heleon (Social Listening)

Dan Gingiss, customer experience expert and author (Customer Experience)

Amrapali Gokani, hospitality professional (Customer Care and Hospitality)

James Gregson, executive brand, creative, and marketing leader. Former Creative Director at LEGO (Marketing, Branding, and Creativity)

Lia Haberman, creator economy expert and UCLA instructor (Creator Economy)

Jehan Hamedi, Founder and CEO of Vizit (Neuromarketing and AI)

Ted Harrison, Founder and CEO of neuemotion. Former Head of Production at Twitter/X (Storytelling)

Guilda Hilaire, Director of Product Marketing at Salesforce (Customer Experience and Advocacy)

Christina Le, Head of Marketing at Plot (Social Media and Brand Personality)

Jenny Li Fowler, Director of Social Strategy at Massachusetts Institute of Technology (Social Media)

Tristan Lombard, developer and engineering community builder and consultant (Community Building and Customer Satisfaction)

John Long, SVP of Creative at Digitas North America (Brand Reputation and Crisis Communications)

Max Pete, Community Lead at Origin. Fomer Community Engagement Program Manager at Square (Community)

Nicole Phillip, travel creator, influencer, and social media strategist (Creator Economy and Social Media)

Tulio Quinones, Chief Solution Architect at Sprinklr (Social Listening)

Vikki Ross, copywriting, brand, and tone of voice expert and consultant (Brand Messaging)

David Meerman Scott, strategist and best-selling author (Fandom)

Adrienne Sheares, entrepreneur and strategist (PR and Crisis Communications)

Joe Teo, CEO and Founder of HeyOrca (Community)

Eli Weiss, VP of Retention Advocacy at Yotpo and former Senior Director of Customer Experience and Retention at Jones Road Beauty (Customer Experience and Retention)

Marianna Whitehurst, Chick-Fil-A Peach Bowl Advisory Board Member and Georgia Sports Hall of Fame Foundation Board Member (Sports Fandoms)

Krystal Wu, Lead Marketing Program Manager at CommonRoom (Community and Social Media)

FOREWORD

Few fields are as misunderstood yet also as consequential as the field of customer experience, or "CX," as it is known amongst practitioners. Part of the challenge is that CX aggregates professional practices such as marketing, community management, frontline employees, corporate communications, product, user experience, or "UX," etc. Yet, in many organizations, it is also a discipline, sometimes led by a head of CX or, on the professional services side, CX strategists. The reason why so many organizations are now treating CX as a key discipline or a more organized aggregation of multiple departments is because of a customer's total experience with a brand, from how it advertises the product or service itself to customer support to the way the brand engages with their community (or not).

Take a brand like Trader Joe's, which enjoys unusually high customer loyalty, engagement, satisfaction, and advocacy levels... Does Trader Joe's stand out because of their unique inventory? What about their price point? How about the in-store experience and staff? What about employee engagement, satisfaction, and corporate culture? How about their social media presence? The reality is that all of these things are key ingredients contributing to the total customer experience Trader Joe's provides to its customers.

In a world where automation and self-checkout are increasingly becoming standard parts of the retail customer experience, Trader Joe's relies on chatty, enthusiastic, and energetic store associates who almost always strike up small talk as your purchases are rung up. This is part of Trader Joe's uniquely ownable experience, and customers reward the company with loyalty and commitment and often view themselves as part of a "community" of like-minded shoppers whose attachment to the brand transcends rational affinity and moves into deep emotional territory.

In my 20-plus years of working with companies ranging from WW Grainger to United Airlines to Kellogg's to the US Dairy Industry and many more, I have come across very few professionals who have become intimately familiar with the relationship between community, marketing, product, and employee engagement as Christina Garnett, who is equal parts practitioner, student, and, possibly most importantly, customer empath. Few companies are heralded for excellence in their customer experience. The ones that often deploy small armies of people like Christina (customer empaths) who become so intimately familiar with their customers' needs, wants, and desires that they become tireless advocates for the customer. Customer empaths understand the value of "micro-interactions," or the little things that make a customer feel valued, unique, and cared for, as many of the examples in this book will illustrate. Advancements in artificial intelligence (AI) technology present considerable opportunities in this space as interacting with large language models today becomes increasingly close to feeling like a natural conversation when compared to the field of conversational AI before the advent of large language models.

But technology alone never represents the total customer experience—it is the combination of your website, app, LLM, customer service agent (human or AI), frontline employees, etc. The result of consistently high-performing customer experiences brings people together! When I meet another Trader Joe's aficionado, it's understood that we are part of something bigger than ourselves. Our shared brand affinity makes us feel like we belong to a club, which is saying something in a world where people increasingly feel isolated and disconnected. Christina's insights will help any professional in any organization become a better customer empath. This quality fosters exceptional customer experiences that build a strong sense of community built on shared loyalty and values. Christina methodically lays out the case for how emotional connection builds relationships and how relationships build community (and advocacy). At the core, none of this is possible without all the mechanisms for CX working together, from customer support to marketing to product to company culture. Empathy is Christina's superpower in providing these business-critical insights; she is uniquely qualified to share this expertise. I am confident that this book will help make you a better "customer empath" as you transform the relationship between the brand you represent and the customers you seek to draw closer to it.

David Armano, Digital Solutions and Innovation Lead,
Launch by NTT Data and CX strategist

PREFACE

Building genuine emotional connections with customers is essential for brands aiming to differentiate themselves in a saturated market. This book serves as your guide to nurturing those connections, fostering loyalty that endures.

The Power of Emotional Connection

People inherently trust and connect with other people. However, brands face the challenge of creating those same connections with their audiences. The goal is not merely to achieve awareness but to drive repeated conversions through trust and, ideally, affinity. Emotional connection transforms a brand from just another name into a beloved part of a customer's life, driving lasting loyalty and advocacy. This book deconstructs how these relationships are forged and strengthened, highlighting what it takes to build brand affinity.

What to Expect

This book is structured to guide you through the multifaceted process of building robust emotional connections between your brand and its customers. This book is your roadmap to harnessing the power of customer voices, leveraging social media, and turning routine customer service into affinity-driving experiences. Discover how to use data and creativity to personalize interactions that leave lasting impressions and explore proven strategies for building loyalty at scale. Through practical case studies and insights into success metrics, you'll learn to captivate your audience with storytelling that resonates and foster communities that amplify your brand's impact. Whether you're aiming to overcome challenges or stay ahead of future trends, this guide offers the tools and insights needed to elevate your brand's customer experience.

Throughout the chapters, we will explore recurring themes such as authenticity, storytelling, and empathy. These elements form the execution plan of creating and maintaining strong emotional connections with customers. The book also features interviews with the world's top subject matter experts in behavioral science, social media, social listening, and storytelling, offering diverse perspectives and deep insights.

Understanding the current climate is critical, as today's consumers demand more than clever advertisements—they seek genuine, transparent, and value-aligned interactions with brands. While the book discusses multiple disciplines and work that you will generally find across departments, the common thread of being unapologetically human is woven through them all. While technology and trends require the need to adapt and remain curious, the desire to understand the human experience is ever-present.

Objective and Scope

The goal of this book is to provide actionable strategies for brands to build and sustain deep emotional connections with their customers. It deconstructs what it truly means to connect with customers and how to create emotional tethers that evolve into brand affinity. Through case studies, interviews, and data-driven insights, you'll learn practical ways to start building and growing your customer–brand relationships.

This book should sharpen your axe, so you have what you need not only to knock down the silos in your organization but also to proactively collaborate across teams to build customer–brand relationships that last. The customer experience and relationship with the brand doesn't live within a singular department but is owned by anyone associated with the brand. Everything the customer encounters impacts their sentiment, experience, and overall perception of the brand and whether they want a relationship with it or not.

PART ONE

Foundational Elements of Customer–Brand Relationships

1

The Power of the Customer

Understanding How Customer Opinion
Can Influence Behavior

What does it take for a brand to last? For it to hold a special place in the hearts of consumers who come back to it time and time again?

Good brands capture attention, tell stories, and sell products. Great brands transcend transactions. They build meaning, emotion, and relationships that make customer feel seen, understood, and deeply connected.

Wanting to transform customer–brand relationships isn't enough to create the connection and affinity brands want and need today. To get started we need to acknowledge the power of the customer and not only their ability in sharing their experiences, but also how they act as the voice potential customers are more likely to believe. This chapter covers the importance of listening to and valuing customer opinions as a foundation for building loyalty and trust. By focusing on authentic feedback, it sets the stage for a customer-centered approach to brand growth and trust.

This approach goes beyond just customer retention to the nurturing of community, providing opportunities for advocacy, as well as what it takes to build brandoms (where customers become active and engaged fans of a brand).

The Influence of the Voice of the Customer Over Time

The concept of the voice of the customer (VoC) is not new; it has existed in various forms for centuries, albeit in much smaller and localized scales compared to the global platforms we see today. In the past, customer feedback was primarily conveyed through word-of-mouth recommendations or complaints within small communities, often influencing only a limited circle of peers. A positive recommendation from a trusted neighbor or a scathing critique from a dissatisfied customer could significantly impact local businesses, but the reach of such feedback was inherently constrained by geography and personal networks.

As with most things, technology and innovation have impacted the reach and power of this word-of-mouth. As businesses scaled up and customer bases expanded, the relationship between companies and their consumers became less personal. For much of the 19th and early 20th centuries, brands relied on sales figures and customer complaints—often submitted via letters or in-store interactions—as the primary indicators of customer satisfaction. The process was reactive and heavily reliant on customers taking the initiative to voice their concerns or praise, leaving companies with a limited and often skewed understanding of their audience.

The mid-20th century saw a significant shift with the rise of consumer advocacy and the proliferation of telephone surveys and focus groups. These methods allowed brands to proactively seek customer input rather than waiting for unsolicited feedback. Businesses began to recognize the value of structured feedback in shaping their strategies, though the process remained largely manual and time-intensive.

The advent of the internet in the late 20th century and its rapid expansion in the 1990s brought about a seismic shift in how customer feedback was collected and shared. Online review platforms like Yelp, TripAdvisor, and Amazon's customer review system gave consumers unprecedented power to publicly share their opinions. For the first time, a single customer's experience—positive or negative—could influence countless potential buyers. This era marked the beginning of the "digital voice" of the customer, where feedback became both a valuable resource for brands and a potential threat to their reputation.

The rise of social media in the early 2000s further amplified the VoC, transforming it into a global force. Platforms like Facebook, X (formerly Twitter), and Instagram provided customers with public forums to express their opinions in real time, often reaching massive audiences. A tweet about a poor customer service experience or an Instagram post praising a product could go viral, with brands needing to monitor and respond quickly to protect or enhance their reputation. The democratization of customer feedback also shifted the balance of power, as brands could no longer control the narrative; consumers became co-creators of brand perception.

In the last decade, advancements in technology have taken the VoC to new heights. Social listening tools, sentiment analysis software, and artificial intelligence (AI) have enabled brands to analyze vast amounts of customer data in real time, uncovering trends and insights that would have been impossible to detect manually. The proliferation of multimedia content, such as video reviews on YouTube and TikTok, has added further complexity, requiring brands to adapt their strategies to include non-text-based feedback.

Today, the voice of the customer is more influential than ever. It is no longer confined to direct feedback channels but is embedded in every online interaction, from reviews and social media posts to user-generated content and forums. Consumers expect brands to listen actively and respond authentically, creating a dynamic where VoC is not just a measure of satisfaction but also a driver of innovation, strategy, and loyalty. By understanding this evolution, brands can better appreciate the significance of customer feedback and its critical role in shaping modern business practices.

Consumers are doing their research. Consumer choices are both extensive and highly informed and the voice of the customer has emerged as a crucial factor for brands seeking to influence behavior and foster loyalty. These VoC insights often encompass expectations, needs, and even requested product improvements. Listening to and acting upon the VoC can turn customers into brand advocates, not only impacting their behavior but also influencing the decisions of their peers.

The customer who specifically requests a product feature that then gets shipped (made and launched) will tell everyone they've ever met that this new feature exists because of them. They become a one-person promotion that highlights both the feature and the fact that the brand listened to them and acted on their needs.

Successful brands recognize that customers want to feel heard and valued. When businesses actively listen to and engage with their customers, they create a sense of trust and loyalty that can significantly affect purchasing decisions. This ongoing dialogue allows brands to remain agile and responsive, adjusting their strategies and offerings to meet evolving customer demands.

The Impact of Social Media

Social media has made the VoC even louder and harder for brands to ignore. Platforms like X, Facebook, Instagram, YouTube, and TikTok provide consumers with public forums to voice their opinions, whether they are positive or negative. A single tweet or post can go viral, impacting a brand's reputation on a global scale in a matter of hours. This makes real-time social media monitoring and engagement vital for modern brands.

Today's consumers are equally aware of their voices' amplification and in many cases create social content to complain about their experience when they have tried traditional customer service channels without having their issue resolved. One viral post ensures that more than the customer service team will see it and usually it is accompanied by senior leadership stepping in to make a statement and/or reach out directly to the consumer. For better or for worse, companies tend to solve issues if the complaint is loud enough. Angry customers realize that while their problem might not be big enough for the company to care, those same brands don't want a PR nightmare.

By actively participating in social media conversations, companies can quickly address complaints, celebrate praise, and humanize their brand. Social listening tools enable brands to track mentions, sentiment, and trends related to their business. This arms brands with the capability to respond proactively rather than reactively, placing them in a better position to build and sustain customer loyalty.

However, being on social isn't enough. It's how you show up that matters. Joe Teo, CEO and Founder of HeyOrca, sees social media as "your front door—it's where you meet people, start conversations, and keep things buzzing. Platforms like TikTok and Instagram Reels are great for getting discovered, while LinkedIn and Facebook Groups are awesome for deeper engagement. The key is knowing where your people are and showing up consistently.

"But remember, these platforms are 'rented' spaces. The real magic happens when you guide your community to your own platforms—like your website, app, or private forum—where you have full control over the experience and can really cultivate those relationships without the fear of changing algorithms."

If a brand uses social media for attention and brand discovery, they have to understand that their customers (satisfied or not) are also welcome and active in those same spaces.

Social media allows brands to show their more personal side, establishing a direct connection with their audience. Customer feedback on these platforms provides invaluable insights that can guide marketing strategies, product development, and customer service improvements.

While the full impact of social media cannot be captured briefly, we will examine its many layers, with Chapter 14 providing a thorough exploration. It delves into how social media drives brand loyalty, encourages advocacy, and challenges companies to respond authentically in real time.

What We Can Learn About the Voice of the Customer From Behavioral Science

Now that we understand what VoC is, we need to get to what is behind that voice. What drives customers to interact and advocate or complain the way they do?

Behavioral science offers profound insights into understanding and leveraging the VoC. By examining how customers think, feel, and act, brands can tailor their approaches to be more aligned with the psychological principles driving consumer behavior. Behavioral economics, for example, suggests that people are more likely to share positive experiences when they feel emotionally connected to a brand.

The voice of the customer is more than just feedback—it reflects the emotions, motivations, and psychological drivers that shape consumer behavior. Customers don't merely express opinions about a product or service; they share their feelings, values, and expectations, which often influence their loyalty and willingness to advocate for or criticize a brand.

At the core of customer behavior is the human need to feel valued and heard. When customers voice their opinions, they are often seeking validation that their experiences matter to the brand. Brands that actively listen and respond to customer feedback fulfill this psychological need, building trust and loyalty in the process. This concept is rooted in reciprocity—a principle of behavioral science that suggests people are more likely to engage positively with those who value their contributions. For example, a customer who receives a thoughtful response to their complaint is more likely to forgive a brand's mistake and remain loyal.

Emotions play a significant role in how customers interact with brands and express their feedback. Positive emotions, such as delight or satisfaction, often lead to glowing reviews and word-of-mouth recommendations. Conversely, negative emotions, such as frustration or disappointment, can result in public criticism or even viral complaints. Behavioral economics highlights this disparity through the concept of loss aversion—the idea that people feel the pain of loss more intensely than the pleasure of gain.[1] This explains why a single negative experience can outweigh multiple positive ones in shaping customer perception. Brands must prioritize resolving negative feedback swiftly and empathetically to mitigate the impact of such experiences.

Another psychological driver is confirmation bias, which influences how customers perceive and interpret their interactions with a brand.[2] Once customers form an initial opinion—whether positive or negative—they are likely to filter subsequent experiences to align with that belief. For example, a customer who sees a brand as reliable may overlook minor issues, while one with a negative impression may amplify even small inconveniences. Brands can combat this by consistently exceeding expectations, creating a cycle of positive reinforcement that strengthens the customer relationship over time.

The principle of social proof also plays a pivotal role in the voice of the customer.[3] People are inherently influenced by the opinions and actions of others, especially when making purchasing decisions. Reviews, testimonials, and social media posts from other customers provide reassurance and credibility, making them a powerful driver of consumer behavior. Brands that showcase positive feedback and actively encourage satisfied customers to share their experiences can leverage social proof to attract new audiences and build trust.

Ultimately, the psychological and emotional drivers behind the voice of the customer emphasize the importance of empathy and authenticity in brand interactions. Customers are more than data points—they are individuals with feelings, expectations, and desires. By understanding the motivations behind their feedback, brands can move beyond transactional relationships and foster deeper, more meaningful connections that drive long-term loyalty and advocacy.

Understanding Neuromarketing: Harnessing the Brain's Influence on Consumer Behavior

While behavioral science explores customer motivations and actions, neuromarketing goes deeper by examining the neurological and biological processes that drive those behaviors. This approach, supported by recent research published by the National Center for Biotechnology Information (NCBI),[4] explores how the brain reacts to stimuli such as visuals, sounds, and emotions, helping brands create more impactful and emotionally resonant customer experiences. Techniques such as brain imaging, eye tracking, and biometric analysis provide measurable insights into how consumers engage with marketing efforts, offering brands a scientific foundation for crafting more effective campaigns.

A key finding from neuromarketing is the role of emotions in decision-making. Research shows that emotional stimuli activate areas of the brain associated with memory retention and reward processing. This explains why emotionally charged campaigns—those that evoke joy, nostalgia, or excitement—are more likely to resonate with audiences and lead to higher brand recall. For example, a vibrant, uplifting advertisement may create a lasting impression by engaging the brain's emotional processing centers, often influencing purchase decisions before rational analysis even occurs.

Visual and sensory cues also play a significant role in shaping customer perceptions. Neuromarketing research reveals that simple, visually appealing designs activate the brain's reward pathways, encouraging higher engagement and positive associations with the brand. Additionally, sensory elements such as touch, sound, and scent can subconsciously impact how customers perceive quality or trustworthiness. For instance, a luxury product wrapped in textured packaging or accompanied by calming background music in a retail setting can create a multisensory experience that reinforces the brand's premium image. Just another reason why we see brands trying to do more with experiential marketing.

According to Vizit Founder and CEO Jehan Hamedi, "visuals have become the primary currency of connection between brands and consumers. Research shows that 93 percent[5] of consumers rely on what they see to make purchase decisions, underscoring the profound role that imagery plays in shaping brand perceptions and driving action. At Vizit, we've found that the most successful brands are those that deeply understand how their visuals resonate—what attracts attention, builds trust, and compels conversion. By leveraging neuromarketing principles and AI-powered insights, we've learned that visual content isn't just a creative asset; it's a data-rich reflection of consumer preferences and behaviors—and a brand's #1 digital sales force.

"One of the most transformative lessons we've uncovered is the importance of seeing through the eyes of your audience. Our research at Vizit reveals that even small adjustments in imagery—whether it's the composition, color palette, or visual hierarchy—can result in dramatic shifts in consumer engagement and sales. For brands, this means adopting a more scientific approach to their visual strategies. AI enables us to move beyond intuition, using predictive insights to understand not just what works, but why it works, and how to replicate success at scale.

"For some of the world's largest brands, including L'Oréal, Mars, and Ghirardelli, the stakes couldn't be higher. These billion-dollar companies now rely on AI-powered visual intelligence to ensure their content connects with audiences *before* it ever goes to market. This is the Vizit effect: brands now 'Vizit' their content in advance because they know first impressions matter, and images are the gateway to consideration. We've seen brands achieve 20–40 percent lifts in sales simply by optimizing visuals based on what resonates most with their target audience. It's a testament to the power of seeing through the eyes of the consumer. By applying a more scientific approach to visual strategy, brands aren't just adapting to changing consumer behaviors—they're actively shaping them, creating stronger and more meaningful relationships in the process. We are all competing in the visual economy now. It's instant, and unforgiving."

Another area where neuromarketing excels is storytelling. Neurological studies show that stories engage multiple regions of the brain, including those associated with empathy and imagination, making them more memorable than purely factual information. Narratives with a clear structure—beginning, middle, and end—are particularly effective at fostering emotional connections and reinforcing brand loyalty. Brands that weave relatable or aspirational stories into their marketing, like showcasing a customer's journey from challenge to success or highlighting the brand's mission in action, can deeply engage customers.

The concepts of scarcity and urgency also align with findings from neuromarketing research. Scarcity triggers neural regions associated with decision-making and risk assessment, creating a psychological effect where customers feel compelled to act quickly, fearing they might miss out on a limited opportunity. For example, language like "Only three left in stock" or "Offer ends tonight" taps into this brain response, motivating faster purchasing decisions. However, it is essential to apply these techniques ethically to maintain long-term trust with customers.

Cognitive load reduction is another important neuromarketing insight. The brain prefers simplicity when processing information, and overly complex choices or unclear messaging can lead to decision fatigue and disengagement. Simplifying the customer experience, through intuitive navigation, minimalistic design, and concise messaging, helps reduce mental effort, making it easier for customers to decide and feel confident about their choices. For example, an e-commerce website with a streamlined checkout process and clear product descriptions ensures that customers stay engaged and complete their purchase.

According to Marketing and SEO Strategist at Under Armour Holly Miller Anderson, the e-commerce experience can make or break the overall customer experience. "Especially in e-commerce, the customer's experience cannot be overstated. They are trusting you with their money to solve a problem or make their life better. It's the reason why customers do or don't buy from you. There are so many people working 'behind the scenes' at major brands collaborating on all aspects of the business but there's only one customer and to them, whatever their personal experience is—be it online or offline (in person)—that's reality to them."

Removing friction for the customer and validating their belief that what they are choosing is right for them shows that the brand understands the consumer, and they can in turn trust the brand.

And finally, we're back to the power of social proof. Observing others' positive experiences triggers reward centers in the brain, providing reassurance and building trust. Prominently displaying customer testimonials, reviews, and user-generated content creates a psychological effect that encourages new customers to engage with the brand. This is particularly effective when paired with endorsements from influencers or satisfied customers, reinforcing the credibility and desirability of the product or service. Not only are customers happy but the internet's "it girls" also love the product. It must be good.

Neuromarketing provides a scientific lens for understanding how customers process and react to marketing efforts. By applying insights from neurological research, brands can design strategies that align with how the brain naturally responds to emotional and sensory stimuli.

Note: Many of the topics introduced here, such as storytelling and leveraging emotional engagement, will be explored in greater depth later in the book. This section lays the foundation for understanding the neurological principles that drive consumer behavior, while subsequent chapters will provide practical frameworks and detailed examples for applying these concepts in specific marketing strategies.

Brands Using the Voice of the Customer for Good

Numerous brands have successfully harnessed the VoC to drive positive change, both for their business and broader society. For instance, companies like Apple frequently use customer feedback to refine their products and services. Apple's approach to customer feedback has seen numerous enhancements in their product lines, often incorporating user suggestions to improve their technology.[6]

Brands like Patagonia leverage customer opinions to bolster their corporate social responsibility initiatives.[7] By listening to their customers' values and concerns, these brands have implemented sustainable and ethical practices that not only enhance their brand image but also contribute positively to society.

The Cultural and Social Implications
of the Voice of the Customer

The VoC extends beyond influencing brand perception and purchasing decisions; it reflects broader cultural and social trends. As customer feedback increasingly shapes public discourse, it becomes a powerful tool for driving societal change and aligning brands with the values of their audiences. In the age of transparency and interconnectedness, brands can no longer ignore the cultural and social implications of the customer voice—they must embrace it as a dynamic force that not only impacts their business but also resonates within the larger social fabric.

It's not enough to be a popular brand. If the brand makes a decision that doesn't align with the values of their customer base, even the most loyal of customers can leave as a loud condemnation of the decision. Consumers not only understand how powerful the VoC can be, they also realize that they have power in their wallet. Many consumers may choose to be a customer for a specific brand purely because their values are aligned with them and vice versa.

For instance, consumers have used social media platforms to call for greater representation in advertising or to challenge companies on their diversity practices. This feedback not only compels brands to act but also catalyzes broader conversations about equity and inclusion in society. Brands that listen to and act on these cultural demands—such as Nike's campaigns highlighting social justice or Fenty Beauty's commitment to inclusivity in cosmetics—become leaders in aligning their business goals with societal values.

Customer engagement and branding expert Kalina Bryant stresses the importance of people feeling included when they see representation. "To effectively engage with diverse communities, brands must prioritize inclusion and make genuine efforts to understand the unique challenges and needs of these groups. It's essential that brands build diverse teams that can create authentic and relevant content. Their messaging should reflect diversity not just in appearance, but also in values and lived experiences. Engagement shouldn't stop at marketing—brands should be proactive in supporting initiatives that empower these communities. Whether through partnerships, sponsorships, or supporting advocacy groups, it's crucial that a brand walks the talk. Customers can tell when efforts are not authentic, and brands must ensure that their actions, communications, and internal policies are consistent with their external messaging."

The VoC also plays a pivotal role in the growing emphasis on sustainability and corporate responsibility. Customers are increasingly vocal about environmental concerns and ethical business practices, influencing brands to adopt more sustainable operations. For example, Patagonia's environmental advocacy and commitment to transparency have been shaped in part by customer voices demanding action against climate change. When brands listen to these calls and implement meaningful changes, they reinforce their credibility and earn the trust of consumers who see their purchases as an extension of their personal values.

Kalina Bryant continues: "Genuine care begins with understanding the deeply held values of the customer base. Brands can show they care by listening actively and responding to the needs of their audience. This involves engaging in meaningful conversations, not just through marketing but through actionable commitments to causes. For example, a brand should prioritize transparency, demonstrate social responsibility, and align their product offerings with their customer values. When brands invest in sustainability, inclusivity, and equity within their operations and communicate this clearly, they establish themselves as partners in the customer's mission, fostering deeper trust and loyalty."

On a societal level, the VoC has democratized power dynamics between brands and consumers. Historically, brands controlled the narrative through carefully curated advertising and PR campaigns. Today, the rise of social media and digital platforms has shifted this balance, giving customers a platform to challenge or co-create the brand narrative. This shift has made transparency and authenticity non-negotiable for companies, as any disconnect between their messaging and actions is quickly exposed by vocal and empowered customers.

In this interconnected and values-driven era, the VoC is not just a tool for understanding customer sentiment—it is a lens into the cultural and social dynamics shaping our world. Brands that embrace this perspective and actively engage with the cultural implications of customer feedback can position themselves as leaders in their industries and contributors to meaningful societal progress.

Measuring the Voice of the Customer

Now that we understand why the VoC is so important, how do we capture and measure it?

Effectively measuring the VoC involves both quantitative and qualitative methods. Surveys, net promoter scores (NPS), and customer satisfaction

(CSAT) scores are traditional tools used to gather quantitative data. These metrics provide measurable insights into customer satisfaction and loyalty, revealing patterns and trends that can inform business strategies.

Qualitative measures, such as in-depth interviews, focus groups, and social media sentiment analysis, provide a deeper understanding of the nuanced experiences and emotions behind the metrics. They offer context that numbers alone cannot provide, helping brands to understand the "why" behind customer behaviors and opinions.

Combining these methods with social listening data offers a comprehensive view of the VoC, enabling brands to develop strategies that are not only data-driven but also empathetic and customer-centric. Regularly reviewing and acting on this data ensures that the brand remains aligned with customer needs and expectations, fostering stronger, lasting relationships.

The methods and tools used to measure the VoC will be explored in greater detail in Chapter 7, where we'll break down how to implement these strategies and maximize their impact on building trust and loyalty.

Future Outlook for the Voice of the Customer

As technology evolves and consumer expectations continue to rise, the future of the VoC promises to be more dynamic, personalized, and impactful than ever before. With advancements in AI, machine learning, and data analytics, the tools and techniques for capturing, understanding, and acting on customer feedback are poised to revolutionize how brands interact with their audiences. This future will not only enhance the efficiency of VoC programs but also deepen the emotional and strategic connections between businesses and consumers.

One major trend shaping the future of VoC is the increasing role of AI and predictive analytics. Tools powered by AI are becoming adept at analyzing vast amounts of unstructured data, including text, video, and audio, to uncover patterns and trends that would be impossible for humans to detect manually. Predictive analytics, in particular, allows brands to anticipate customer needs and preferences before they are explicitly voiced. For example, AI can analyze past feedback and current trends to predict product demand, identify potential issues, or even suggest new features that would delight customers. These capabilities will enable brands to move from a reactive stance to a proactive approach, addressing needs and opportunities in real time.

Another transformative development is the growing importance of multi-media feedback. As platforms like TikTok, YouTube, and Instagram dominate digital engagement, traditional text-based feedback is increasingly supplemented—and in some cases, replaced—by visual and video content. Consumers are sharing their experiences through vlogs, unboxings, and social commentary, providing brands with richer, more authentic insights. However, analyzing this type of content requires sophisticated tools equipped with image and video recognition technologies. Brands that invest in these tools will gain a competitive edge by accessing nuanced, emotion-driven feedback that goes beyond words.

Blockchain technology also holds promise for the future of VoC, particularly in addressing issues of trust and authenticity. Fake reviews and manipulated feedback have become concerns, eroding consumer confidence in traditional feedback mechanisms. Blockchain's decentralized and transparent nature can be used to verify the authenticity of reviews, ensuring that they come from real customers with genuine experiences. This technology has the potential to restore trust in customer feedback systems, making them more reliable for both consumers and brands.

With the rise of smart speakers and voice-controlled devices, customers are increasingly using voice commands to express preferences, make purchases, and provide feedback. These interactions represent another layer of VoC data, requiring brands to adapt their listening strategies to capture and analyze spoken feedback effectively.

Personalization will also define the future of VoC, as consumers continue to demand interactions that feel tailored to their unique needs and preferences. Advanced analytics and customer data platforms will enable brands to segment feedback and deliver hyper-personalized responses, demonstrating a deeper understanding of each customer's individual journey. For instance, brands might use VoC insights to create personalized loyalty programs, curate product recommendations, or proactively resolve issues before customers voice complaints.

Finally, the future of VoC will be marked by a stronger focus on ethical and inclusive practices. As customers become more aware of how their data is used, they will demand greater transparency and control over their information. Brands that prioritize ethical data collection, comply with evolving privacy regulations, and foster inclusivity in their feedback mechanisms will stand out as trusted partners. For example, ensuring that feedback tools are accessible to people with disabilities and available in multiple languages will help brands capture a more diverse range of voices.

KEY TAKEAWAYS

- **Voice of the customer:** VoC encompasses all feedback and opinions from customers about their experiences, shaping brand perception and influencing peer decisions.

- **The influence of social media:** Social media amplifies the VoC, giving customers a platform to praise or criticize brands publicly, with the potential for posts to go viral and impact brand reputation quickly.

- **Behavioral science insights:** Techniques from behavioral science, like social proof and reciprocity, can encourage feedback and engagement by tapping into emotional and psychological motivators.

- **Brands leveraging VoC effectively:** Leading brands like Starbucks and Apple use customer feedback as a foundation for product innovation, brand loyalty, and corporate responsibility.

- **Measuring VoC:** Quantitative tools (e.g., net promoter scores) and qualitative analysis (e.g., sentiment analysis) provide a balanced view of customer sentiment and the drivers behind it.

- **Advancing technology:** The future of VoC will be increasingly shaped by advancements in technology, the rise of multimedia and immersive feedback channels, and a growing emphasis on personalization, trust, and inclusivity.

Notes

1 C. Back and M. Spann. The impact of uncertainty on customer satisfaction (No 343), discussion paper, EconStor, 2022. www.econstor.eu/handle/10419/282035 (archived at https://perma.cc/99RU-7GJ4)

2 G. Kihlstrom. How cognitive biases can create a negative customer experience, Forbes, September 10, 2021. www.forbes.com/councils/forbesagencycouncil/2021/09/10/how-cognitive-biases-can-create-a-negative-customer-experience/ (archived at perma.cc/G2U6-QTBY)

3 S. Park and J. McCallister. The effects of social proof marketing tactics on nudging consumer purchase, *Journal of Student Research*, 2023, 12(3). www.jsr.org/hs/index.php/path/article/view/4887 (archived at https://perma.cc/QNG4-2UAU)

4 G. R. Foxall. The neurophysiological Behavioral Perspective Model of consumer choice and its contribution to the intentional behaviorist research programme, *Frontiers in Human Neuroscience*, 2023. pmc.ncbi.nlm.nih.gov/articles/PMC10427341/ (archived at https://perma.cc/79T7-SPJA)

5 L. Smith. The effects of color on consumer behavior, Inverve Marketing, 2021. www.invervemarketing.com/blog/the-effects-of-color-on-consumer-behavior (archived at perma.cc/P4ET-BQWN)

6 A. Patov. How Apple elevates customer experience (CX) through ecosystem integration, Renascence Journal, 2024. www.renascence.io/journal/how-apple-elevates-customer-experience-cx-through-ecosystem-integration (archived at perma.cc/4L9C-6VHN)

7 V. Stanley. How Patagonia learned to act on its values, Yale Insights, 2021. insights.som.yale.edu/insights/how-patagonia-learned-to-act-on-its-values (archived at perma.cc/6GQF-K9P9)

2

From Loyalty to Fandom

How Brandoms are Redefining Engagement

If a brand wants consumers to love them and be their biggest fans, they need to give them something that is worthy of that love and devotion. One has to become a fan of the fans.

Brands are no longer just selling products or services—they are building communities, identities, and experiences. The emergence of *brandoms* (brand fandoms) signifies a deeper level of customer engagement, where consumers don't just buy from a company but form a deep emotional bond, similar to how fans engage with entertainment franchises or celebrities. When a brand achieves brandom status, it signifies more than customer satisfaction; it represents the pinnacle of emotional loyalty, cultural connection, and advocacy.

Understanding Fandoms and Brandoms

Fandoms are passionate communities centered around shared interests, often tied to entertainment mediums like movies, music, or books. These groups form a strong identity around the object of their devotion, actively promoting and defending it. When this concept translates into the commercial world, it becomes what is known as a "brandom," where fans of a specific brand exhibit similar passionate behaviors. Tesla enthusiasts, Apple devotees, and Nike sneakerheads, for example, are more than just consumers—they integrate the brand into their personal identity, championing it as an essential part of who they are.

At its essence, a brandom represents the ultimate aspiration for companies, signaling that they have surpassed mere transactional relationships to achieve an emotional loyalty that is rare in the marketplace. Unlike a typical loyal customer who makes repeat purchases, members of a brandom advocate, evangelize, and sometimes even help co-create the brand's future. This elevated form of loyalty means the brand has become integral to the customer's personal narrative and sense of self.

For Dr. Georgie Carroll, a fan culture expert, the difference between fandom and brandom comes down to control. "Fandoms are organic and fan-led rather than being created and controlled by brands. Think about how fans build community around television shows or books that continue years after they've been released. They're engaging with the product, but in their own, participatory spaces. They don't necessarily need the brand, and the brand has no say over what they're saying or doing (which is often how fans like it—never forget the fourth wall!).

"Brandoms, however, are marketing-led spaces where brands are able to control (to a degree) the participation and engagement practices of their fans. This occurs primarily through a brand offering a 'reward' system that encourages participation. The exact nature of the reward varies based on what exactly it is that your customers value, which is why understanding your audience is so important. Taylor Swift fans, for example, engage in her brandom in the hopes of receiving a social media like or reply, but that's not going to work for everyone. You don't want to be the uninvited guest amongst your customers: you need them to see you as adding value to the community, and giving them a reason to stick around."

Dan Gingiss, customer experience expert and author, has spent years researching and exploring what makes customers feel like they have a relationship with a brand instead of being treated like a transaction. Surprisingly, the biggest brand fans he's interviewed shared that their loyalty was built off something going wrong. "I believe that one of the core human desires we have, first of all, we don't look at it as a transaction. We look at it as a relationship. Companies tend to look at it as transactions. But in a relationship, in any relationship, you want to make sure the other person has your back.

"And if your relationship is with a brand, you want to make sure the brand has your back when you need them. And one of my favorite ways to sort of look at this is if you think about the insurance industry. Think about your auto insurer, whoever it is, you pay them a premium every month, clockwork, money out the door. It's this one-way relationship. And then, all of a sudden, you need them to actually have your back. And it's just the worst time to find out whether they have your back or not, which is why insurance companies should be doing a better job to show you that before you have an accident.

"It's: 'I want to work with you, I like your product, I like your salesperson—whatever it is. But if something goes wrong and the you-know-what hits the fan, I want to make sure you're going to take care of me. And once I learn that you're going to take care of me, then you become one of my favorite brands.' And that's why, when I ask people what their favorite brand is and why, three-quarters of the time they tell me about a problem they had with the brand. It's just so fascinating."

This breakdown of what makes the relationship work is powerful as it isn't built on perfection. Mistakes can happen and brands won't always get it right the first time. The loyalty comes from the brand making it right for the customers. Does the brand make the customer feel like they'll be taken care of in the end? Does the brand have their back, as Gingiss suggests?

Traditional customer loyalty often relies on incentives like discounts or perks, aiming to encourage frequent purchases or brand preference. A brandom, however, encompasses a far deeper, more complex relationship. Several unique factors contribute to this phenomenon. The first is emotional investment: unlike loyalty programs, which reward frequent buyers, brandoms foster a genuine emotional connection. Customers become deeply invested in the brand's story, mission, and ethos, seeing it as an extension of their own values. For instance, Patagonia's dedication to environmental activism has drawn a customer base that views the brand as a mirror of their commitment to sustainability, forming a loyal community around shared principles and purpose. By continuing to buy from Patagonia they are essentially advocating for the brand and their purpose of sustainability.

A second characteristic of brandoms is identity and self-expression. Customers in a brandom don't just buy products for their functional benefits; they choose them as symbols of who they are and what they value. Wearing an Apple Watch or riding a Harley-Davidson motorcycle goes beyond utility—it's a statement of lifestyle, values, and self-image. For these customers, the brand relationship is a part of their personal identity, serving as a visible marker of the way they see themselves and wish to be seen by others.

A third vital component of brandoms is community and social belonging. Just as fandoms thrive on collective experiences, brandoms also foster a sense of community built around shared experiences, values, and interests. These communities form both online and offline, creating spaces where fans can interact, share experiences, and even celebrate the brand together. Companies like LEGO actively nurture these communities, recognizing the value of spaces where fans can engage not only with the brand but with each other. This sense of belonging strengthens the emotional bond as fans feel connected not just to the brand but to others who share their passion.

Finally, a hallmark of any strong brandom is advocacy and word-of-mouth. Fans within a brandom naturally become brand ambassadors, spreading the word through social media, user-generated content, or personal recommendations. This type of advocacy is invaluable to businesses because it is perceived as authentic, trustworthy, and free from commercial bias—qualities that traditional advertising often lacks. These brand advocates serve as an organic, self-sustaining marketing force, attracting new customers while reinforcing their own connection to the brand.

Brandoms transform customer loyalty into an experience rooted in emotional resonance, personal identity, and shared community. By achieving this level of relationship, brands not only secure long-term support but also cultivate a group of individuals who see the brand as an essential part of their lives. This unique blend of personal attachment, communal engagement, and organic advocacy positions brandoms as a powerful force, driving both business success and cultural relevance.

So how do brands turn a customer's "like" into "love"? Marketing strategist and best-selling author David Meerman Scott sees two main elements. "The first thing is that it seems like it requires humanity. And what I mean by that is it seems like it requires that organizations have an approach to the way they do business that feels authentic; it feels real.

"It feels like there are people behind it that care. That's not to say that things like AI or other technologies can't help because I think they can. But people generally don't want to be treated like they're a number. They don't want to be treated like they're just a customer to extract money from.

"So, there's that idea of humanity. The second thing, which kind of was surprising when I was originally doing my research but in hindsight makes total sense, is that we all want to belong to a tribe of like-minded people."

Authenticity and connection forge the road to affinity and brandoms.

Business Relevance: Why Brandoms Matter

For brands, building a "brandom"—a dedicated community of passionate brand fans—is more than a badge of honor. It's a powerful business strategy with tangible benefits. A well-nurtured brandom drives organic growth by reducing customer acquisition costs. When fans share their enthusiasm, they create a wave of authentic word-of-mouth advertising that brings in new customers without the need for extensive and costly marketing efforts.

Customers within a brandom have higher lifetime value, making repeat purchases and engaging with premium or new products. Their emotional connection to the brand leads to consistent spending, seeing it as part of their lifestyle rather than just a purchase. This loyalty gives brands resilience in competitive markets, where others rely on discounts to retain customers. Apple exemplifies this, with users choosing its products despite lower-cost alternatives because the brand feels integral to their identity.

Beyond loyalty, brandoms foster collaboration, turning customers into contributors. These fans actively participate in product development, offering feedback, ideas, and design input. This co-creation strengthens the relationship between brand and consumer while driving innovation.

Passionate fan communities also elevate brands beyond their industry, shaping culture and embodying values that resonate deeply with consumers. Nike, for example, is more than a sportswear brand—it symbolizes empowerment and personal achievement. A strong brandom not only provides a competitive edge but also positions a brand as a cultural icon, standing out in both its industry and broader society.

Challenges in Building and Maintaining Brandoms

Building and sustaining a brandom is akin to nurturing a long-term relationship rather than simply closing a transaction. Brandoms are not built overnight. They require authenticity, consistency, and an ongoing dialogue with their audience. Moreover, the most powerful brandoms often emerge not solely from the efforts of the brand itself but also through the active participation and advocacy of superfans who feel truly seen, heard, and valued.

For customer engagement and branding expert Kalina Bryant, "culture plays a pivotal role in creating an emotional connection between brands and their customers. A brand that reflects the cultural nuances and values of its audience will foster a sense of belonging, which is critical in building loyalty. As a community curator, I know that brand culture should resonate with the target community's identity and values, whether it's sustainability, social justice, or empowerment. Brands should ensure that their marketing and products not only represent diverse cultural backgrounds but also integrate cultural awareness into their internal decision-making processes, fostering an environment of inclusivity. This not only enhances brand perception but also strengthens the bonds with customers who see their experiences and values reflected in the brand."

Nike didn't become a brandom simply by selling shoes; it became one by consistently aligning itself with powerful narratives of empowerment, self-determination, and athletic excellence over decades. From the "Just Do It" campaigns to partnerships with iconic athletes like Michael Jordan and Serena Williams, Nike didn't just market products; it created an emotional connection.

Similarly, LEGO offers another example. The brand's rebirth as a cultural and creative phenomenon was no accident. It took years of listening to and collaborating with its community. From fostering user-generated content to creating platforms like LEGO Ideas, where fans can submit and vote on new designs, LEGO didn't just sell toys—it cultivated a co-creative relationship with its audience. Through these initiatives, LEGO's superfans felt involved in the brand's journey, creating an ecosystem where consumers felt empowered and invested.

For fan culture expert Dr. Georgie Carroll it comes down to communities being at their most human. "Community is at the heart of human experience, and it's also at the heart of both fandoms and brandoms. We're social creatures, and we want to forge connections. In order to forge these connections, brands need to undertake qualitative research to ensure they truly understand who they're speaking to, what role they play in their customers' lives, and how they're engaging when they're not around. If you're attempting to build a community based on assumptions, purely quantitative data, or someone else's playbook, you're going to have a hard time. If you know who is in your community, you can find authentic ways to join conversations, add value, and reward and encourage participation. That's going to look very different if you're a hip beverage brand vs. an entertainment organization vs. a business-to-business software company, but if the research and insights are there, your community can evolve."

Brandoms thrive at the intersection of authenticity, consistency, and fan empowerment. They aren't created by accident or through a single marketing campaign but through years of deliberate effort, transparency, and co-creation. When brands nurture their relationships with superfans—by listening to them, acting on their feedback, and staying true to shared values—they transform from companies selling products into cultural touchstones.

Clement Bryant, a TV and film marketer, sees brands getting closer to fans and turning them into influencers. "Make superfans your 'influencers.' A standout example of this is how Marvel compiled clips of fans alongside footage from their films into a 'trailer tomorrow' teaser for *Avengers: Infinity War*. This asset not only showcased the excitement of their dedicated fanbase but also demonstrated Marvel's appreciation for their fans' contributions to the brand's success. By acknowledging the fans' role in their journey, Marvel reinforced loyalty, fostered a deeper connection with their audience, and garnered excitement for their trailer release."

What Can Brands Learn From Sports Fandoms?

When we talk about love and fandom, we have to talk about sports.

Sports fandoms offer a masterclass in building deep emotional connections that inspire unparalleled loyalty and passionate engagement. Unlike casual brand interactions, sports fans forge intense, lifelong bonds with their teams, often going to extraordinary lengths to demonstrate their devotion. These fans not only watch games from the comfort of their homes or favorite bars but also travel great distances to attend games in person, transforming stadiums into electric arenas of shared enthusiasm. Their loyalty drives their own economy, from purchasing tickets and merchandise to subscribing to exclusive content and celebrating their teams at tailgates and viewing parties.

What sets sports fandoms apart is the emotional intensity they bring to every interaction. Fans wear their allegiance like a badge of honor—literally, through jerseys, hats, and memorabilia, and figuratively, through impassioned debates, team chants, and the rituals that define game days. Even during moments of defeat, this passion endures, often strengthening their connection to the team. For brands, this unwavering loyalty is a model of how emotional investment can translate into a lifetime of engagement and spending.

According to University of Miami sports management professor and Graduate Program Director Dr. Windy Dees, "Sports fandom is all about three things: passion, loyalty, and fun. No matter the ups and downs of supporting a favorite team or athlete, die-hard fans love the comradery and community that develop through the shared experiences of sport. Brands communicating with consumers can take a page out of the sports marketing handbook by focusing on the same three prongs of passion, loyalty, and fun. Brands should find the passion points that truly connect consumers with their products and services and focus their storytelling there. Creating loyalty programs that reward purchase behavior and ambassadorship keep consumers engaged for the long run. Lastly, making the journey or brand relationship fun is the cornerstone of an effective marketing process. In branding just like sports, there will be wins and losses, but fandom and brandom are built on a strong combination of sustained performance and strategic marketing!"

The lessons for brands are clear: building a community around a shared identity or purpose can inspire behaviors like those of sports fans. By creating touchpoints that allow customers to express their enthusiasm—whether through branded merchandise, experiential events, or opportunities to connect with other fans—brands can transform casual buyers into deeply committed advocates. Just as sports teams thrive on fostering emotional investment, brands that tap into this energy can build "brandoms" that mirror the loyalty and passion of sports fandoms, turning customers into enthusiastic participants in the brand's story.

Nothing highlights this ability to connect and build community through fandom more than Ireland embracing college football. Chick-Fil-A Peach Bowl Advisory Board and Georgia Sports Hall of Fame Foundation Board Member Marianna Whitehurst saw this first-hand in 2024. "I wish I could have bottled the energy of the fans who traveled and the Dubliners falling in love with college football. This season the fandom feels like it's been on overdrive. We were graced with upsets, field rushes, and my beloved Tennessee Volunteers trying to take over the famous Horseshoe of Ohio State."

Whitehurst particularly loves how fandom creates impact. "The fans drive the market, and the marketing. Each new activation that arrives and delights us—well, it's a nod to our humanity because it's tying us together. Our shared love of this tremendous sport creates a community. That's probably why this fandom is my favorite-there's a place for everyone."

In the end, fandom connects, and connection is a hard lever to beat.

Bonding Content

We are increasingly seeing brands create content designed to forge stronger connections with their consumers, yet it's not always recognized for what it is: content intentionally crafted to help consumers bond with a brand. This is more than a passing trend; as AI-generated content and misinformation continue to erode trust between brands and their audiences, the need for genuine human connection is becoming critical. Consumers crave authenticity, and they look for relatable, human elements to rebuild trust. Brands that want to foster deeper relationships will lean even more heavily into creating this type of content, ensuring their humanity is at the forefront of their messaging.

Dr. Georgie Carroll sees this as an extension of getting to know who you want to connect with. "Once you know who you are, the most important strategy is to invest time and resources into understanding your customers and their habits. Connecting with fans involves knowing who you're speaking to, what conversations are already happening, and how your input could be seen as valuable vs. intrusive. You want to encourage your customers to be engaging where you are and to see you as a source of more than just troubleshooting. But you need to stay true to your brand identity: too often brands try to culture-jack or jump quickly between trends, trying to copy the success of others. What makes someone else successful isn't going to create a community for you. Yes, memes may bring laughs and be relatable in the short term, but they can't replace the importance of authenticity and reliability."

Founder-Led Content: Relating Through Vulnerability

Founder-led content creates a unique opportunity for brands to humanize themselves by showcasing the personal stories, struggles, and successes of the individuals behind the business. When founders step forward to share their journeys, they provide a face and personality for the brand, transforming it into something relatable and genuine. Transparency and vulnerability are key. Consumers are drawn to stories of overcoming challenges and achieving success because they see the humanity in them. This type of content allows brands to communicate their values through personal anecdotes, building emotional connections that resonate on a deeper level.

Influencer Marketing and the Creator Economy: Relatable Advocates

Influencers often act as a bridge between brands and consumers, providing a trusted, familiar voice that makes a brand feel accessible and relevant. These individuals build their careers on connecting authentically with their audiences, and their recommendations are often seen as more credible than traditional advertising. When influencers share their personal experiences with a product or service, it feels personal, relatable, and authentic.

Creator economy expert and UCLA instructor Lia Haberman sees the use of influencers as a core way to bridge the divide between brands and their audience, but they need to be treated as more than an advertising tactic. "Creators and influencers command the attention of social audiences. Pure and simple. Their content is raw, relatable and authentic. And these days, its what consumers want to see—not just on social media but everywhere.

"The shift has revolutionized brand marketing, changing who owns the message, who controls the mic, and who gets to shape consumer perception. Influencers should no longer be simply considered as billboards or ad units;

they're creative collaborators and trusted distribution partners. Brands that recognize influencers as valuable partners can leverage their expertise to create and share engaging, relatable content. This approach often outperforms traditional marketing tactics, especially on platforms like TikTok, where raw, authentic content resonates more strongly with audiences than traditional brand messaging."

Partnering with influencers allows brands to tap into preexisting trust and engage with audiences that might otherwise remain skeptical. The human touch that influencers bring to branded content helps consumers feel connected, reducing barriers to trust.

According to social media strategist and travel creator Nicole Phillip, "Brands can build trust by partnering with creators who genuinely represent the customer base they're trying to reach, not just throwing money at any person with a large following. Creators already have a unique bond with their audience—one built on trust and familiarity that's hard to replicate, especially for a corporation.

"The key is to work with people who also align with your brand so the connection feels natural, not forced. Then, give them the freedom to create content in a way that resonates with their audience, rather than imposing strict brand guidelines. People can always tell the difference between authenticity and a forced ad.

"When done properly, the right creator can humanize a brand, transforming it from just another company into something their audience can connect with and trust."

User-Generated Content and Reviews: Trust Through the Voice of the Customer

User-generated content (UGC) and reviews bring unparalleled authenticity to a brand's story because they come directly from the customers themselves. This content is inherently relatable. Consumers see people like themselves using and benefiting from a product or service, which makes the brand feel more approachable and credible. UGC and reviews create an emotional resonance that polished, brand-generated content often cannot achieve. Whether it's a simple social media post, a heartfelt review, or a video showing how a product is used, these forms of content demonstrate real-world applications and experiences, reinforcing trust in the brand.

As Lia Haberman stresses, "People want to be heard. Not only do audiences expect brands to reply in the comments, but they also want to be featured on the feed and have their feedback incorporated into the brand's social strategy. Audiences want and expect to be collaborators in their online experience.

"So it's vital that brands prioritize the cues audiences are sending them.

"Brands need to remember that it's not just about broadcasting corporate messaging but participating in cultural conversations and trends already happening online and practicing active social listening to fuel faster and smarter business decisions.

"Giving audiences a seat at the table—and a starring role in UGC content—is a shift from brands being the star of the show, to becoming partners to people's online experiences."

Community: Building Relationships Between Consumers

Community-building extends bonding content beyond individual relationships, fostering a sense of belonging among consumers themselves. By creating spaces where customers can connect with one another, brands transform themselves into facilitators of shared experiences and values. These communities strengthen the emotional bond between customers and the brand while allowing the relationships between consumers to grow organically.

Joe Teo sees community as connection. "When people feel like they belong to a community, they stick around—and they're more likely to spread the word. That sense of belonging creates emotional connections that go beyond just buying a product. At HeyOrca, we make sure our community members feel valued, heard, and involved. We've set up ways to recognize and celebrate different types of members—from casual followers to our most dedicated super-users and creators.

"This personal touch not only boosts retention but also turns members into vocal advocates. By giving our community a sense of identity and ownership, we keep them engaged and loyal, driving long-term relationships that are way more valuable than any single transaction."

Whether through online forums, dedicated social media groups, or in-person events, communities help brands scale the feeling of connection and make consumers feel like part of something larger.

Marjorie Anderson, Director of Community at Exos, sees this connection through the human need to not be alone. "People are lonelier in this world than ever before. Meaningful connection is more important than ever and in a time where the agency to make decisions to spend time with people/places/ things that connect to their own values is incredibly important to people, brands can't just think about the success of their business and that their name/product alone will do the trick. They need to be an enabler of that meaningful connection that lets others know they are seen, heard, and considered in everything that the brand does."

REAL-WORLD SUCCESS STORIES: APPLE

According to Marjorie Anderson, the latest Airpod with hearing aid assistance was the perfect example of this. "I saw an ad for Apple for their newest version of the Airpods. It didn't talk about the sleek design or the cool accessories. Instead, it showed a man sitting in the living room with his wife and daughter. His daughter was about to play a song on her guitar and when she started to play, suddenly the sound in the commercial became muffled as they panned to the man. His wife tapped him on the shoulder and pointed to their daughter and he put his Airpods in. Suddenly the sound became clear again and *then* Apple pointed out its new hearing aid feature as part of the new Airpod Pro. They didn't lead with the product. They led with how it makes life more rich for people with hearing disabilities.

That's connection. Provide people avenues to talk about their experiences in a human way, share stories, swap tips and tricks in an organic way because you made their life better. Tactically, that could look like online communities, special events, or focus groups, but lead with helping them find commonality *because* of how what you offered contributed to the enrichment of their lives—not with how cool you think they should think you are."

Elements for a Consumer Bond

To transition from customer loyalty to true fandom, brands need to engage customers on a deeper emotional level, creating a connection where customers don't just buy the product—they believe in the brand's mission and feel part of its journey.

What elements do you need to consider when creating bonding content and building customer relationships?

Authenticity and Transparency

Customers today value brands that are transparent and consistently authentic. They want brands to stand by their mission and values in everything they do—from product sourcing to social responsibility efforts. Brands like Patagonia and TOMS have built strong fan bases by aligning their actions with their stated missions. Patagonia's environmental stance, for example, permeates not only its products but also its activism, creating a community of customers who view their purchases as contributions to a shared cause.

To implement authenticity and transparency, brands can start by openly sharing their processes and decision-making. Create regular communication touchpoints, such as newsletters, blog posts, or social media updates, that highlight behind-the-scenes operations, including ethical sourcing, sustainability practices, and charitable initiatives. Publicly address customer concerns or challenges the brand is facing, demonstrating humility and a commitment to continuous improvement. Incorporating real-time updates on progress toward stated goals—such as a sustainability report or donation tracker—can make customers feel connected to the brand's journey and assured of its integrity.

Customer engagement and branding expert Kalina Bryant sees transparency and genuine care as a must-have instead of a nice-to-have for brands. "Many brands falter in the area of consistency and authenticity. Trust isn't built overnight; it requires long-term, consistent actions that align with brand messaging. Brands often make the mistake of engaging in one-off campaigns or token gestures that don't reflect their true business practices. To build lasting trust, brands must embed their values into every facet of the customer experience, from product development to customer service to community involvement. Customers are discerning—they can sense when actions don't align with words. Being genuine, transparent, and consistently living the brand's values over time is essential in earning trust."

Purpose-Driven Storytelling

Great brands tell stories that resonate deeply with their customers' values and aspirations. Nike's storytelling, centered around resilience, personal triumph, and self-improvement, inspires customers to see the brand as a partner in their personal journey. Purpose-driven storytelling doesn't just convey what the brand offers; it creates an emotional connection by reflecting the struggles, dreams, and ambitions that customers identify with.

By sharing narratives that align with customers' values—whether through ads, social media, or brand campaigns—brands can create a sense of shared purpose that transforms customers into fans who see the brand as an extension of their own identity.

Spaces for Community Engagement

Brands that create dedicated spaces for customer engagement foster a sense of belonging that strengthens loyalty. These platforms make customers feel like part of a special community, turning a product purchase into a lifestyle. Brands can leverage online communities, in-person events, and user-generated content to encourage fans to share their stories and interact with each other, deepening emotional connections. A thriving community space encourages customers to feel part of something larger than themselves, which is essential to building brand fandom.

Brands can start by identifying the most active and engaged segments of their audience and creating dedicated spaces for them to interact. Launch a branded Facebook group, Discord server, or subreddit where fans can share their experiences, ideas, and enthusiasm. For in-person engagement, consider organizing local meetups, workshops, or larger-scale events tied to the brand's mission. To increase participation, offer incentives such as exclusive content, discounts, or merchandise for members who actively contribute. Regularly feature user-generated content on the brand's official channels, highlighting standout stories and reinforcing the sense of community.

Responsive and Collaborative Customer Service

Customer service plays a vital role in turning loyalty into fandom, especially when it's proactive and collaborative. Customers appreciate when brands treat them as partners rather than just consumers, especially in times of issue resolution. When a brand swiftly addresses a complaint and engages the customer as a collaborator in finding a solution, it can turn a negative experience into a positive memory and story of loyalty. This approach creates "brand heroes"—customers who feel valued and respected and who will eagerly share their positive experiences with others. When service teams engage with customers in ways that show genuine respect and empathy, they build strong emotional bonds that transcend typical brand interactions.

Exclusivity and Access

Providing exclusive access to products, events, or content can make customers feel valued and deepen their connection to the brand. Limited-edition releases, early access to sales, or members-only experiences give loyal customers a sense of special status and strengthen their sense of community within the brand. Giving loyal customers exclusive perks not only enhances their feeling of belonging but also rewards their loyalty, making them more likely to advocate for the brand.

Brands can implement exclusivity by offering loyalty programs with tiered benefits, where higher levels unlock special perks such as early access to sales, limited-edition products, or private events. Use email or app notifications to alert customers to these opportunities, creating a sense of urgency. Host members-only events or livestreams where top customers can interact with brand leaders or influencers. For product launches, create pre-sale opportunities for loyal customers or offer exclusive merchandise that is only available to program members.

Sometimes this looks like attending what feels like a once-in-a-lifetime experience. David Meerman Scott, an avid Grateful Dead fan, loves seeing how the Sphere, and its technology, has reinvigorated audiences that had grown tired of concerts. "Dead & Company, I think, was the third act to book the Sphere. That technology has brought in more fans. Because people said, maybe I should go check out the Sphere, maybe I should go check out Dead & Company, I've never seen them before, or they might say, oh yeah, remember when I was a kid, I liked them, or I've lost track of them for the last 30 years, maybe I should go check this out, because of that technology."

Involving Customers in Brand Development

When customers are invited to contribute to a brand's growth, they feel a sense of ownership and pride in its success. This participatory approach transforms the customer–brand relationship into a partnership. LEGO exemplifies this strategy through its LEGO Ideas platform, where fans can submit designs for new sets, some of which are later produced and sold. As their ideas are brought to life, customers feel empowered and invested, increasing their loyalty and likelihood of advocating for the brand.

Celebrating Customer Success Stories

Highlighting the achievements and stories of customers who align with the brand's mission creates a powerful sense of connection and community. By showcasing real customers as heroes, brands can inspire others while reinforcing their shared values. Nike has excelled in this area by featuring everyday athletes in its campaigns, celebrating their stories of perseverance and determination. Brands can incorporate customer success stories into social media posts, email campaigns, or website features, making these individuals feel recognized and valued. This practice not only strengthens the bond with existing customers but also inspires others to see themselves in the brand's narrative, driving deeper engagement and loyalty.

Rewarding Advocacy

Brands that recognize and reward loyal advocates strengthen the bond between customer and brand. Customer referral programs, loyalty rewards, and public recognition can go a long way in encouraging fans to spread the word. When fans feel that their support is acknowledged, they're more likely to act as brand ambassadors. Programs that offer unique rewards for advocacy—such as exclusive content, early access, or discounts—motivate customers to take pride in their association with the brand, creating a self-reinforcing cycle of fandom.

These tactical steps work together to deepen emotional connections and transform loyalty into fandom, creating a community of customers who feel connected to the brand's mission, values, and future. By focusing on authenticity, engagement, and inclusivity, brands can cultivate passionate fans who see themselves not just as customers, but as an integral part of the brand's journey.

KEY TAKEAWAYS

- **Brandoms vs. fandoms:** Fandoms form organically, while brandoms are strategically built by brands to foster deep emotional connections.

- **Emotional investment:** Customers in a brandom integrate the brand into their identity, leading to loyalty and advocacy.

- **Community building:** Strong brandoms create spaces where customers engage, connect, and feel a sense of belonging.

- **Superfans drive growth:** Passionate customers act as organic influencers, spreading word-of-mouth marketing.

- **Lessons from sports fandoms:** Brands can learn from sports by fostering loyalty, gamifying engagement, and creating shared rituals.

- **Authenticity matters:** Transparency, purpose-driven storytelling, and consistent engagement sustain long-term brand relationships.

- **Influencer and UGC power:** Collaborating with influencers and leveraging user-generated content strengthens credibility and trust.

- **Exclusivity enhances loyalty:** Early access, VIP treatment, and special events create deeper emotional bonds with customers.

- **Co-creation boosts engagement:** Involving customers in product development increases their sense of ownership and brand advocacy.

- **Customer service builds advocates:** Resolving issues with empathy and care turns casual buyers into lifelong fans.

3

The Art of Social Listening

Leveraging Social Media for Affinity

To fully understand the power and purpose of social listening, it is essential to distinguish it from related practices such as social monitoring and sentiment analysis. While these terms are often used interchangeably, they represent distinct processes that serve different objectives within a brand's digital strategy.

Social monitoring is the foundational layer of digital observation, focusing on tracking mentions of a brand, product, or keyword across social media platforms. The goal of monitoring is to identify when and where conversations happen, providing a surface-level understanding of what is being said. For instance, social monitoring might reveal that a brand's new campaign is being discussed frequently on Twitter/X, but it does not provide the context or emotional nuances of those conversations. Monitoring is reactive in nature, designed primarily to flag mentions for immediate response or categorization.

Social listening, by contrast, goes deeper. It not only tracks what is being said but also analyzes the underlying sentiment, motivations, and context driving those conversations. Social listening transforms raw data into actionable insights, enabling brands to understand why customers feel the way they do. For example, if monitoring reveals a spike in negative mentions about a product, social listening can uncover that the dissatisfaction stems from a specific issue, such as packaging flaws or unmet expectations. This deeper understanding empowers brands to address root causes rather than just symptoms. Social listening is proactive, allowing businesses to anticipate trends, identify opportunities, and refine their strategies based on nuanced consumer insights.

Sentiment analysis, a subset of social listening, zeroes in on understanding the emotional tone of online conversations. It uses artificial intelligence or machine learning to classify mentions as positive, negative, or neutral. While sentiment analysis provides a valuable snapshot of customer feelings, it has its limitations—such as difficulty detecting sarcasm or cultural nuances. As a component of social listening, sentiment analysis contributes to the overall picture but needs to be complemented by qualitative analysis to ensure accuracy.

According to Danny Gardner, Head of US and North America Social Intelligence at Haleon, "Social listening is the process of collecting, analyzing, and summarizing digital conversations to understand what consumers are saying about a brand, industry, or topic online. It's one step above your traditional monitoring, where the intent is to flag if something comes up, and then essentially count how many times it comes up. Social listening is more hands-on and deliberate, because it's not quite monitoring, it's analysis, the *why* someone said something as opposed to *what* they said."

Social listening is a necessary strategy for brands aiming to cultivate meaningful connections with their audiences. It surpasses mere monitoring of social media mentions and focuses on analyzing the sentiments, conversations, and trends that shape consumer perceptions and behaviors. In this chapter we will explore the intricacies of social listening, supported by insights from industry experts, and provide a step-by-step guide for how brands can build and stand up a social listening plan.

Understanding Social Listening

Gardner has witnessed social listening become more and more necessary and difficult for brands. "Social listening of course has its cons, the data lacks demographics (age, gender, affinities, income, ethnic background, etc.). Some of this data can be inferred or surmised with a little extra analysis, but privacy matters a lot today and people limit what they self-disclose."

While an increasing number of brands have realized that social engagement has become more of a must-have rather than a nice-to-have, social listening has equally grown and adapted to more consumers talking about brands online, while brands tap into these learnings.

Gardner believes "social listening is also a highly innovative field, the velocity and complexity of video and image content in social feeds today makes traditional text-based listening look like a walk in the park. There's just so much data, and it's getting exponentially harder to analyze. This is where social listeners will become arguably the most valuable roles in marketing organizations over the next 10 years, people with a mix of data analytics, digital marketing, and insights skills."

Social listening is a pivotal tool for brands aiming to develop a nuanced and profound understanding of their customers. By meticulously monitoring and analyzing conversations across social media platforms, forums, and additional digital spaces, brands can extract invaluable insights into customer sentiments, preferences, and pain points. This enhanced understanding empowers brands to curate personalized experiences that resonate emotionally with their audience, fostering stronger brand affinity—a deeper emotional connection that transcends mere transactions.

The Importance of Social Listening

It's practically impossible to scroll through social media without encountering consumers being vocal about their experiences, opinions, and expectations. Regardless of whether a brand is actively social listening, the brand's audience and potential target market is seeing this content, often only seeing the experience from the consumer's perspective—one key reason why social listening is crucial for brands. Brands want to be at the top of search results for certain keywords and spend a ton of money on advertising spend and yet it's the voice of the customer that has the strongest influence on other consumers. You need to know and understand what your current customers are saying about you and realize that it is a core part of your brand perception and messaging.

People trust people, not brands. If the customer's experience is counter to what the brand promises in its messaging, it's the consumer who is believed. Of course, the brand is going to tell you how great they are. You believe the consumer first, waiting to see if the brand can resolve the issue and either prove it's a one-off occurrence or a trend that speaks to the true customer experience you can expect.

It provides real-time insights into customer sentiment, enabling businesses to respond promptly and appropriately. By understanding what customers are saying and feeling, brands can refine their strategies, products, and services to better meet consumer needs, thus fostering loyalty and affinity.

If you truly want to build relationships with your customers, social listening needs to be a key part of your strategy. Sprinklr's Chief Solution Architect Tulio Quinones understands the impact social listening can have for fostering those customer–brand relationships. "Social listening is the foundation of creating impactful conversational experiences, but its true power lies in combining it with context, semantics, accuracy, and trust. By applying these layers, brands can transform unstructured conversational data into actionable and insightful interactions. This approach enables meaningful, personalized customer engagements that go beyond listening— driving loyalty and fostering deeper connections through every interaction."

Challenges in Social Listening

Differentiating Between Actionable Insights and Noise

While social listening is an indispensable tool for modern brands, it is not without its challenges. The sheer volume of data available, the nuances of human communication, and the evolving nature of digital interactions can make social listening a complex and demanding task. For brands to fully leverage its potential, they must first understand these challenges and develop strategies to address them effectively.

One of the most significant challenges in social listening is distinguishing meaningful insights from the overwhelming noise of digital conversations. Social media platforms generate vast amounts of data daily, and not all of it is relevant to a brand's objectives. Irrelevant mentions, duplicate posts, and generic comments can cloud the data, making it difficult to extract actionable insights. To overcome this, brands need to refine their data collection processes. This includes using advanced social listening tools to set up precise filters, keywords, and exclusions to focus only on conversations that matter. Additionally, brands should regularly audit their monitoring criteria to ensure they remain aligned with specific goals, such as tracking campaign performance or understanding sentiment around a product launch.

Gardner sees many brands struggle with this. "This is a pretty common hurdle for companies who are just starting out, where they are too easily discouraged by poor data quality. Which can be resolved! There's a misconception that these tools and datasets are ready to use out of the box, but there's quite a bit of skill required to get to those juicy actionable insights. Many tools today use what's called Boolean logic, a way to search for keywords using a combination of AND, NOT, and OR operators. For example, (Apple) NOT (MacBook), (Apple OR Orange), (Apple AND Sauce). This is how you tidy and clean your data, which can get really complex depending on what you're searching for."

Two contrasting case studies—the *Morbius* movie re-release and the redesign of *Sonic the Hedgehog*—highlight the importance of effective social listening and contextual understanding.

REAL-WORLD EXAMPLE
Morbius: Misinterpreting Social Buzz

In June 2022, *Morbius* was re-released in theaters by Sony, fueled by a surge in social media buzz characterized by the "it's morbin' time" meme.[1] Despite the meme's popularity, the significant social media activity did not equate to positive engagement or genuine interest in the film. Instead, much of the buzz was negative or ironic.

The result was a disastrous box office performance, with the film making just $85,000 on its first day back in over 1,000 theaters. The re-release failed because Sony misinterpreted the nature of the social media buzz. They saw the volume of mentions and assumed it indicated positive interest. In reality, the mentions were largely mocking the film, and the audience had no genuine interest in revisiting it. This situation underscores the necessity of analyzing sentiment and understanding the context behind social media activities.

Repeat after me: quality over quantity.

REAL-WORLD EXAMPLE
Sonic the Hedgehog: *A Masterclass in Social Listening*

In stark contrast, Paramount's handling of the social media backlash for *Sonic the Hedgehog* serves as a prime example of the effective use of social listening.[2] The initial trailer for the movie was met with overwhelming negativity. Fans expressed visceral contempt for Sonic's design, particularly critiquing his fur and human-like teeth. The backlash was immediate, widespread, and rooted in genuine emotional responses from a passionate fan base.

Paramount listened. Rather than dismissing or ignoring the feedback, they acknowledged the fans' concerns and made a bold decision to redesign Sonic. This move delayed the film's release and reportedly cost an additional $5 million, but it proved to be a priceless investment in community trust and brand loyalty. The action underscored Paramount's commitment to their audience, demonstrating that they valued fan feedback and were willing to take significant steps to address it. When the redesigned Sonic was revealed, the positive response from fans not only salvaged the film but also galvanized a supportive and appreciative community.

Clement Bryant, TV and film marketer, shares this as the perfect example of listening to fans. "What they did right was responding to the criticism within a couple of days through the Director, Jeff Fowler, who expressed an understanding of the concerns. I was impressed that instead of doubling down or ignoring the backlash, they committed to redesigning Sonic and delaying the movie to accommodate the changes. By allocating millions in additional funds to the production budget and pushing the film back, they showed a clear responsiveness and a willingness to listen to their audience. Ultimately, this communication and action diffused the backlash by showing they valued fan input. It turned what could have been a messy and negative situation into a positive one, resulting in a successful box office run and the start of a successful franchise."

Nuance and Content

Interpreting human sentiment remains a challenge for automated tools, as they often misread sarcasm, slang, and cultural nuances. A sarcastic tweet, for example, may be flagged as positive despite its critical intent. To improve accuracy, brands should supplement AI-driven sentiment analysis with human oversight. A dedicated team can review data samples for context while refining AI models with custom datasets tailored to the brand's audience and language patterns.

The rise of multimedia content on platforms like TikTok, Instagram, and YouTube further complicates traditional text-based social listening. Visual media requires advanced AI for image and video recognition, which is still developing. Brands should invest in AI tools capable of detecting logos, analyzing brand mentions in videos, and interpreting visual tone to gain deeper insights into consumer perception beyond text-based content.

Privacy Concerns

Privacy concerns and data limitations are also significant challenges in social listening. With increasing awareness and regulations surrounding data privacy, such as the General Data Protection Regulation (GDPR) and California Consumer Privacy Act (CCPA), brands face constraints in accessing detailed demographic information. For example, age, gender, and income data are often unavailable or must be inferred indirectly. To ethically navigate these limitations, brands should focus on the insights they can derive from aggregate and anonymized data rather than attempting to access personal details. Communicating openly with consumers about how their data is used for analysis can also help build trust and foster transparency.

Taking Necessary Action

Finally, the challenge of responding effectively to insights is a common hurdle for brands. Social listening is only as valuable as the actions it inspires. Without a clear process for turning insights into strategies, brands risk missing opportunities or failing to address critical issues in a timely manner.

To overcome this, companies must establish workflows for acting on social listening data. This involves creating cross-functional teams that include marketing, PR, customer service, and product development, ensuring that insights are shared and acted upon quickly and efficiently. For example, if social listening identifies a widespread customer complaint, customer service teams should address it immediately, while product teams work on a long-term fix.

Tips for Effective Social Listening

Sentiment Analysis

One of the primary differentiators between actionable insights and mere noise when conducting social listening is sentiment analysis. While it's important to track the volume of mentions your brand receives, it's even more crucial to determine whether these mentions carry positive, negative, or neutral sentiments. Sentiment analysis tools are imperative as they get into the emotional tone of conversations, offering a layer of context that raw numbers alone cannot provide. Understanding the underlying emotions allows brands to prioritize issues effectively and respond in a manner that aligns with customer sentiments, enhancing overall customer experience and brand perception.

Engagement Quality

The quality of engagement is a more reliable indicator of genuine interest and potential influence than sheer volume. High engagement rates characterized by constructive comments and thoughtful discussions signify meaningful interactions that should capture a brand's attention. For instance, in analyzing the case of the movie *Morbius*, while there was a notable volume of engagement, much of it was superficial or negative. Conversely, when the initial feedback for *Sonic the Hedgehog* was negative, it was constructive, heartfelt, and indicative of a genuine desire for improvement. Evaluating the quality of discourse helps brands focus on effective engagement, fostering a responsive and adaptive communication strategy.

Source Credibility

The credibility of sources can greatly influence the weight of insights. Trusted and influential voices, including industry experts, credible media outlets, and prominent influencers, provide insights that carry more significance than those from random or less reliable accounts. Paramount Pictures' response to fan criticism regarding the *Sonic the Hedgehog* design changes illustrates the importance of acknowledging feedback from credible sources. Much of the feedback came from long-time fans and respected voices in the animation community, guiding the studio in making impactful changes that resonated positively with the audience.

Contextual Relevance

Contextual relevance informs the effectiveness of social listening strategies. Understanding the nuances of why discussions are happening, identifying who the key influencers are, and grasping the prevailing sentiments provide necessary context for informed decision-making. Sony's oversight in interpreting the ironic undertones of the *Morbius* memes within the broader cultural context led to decisions that did not resonate well with the audience. In contrast, Paramount Pictures' comprehensive understanding of the genuine fan outrage surrounding *Sonic*'s design led to strategic decisions aligned with audience expectations. Proper contextual interpretation allows brands to adapt strategies in ways that reflect the true sentiments and preferences of their audience, ultimately fostering a more authentic and engaging brand experience.

Strategies for Successful Social Listening

Combine Quantitative and Qualitative Methods

To effectively combine quantitative and qualitative methods, brands should begin by investing in robust social listening tools. These platforms provide essential quantitative data, including sentiment analysis, share of voice, and engagement trends across social media. While these metrics offer a high-level overview of customer sentiment, qualitative insights add critical depth by exploring the reasons behind the numbers.

For instance, a sudden spike in negative sentiment might be tied to a product issue or a campaign misstep, which can only be fully understood by diving into individual comments and discussions. Brands should also segment their audience data by demographics or regions to uncover unique insights about how different customer groups perceive the brand.

Cross-functional reporting is vital here: sharing combined insights with teams across marketing, product development, and customer service ensures that the data informs every aspect of the business. For example, presenting sentiment trends alongside specific customer feedback allows teams to take targeted actions that resonate with the audience's needs and concerns.

Implement Feedback Mechanisms

Direct feedback mechanisms such as surveys, polls, and focus groups play a crucial role in complementing social listening by providing more structured and actionable customer insights. Brands should embed surveys at critical touchpoints in the customer journey, such as after a purchase, interaction with customer service, or participation in a campaign.

Social media platforms also offer powerful feedback opportunities through native features like Instagram Stories polls, LinkedIn surveys, or Twitter/X polls, allowing brands to gather quick input from engaged audiences. Additionally, brands can organize focus groups, selecting participants who are active in online conversations about the brand, and use these sessions to explore complex topics in depth. Open-ended questions, whether in surveys or focus groups, allow customers to express their thoughts in their own words, revealing insights that structured data might miss. These insights can then be cross-referenced with social listening data to confirm trends or explain surprising findings, creating a comprehensive understanding of customer sentiment and preferences.

Regularly Review and Act on Data

Social listening must be an ongoing effort, with continuous monitoring and timely responses to emerging trends and customer feedback. Brands should set up real-time alerts using tools like Google Alerts to immediately identify spikes in activity, whether due to positive buzz or potential crises. These

alerts allow teams to address issues as they arise, preventing negative sentiment from escalating. It's also important to monitor industry-wide trends
and competitor activity, which can provide valuable context for interpreting
customer feedback and identifying new opportunities. Monthly audits of
social listening tools ensure that tracked keywords, hashtags, and sentiment
parameters remain relevant and aligned with the brand's evolving goals.

When actionable insights arise, brands should have a workflow in place
for swift responses, with clearly defined roles and responsibilities for marketing, PR, and customer service teams. For example, if a campaign receives
backlash, these teams should collaborate immediately to address customer
concerns through transparent communication. Finally, brands should measure the impact of any changes made in response to feedback by tracking
post-action sentiment and engagement data. This process demonstrates that
the brand listens to and values its customers, fostering greater trust and
loyalty.

In addition to all of this, you need to ensure that you are setting up your
social listening program for success. Danny Gardner shares that "the reality
of most searches is that 50 percent or more of your data will be noise, or
what I call 'for your information (FYI)' mentions. I run the social listener for
our Advil brand and regularly see 'My head hurts but I took Advil and now
I'm better,' very FYI, and nothing I can take action on. It still counts, and
we'll still include it in our analytics, but it's 'business as usual.' You'll need
analytics and data visualization to identify underlying trends in a dataset as
big as Advil (~300 mentions a day) or total pain mentions, the latter of
which when executed correctly would lead you to a 17 percent year-to-date
increase in menstrual pain mentions, a growing and untapped segment of
the pain category. That's why I laugh at job descriptions that have social
media managers doing social listening among 10 other things, all of which
require specialized expertise. Social listening at its core is data mining and
business intelligence, a highly technical role."

Techniques to Identify Actionable Insights

Effective social listening involves more than merely monitoring social media
conversations—it requires the ability to filter, analyze, and act upon the
gathered data to derive meaningful insights. By embracing these strategic
techniques, brands can refine their social listening approaches to extract
actionable intelligence that can enhance customer experience and drive strategic decision-making.

Relevance

Begin by focusing on conversations that directly pertain to your brand, industry, or specific marketing campaigns. Concentrating on relevant discussions allows you to gather valuable feedback while avoiding the pitfall of information overload.

To achieve this specificity, identify key topics such as brand mentions and industry-related keywords. Establish alerts for direct mentions of your brand name across social media platforms. Additionally, track industry-relevant keywords and phrases to monitor the wider context in which your brand operates. Pay particular attention to campaign-specific hashtags and phrases to assess the impact of your marketing efforts.

Regularly review and update your list of keywords to maintain relevance and comprehensiveness. Organize this information into separate streams or dashboards dedicated to each category, ensuring efficient access to critical insights.

Sentiment Analysis

Understanding the emotional tone of conversations is paramount. Employ sentiment analysis tools to distinguish between positive, negative, and neutral mentions, which aids in prioritizing issues that require immediate attention.

Develop a robust protocol for addressing negative mentions promptly, such as escalating pressing issues to a specialized customer support team. Conduct periodic audits of sentiment analysis results to guarantee accuracy and make necessary adjustments.

Trend Identification

Identifying patterns and emerging trends across different platforms and timeframes can unveil insights into evolving customer preferences and highlight potential opportunities. Regularly analyze data to recognize recurring themes and monitor spikes in specific topics. Compare information across various timeframes—daily, weekly, monthly—to spot persistent trends. Ensure you are monitoring trends across all pertinent platforms to capture a comprehensive understanding of your audience's evolving interests. Utilize trend analysis features in your social listening tool to identify and interpret these patterns. Establish a routine for generating regular reports, whether weekly or monthly, that summarize key trends and insights. Share these reports with relevant departments, such as marketing, product development, and customer service, to inform strategic planning and operations, ensuring that your team is well-equipped to capitalize on emerging opportunities.

This needs to be a part of a larger and more holistic social listening plan. Let's build it.

Nine-Step Guide to Setting Up a Social Listening Plan

Step 1: Define Your Objectives

Initiating a social listening strategy begins with an in-depth understanding of what you hope to accomplish. Start by gathering your team and discussing what success looks like for your social listening efforts. Are you focusing on understanding your customers' overall sentiment towards your brand, or are you trying to spot emerging trends within your industry? Perhaps your aim is to keep a vigilant eye on your competitors or to improve the quality and responsiveness of your customer service. Setting clear objectives can also help tailor your overall marketing strategy. For instance, if crafting personalized marketing strategies is your goal, focus on detailed customer profiles and preferences. By articulating these objectives clearly, you ensure that your social listening activities are purposeful and targeted, laying the foundation for actionable insights.

Step 2: Choose the Right Tools

With objectives in hand, the next step is to arm yourself with the right tools. Consider your budget and the complexity of the features you require. Evaluate the available tools not only on their current capabilities but also on how they integrate with your existing systems and their scalability for future needs. A trial period is usually a wise investment to ensure the usability and effectiveness of the tool align with your team's workflow.

Step 3: Set Up Keywords and Topics

Now it's time to outline exactly what you want to monitor. Brainstorm with your team to create a list of keywords and topics that perfectly encapsulate your brand and its environment. These include obvious terms like your brand and product names, but should also cover industry jargon, competitor brands, and trending hashtags. It might also be beneficial to monitor common pain points and frequently asked questions in your industry. Explore which influencers and opinion leaders resonate most with your audience and track conversations around them as well. Crafting a robust keyword strategy ensures that you capture a broad spectrum of social media chatter relevant to your brand.

Step 4: Monitor Multiple Channels

Diversity in channel monitoring is key to the effectiveness of your social listening plan. While platforms like Twitter/X and Instagram are dynamic and highly engaging, don't neglect other influential channels such as LinkedIn, forums, blogs, and review sites. Conduct initial research or surveys to understand where your ideal customer profile frequently engages, and tailors your monitoring activities accordingly. This informed channel selection allows you to tap into a rich stream of insights, providing a fuller picture of public sentiment and trend dynamics across diverse platforms. Remember, it's not about being everywhere, but being present where it counts most.

Step 5: Analyze Sentiment and Context

Beyond just tracking mentions, focus on the nuance of sentiment and contextual analysis to derive more profound insights. Sentiment analysis helps you understand the emotional tone of the conversations—whether positive, negative, or neutral. However, while automated tools provide a significant starting point, they may lack the finesse to grasp context intricacies fully. Regularly collaborate with a multi-disciplinary team comprising social media experts and customer service representatives. This collaboration is vital, especially during crises or the launch of campaigns, ensuring that any anomalies are thoroughly vetted and addressed efficiently. These insights are not just about understanding what is said, but interpreting why it is said, helping inform strategic adjustments.

Step 6: Identify Trends and Patterns

With consistent data input, establish a routine for analyzing this information to discover patterns, trends, and recurring themes. This practice is not only about understanding the data at face value but involves identifying the underpinning triggers of both positive and unfavorable brand perceptions. Is there a recurring complaint about a specific product feature? Are there emerging themes, like sustainability, that are gaining traction among your audience? Recognizing these patterns early on can guide necessary operational changes, product developments, or shifts in marketing focus, ensuring your brand maintains its relevance and resonance with your audience.

Step 7: Engage and Respond

Engagement is the bridge that connects insights with actionable outcomes. Utilize the intelligence gathered to interact meaningfully with your audience—quickly addressing complaints, expressing appreciation for positive mentions, and adding value to ongoing conversations. This approach shows a commitment to listening and adapting based on customer feedback. Have a strategy in place for crisis management, including set procedures and scripts to ensure consistency and appropriateness of responses. Proactively engage with your community to foster a positive brand image that is transparent and approachable.

Step 8: Apply Insights to Strategy

The culmination of your social listening efforts lies in applying the insights to sharpen your overall business strategy. These insights should ripple across various functions—informing your marketing campaigns to be more aligned with audience expectations, optimizing customer service processes for efficiency and empathy, and guiding product innovation that meets consumer needs. The ability to pivot and adapt strategies based on the latest insights ensures your brand remains dynamic and customer-centric.

Step 9: Measure and Refine Your Approach

Continual measurement and refinement are key to the longevity and effectiveness of your social listening strategy. Define and track key performance indicators (KPIs) such as the volume of brand mentions, changes in sentiment scores over specific periods, engagement rates, and time taken to address and resolve issues. Regularly review these metrics to assess what's working and identify areas for improvement. Encourage a culture of iteration—where feedback from these metrics leads to constructive refinement of tactics and approaches. This ongoing cycle of measurement and adjustment keeps your social listening strategy agile and responsive to evolving market dynamics and consumer expectations.

How Social Listening Builds Brand Affinity

Fostering Loyalty Through Social Listening

Social listening allows brands to address issues proactively and continuously refine the customer experience, converting satisfied customers into loyal advocates.

Customer loyalty is built through consistent, positive interactions over time. For instance, Chewy leverages social listening to deliver an exceptionally personal customer experience.[3] When the brand detects through social media posts that a customer's pet has passed away, they often send handwritten condolence cards or flowers. This level of empathy and attention has garnered Chewy not only loyal customers but also widespread social media acclaim, showcasing the power of personalized, empathetic responses in fostering loyalty.

REAL-WORLD EXAMPLE
Chewy[4]

Chewy's use of social listening exemplifies how brands can offer deeply personal experiences. When they become aware of a customer's grief over a pet's passing, Chewy sends handwritten condolence cards or flowers, demonstrating empathy and garnering widespread admiration. This reinforces their emotional connection with customers. They respond across social when customers share these stories with compassion and grace.

Audience Intelligence

Audience intelligence helps brands understand who their customers are, what they care about, and how they engage with content. By analyzing social media data, brands can gain insights into demographics, behaviors, and preferences, allowing them to refine market segmentation and create more relevant messaging.

With a clearer picture of their audience, brands can design targeted campaigns that feel more personal and meaningful. Engaging with social media mentions and responding to feedback—both positive and negative— shows customers that their voices matter, helping to build trust and long-term connections.

Fostering a Sense of Fandom

Social listening goes beyond understanding customer preferences—it enables brands to create a devoted fan base by identifying and nurturing brand enthusiasts. Recognizing and celebrating the most loyal and passionate customers can transform ordinary customers into brand advocates.

For instance, when brands spotlight fan creations or stories on their social media pages, it not only celebrates their customers but also shows appreciation for their engagement. Social listening helps identify these enthusiastic customers, allowing brands to foster and grow their fandom effectively.

Understanding Customer and Fan Desires

By using social listening to comprehend customer desires, brands can tailor their products, services, and interactions to meet and exceed these expectations. For example, LEGO frequently pays attention to customer suggestions and incorporates them into new product lines or marketing campaigns, solidifying their customers' sense of involvement and appreciation.

As Krystal Wu, Lead Marketing Program Manager at CommonRoom, states, "The LEGO Ideas platform invites fans to submit their own designs, some of which even get turned into official products. This is the pinnacle of user-generated content—LEGO isn't just building toys; they're building dreams alongside their community. This mirrors something I've focused on in my career: giving your audience ownership (never lose sight of this). When people feel like they're co-creators in your brand's journey, their connection to your community—and to you as a brand—deepens immeasurably."

This practice of listening and responding to customer feedback ensures that brands remain relevant and responsive to customer needs. When customers see that their suggestions influence tangible changes, it enhances their loyalty and commitment to the brand. This active engagement transforms the customer–brand relationship into a collaborative partnership.

Fostering Community Through Engagement

By focusing on customer engagement and fulfilling their emotional and practical needs, brands create a robust sense of fandom. This strong connection encourages customers to actively promote the brand within their networks, effectively turning them into brand ambassadors. The emotional investment fostered through attentive engagement and community-building strategies ensures long-term loyalty and brand advocacy.

Brands can foster a sense of community by creating spaces for customers to interact with each other and the brand. Online forums, social media groups, and community events can serve as platforms for these interactions. When customers feel part of a community, their loyalty extends beyond the product to the brand and its values, encouraging them to advocate for the brand within their circles.

KEY TAKEAWAYS

- **Focus on the "why" behind conversations:** Social listening goes beyond traditional monitoring by analyzing digital conversations to understand customer sentiments and motivations, focusing on the "why" rather than just the "what."

- **Enhanced consumer insight:** Provides deep insights into customer sentiments, preferences, and pain points, enabling brands to curate personalized experiences that foster stronger brand connections.

- **Real-time response:** Enables businesses to respond promptly to customer feedback, enhancing satisfaction and fostering long-term loyalty through timely and appropriate actions.

- **Leverage customer voice:** Customers' experiences and opinions, often shared on social media, have a strong influence on brand perception, sometimes more effectively than traditional advertising.

- **Proactive problem resolution:** Actively listening to and addressing customer issues in real time can mitigate negative experiences and enhance the overall perception of a customer-centric brand.

- **Build emotional connections:** Personalized and empathetic responses to customer feedback can build deep emotional connections with customers.

- **Engage with enthusiasts:** Recognizing and celebrating loyal and passionate customers can transform them into brand advocates, helping to amplify the brand's reach and credibility.

- **Understand audience demographics:** Analyzing social media data helps in understanding the demographics, behaviors, and preferences of the audience, enabling effective market segmentation and personalized marketing efforts.

- **Contextual analysis of trends:** Regularly review and analyze data to identify trends, recurring themes, and patterns. Understanding the context behind social media mentions prevents misinterpretation of data.
- **Collaborative engagement:** Creating platforms for customer interaction, such as online forums and social media groups, builds a supportive community that strengthens customer loyalty and encourages brand advocacy.

Notes

1 E. Roth. *Morbius* meme flop: First day back in theaters, The Verge, June 4, 2022. www.theverge.com/2022/6/4/23154631/morbius-meme-flop-first-day-back-theaters-jared-leto-sony (archived at perma.cc/5YFU-HXCG)

2 C. Garnett. Saving *Sonic*: The power of social listening, Medium, 2020. medium.com/swlh/saving-sonic-the-power-of-social-listening-aed1dd37c4d4 (archived at perma.cc/DRV6-J554)

3 C. Garnett. 10 takeaways from Chewy's master class on customer care, *Adweek*, June 15, 2022. www.adweek.com/brand-marketing/10-takeaways-from-chewys-master-class-on-customer-care/ (archived at perma.cc/M9GA-B8PV)

4 The Social Intelligence Lab. Ari Weiner, Social Intelligence Insider 50, 2024. www.thesilab.com/social-intelligence-insider-winners/ari-weiner (archived at perma.cc/43YP-B3XU)

4

From Satisfaction to Affinity

The Role of Customer Service

Exceptional customer service is not just about resolving issues or answering questions; it's about creating emotional connections and demonstrating empathy. These elements can transform mere customer satisfaction into true brand affinity.

This chapter delves into the critical role empathy plays in transforming customer interactions into meaningful experiences, introducing the building blocks of emotional engagement—active listening, personalization, empathy, and timeliness—and how they work together to nurture trust, loyalty, and advocacy.

Additionally, the chapter provides actionable insights into cultivating a culture of empathy within customer service teams, empowering representatives to deliver personalized, timely, and emotionally engaging support. It examines how creating psychological safety encourages customers to share feedback openly, reinforcing their role as valued partners in the brand's growth. By combining empathy, proactive communication, and thoughtful gestures, this chapter illustrates how customer service can transform satisfaction into lifelong loyalty and advocacy.

The Power of Emotional Connection

Exceptional customer service leverages emotional connection and empathy to transform moments of interaction into memorable experiences. By showing genuine understanding and care, customer service representatives can make customers feel valued and heard.

Experts agree that empathy—the ability to understand and share the feelings of another—is a key element in elevating customer service.[1] When customers feel that a brand cares about their individual needs and concerns, their satisfaction levels increase.

Guilda Hilaire, Director of Product Marketing at Salesforce, sees emotional connections and customer relationships as proof that you are taking care of the customer. "Building an emotional connection with your customers means you have to 'Treat Customers Well'… treat them with genuine care and empathy. This will help to influence culture and connectedness in a powerful way. It's deeper than 'How can I help you today?' It's remembering 'How was your daughter's wedding?' or asking 'Is your son feeling better?' It's knowing your customers morale is low and sending them a gift card to their local coffee shop to brighten their day. It's going above and beyond to ensure they have a thorough understanding on how you use your product and celebrating each milestone.

"When your customers feel heard, understood, and valued, this creates a bond that will last a lifetime. It creates a sense of trust and loyalty, turning one-time buyers into lifelong advocates and friends. This is the foundation of a community."

REAL-WORLD EXAMPLE
Delta Airlines

When Amrapali Gokani, a hospitality professional, kept experiencing flight delays, an employee in the Delta Lounge continued to go the extra mile to make sure she was ok. "I was flying every week and I'm at the airport sitting in the Delta lounge just waiting and all of a sudden my phone starts blowing up with, like, 'Delay, delay, delay,' with no reason why. Nothing, and then another flight that was flying later wasn't being delayed.

"So I changed and I put myself onto that flight and then that one got delayed. So then I got back on my original flight and it was just chaos, and then I couldn't do anything. I went up to this really sweet lady at the lounge, and I think I still have her name, because I think I stored it, and I felt like, that's how much of an impression it left. I told her what was happening. And she said, 'You know what, give me a second.' She said to call the diamond medallion line.

"I told her I'm not a diamond medallion. That I had status, but I wasn't anywhere up there.

"She gave me the phone number. I called and they let me know there was a storm in Florida, which was causing all the delays.

"They let me know they would do what they could to get me on a flight. All I could think was that there is no way we can't make this happen. So they helped me out. She kept an eye on the situation and on me. It was just one of those waiting games, then throughout the next few hours I just sat there longer and longer, hoping to get on a plane.

"The lady in the lounge kept coming back and checking in. She would ask, 'Did you get an update on the call? What do you like? Would you like to grab a snack?' There's just that care and attention.

"When I finally left for my flight, I gave her a huge hug and she said, 'It's people like you who make me feel that like even though something went wrong, you didn't lose your cool and it all worked out.' It was just one of those things and because at that point I think I had her number, she asked me to text her to let her know I had landed safely. It was so sweet."

Building Blocks of Emotional Engagement

To build meaningful, long-lasting customer–brand relationships, it's essential to focus on emotional engagement. This approach shifts the interaction from a one-time transaction to a valued, long-term partnership.

The truth is that customers can tell when you care, and while I can't give you a framework that makes someone care, the following gives you a breakdown of how to put that care into action.

Brands want to be loved but they don't realize they need to treat it like a human relationship, because it is just that. If you want someone to love you, what is there to love about you, and why would someone love you in the first place? How do you show up and show your love in return?

As we break down all of these building blocks, don't think of them just as brand activations, but as love languages that draw people closer and closer to brands.

Active Listening

Active listening is about fully engaging with the customer and ensuring they feel truly heard.[2] When we take the time to listen without interrupting, we're showing that we respect the customer's voice and are committed to understanding their experience. This approach allows us to respond to their concerns with accuracy and empathy, addressing both immediate issues and any underlying needs. These interactions are not simply listening to know when the employee can respond in a reactive way, but to take the time to understand the problem, and just as importantly, why it's a concern for the customer. When customers feel understood and genuinely valued, trust builds naturally, and they're more likely to remain loyal, recommend a brand to others, and give them constructive feedback.

Personalization

Personalization creates a stronger, more relevant connection with each customer. It means more than just using their name—it's about recognizing past interactions, acknowledging preferences, and offering recommendations or support that align with their unique needs. By tailoring our communications and offerings, we reinforce that each customer is valued as an individual, not just a number in our system. When customers experience this level of personalization, they know that we're paying attention, that we remember them, and that we're working to meet them where they are. This also drives efficiency and minimizes cognitive overload. The customer doesn't need to know about every problem and solution. They just need to know what is recommended for them to get to their desired outcome.

Empathy

Empathy is central to how we engage with customers, especially in challenging situations. It's about showing that we're not only aware of what they're experiencing but that we genuinely understand the impact it has on them. Empathy goes beyond fixing a problem—it acknowledges the customer's feelings and supports them emotionally. This is where a brand can be their most unapologetically human. A representative who first acknowledges a customer's frustration before offering solutions demonstrates respect and understanding, which can transform a potentially negative experience into a positive one.

Timeliness

Timeliness demonstrates respect for our customers' time and reinforces our commitment to providing responsive service. We know that a quick, thoughtful response can make all the difference, especially when an issue is urgent. Responding promptly shows that we take their needs seriously, and that we value the opportunity to support them effectively. Whether resolving an inquiry or simply following up on a past interaction, our timeliness reflects our dedication to the customer's experience and shows that we are always here for them.

Cultivating Empathy in Customer Service

Empathy in customer service is a powerful catalyst for building meaningful, lasting relationships between customers and brands. When empathy is genuinely practiced within a company, it moves customer interactions beyond transactional exchanges and into the realm of human connection. Here are four key ways to cultivate empathy within a customer service team, ensuring it becomes a core part of the brand's relationship with its customers.

Comprehensive Training Programs

Effective empathy training goes beyond simply teaching technical skills or standard responses. True empathy requires a foundation in emotional intelligence, active listening, and perspective-taking. This is why training programs should include role-playing exercises and real-life scenario simulations. By immersing representatives in realistic situations, these exercises help them experience customer challenges first-hand, gaining insight into the emotions behind each inquiry or complaint. Group discussions and empathy exercises further build a shared understanding of what it means to listen, understand, and respond with compassion. When customer service representatives develop these empathetic skills, they're equipped not only to resolve issues but to do so in a way that leaves the customer feeling genuinely understood and valued.

Empowerment

Empathy in customer service also relies on giving teams the freedom to make customer-centric decisions. When representatives are empowered to act in the best interests of the customer, they can respond promptly and thoughtfully without needing multiple layers of approval. This flexibility allows them to make real-time adjustments, offer tailored solutions, and provide goodwill gestures that can transform challenging situations into positive, memorable experiences. Empowerment builds a culture of trust and respect, motivating team members to go beyond standard responses. When representatives know they're trusted to handle situations with empathy, they bring a deeper level of care and consideration to each interaction.

Recognition and Feedback

Recognition reinforces empathetic behaviors, helping to make empathy a shared cultural value. By celebrating examples of exceptional empathy in action—through verbal acknowledgment, team highlights, or formal rewards—organizations encourage a compassionate approach to customer interactions. These examples set a benchmark and remind everyone of the value that empathy brings to both the customer and the brand. Additionally, consistent feedback on interactions helps representatives refine their empathetic approach, allowing them to reflect on what went well and where they can grow. A feedback-rich environment, combined with positive reinforcement, makes empathy a clear, achievable goal that becomes part of the daily rhythm of customer service.

Continuous Improvement and Support

Empathy is a skill that requires ongoing development and support. For customer service teams to provide empathetic care consistently, they need access to continuous training, coaching, and mental health resources. Customer service can be emotionally demanding, and burnout can impact empathy. By providing resources that address the mental and emotional well-being of representatives, brands ensure that their teams can engage meaningfully with customers day after day. Continuous improvement programs and support allow representatives to sustain a high level of empathy, so it becomes a lasting, authentic component of their service.

Sustaining Loyalty Through Emotional Engagement

Emotional engagement creates the foundation for long-term loyalty by turning everyday interactions into meaningful connections. When brands prioritize these connections, they inspire customers not only to return but also to advocate for the brand. Here's how to foster that level of loyalty through emotionally engaging experiences.

Consistent Follow-Up

Following-up after an issue has been resolved is a great way to show that the customer's experience matters beyond the initial interaction. This proactive approach communicates ongoing commitment and care, reinforcing that the brand values the customer's satisfaction and peace of mind. Whether it's a quick message to confirm that everything is working as expected or an invitation to reach out with further questions, consistent following-up shows customers that their relationship with the brand is not transactional but rather an evolving connection built on genuine care and attentiveness.

Customer Feedback

Actively encouraging customer feedback—and, importantly, acting on it—demonstrates that the brand is listening and committed to improving. When customers feel their voices make an impact, they're more likely to feel connected to the brand and invested in its success. Collecting feedback isn't just about gathering data; it's about showing customers that their experiences matter and that the brand is willing to adapt and grow based on their insights. Regularly communicating how customer feedback has led to positive changes enhances transparency and reinforces trust, creating a cycle of loyalty driven by shared commitment to improvement.

Storytelling and Customer Success Stories

One of the most compelling ways to showcase a brand's commitment to its customers is through storytelling. Sharing stories of how customer interactions have inspired innovations, changes, or enhancements highlights the brand's dedication to listening and improving. These stories can be shared through social media, newsletters, or on the company's website, showing customers that they are a vital part of the brand's journey. When customers see that their feedback or a situation they experienced led to tangible changes, it strengthens their emotional bond with the brand. This approach also demonstrates that the brand's success is interwoven with its customers' satisfaction, creating a narrative of partnership rather than mere service.

Chapter 8 provides a deeper look at storytelling principles and how brands can better utilize it for connection. This focus will aid brands who are unsure of how to use storytelling not only for attention, but also for staying relevant and sticky in the minds of customers.

Personalized Engagement

Personalization adds a layer of intimacy to the customer–brand relationship, signaling that each customer is valued as an individual. Sending personalized offers based on purchase history, remembering important dates like anniversaries with the brand, or even acknowledging significant milestones in the customer's journey enhances emotional engagement. Small touches—such as addressing the customer by name in follow-ups or recognizing a past issue and ensuring it's been fully resolved—go a long way in making the customer feel appreciated. Personalized engagement shows customers that they are known, valued, and central to the brand's approach to service.

Chapter 5 offers a focus on personalization and how it can be utilized by brands to foster trust and a sense that brands truly understand their customers and their needs.

Proactive Communication

Reaching out proactively—whether to share a helpful tip, introduce a new product feature, or alert customers to relevant updates—demonstrates that the brand is thinking ahead on customers' behalf. Proactive communication can prevent potential issues and add value to the customer's experience before they even think to ask. This level of care creates a sense of security and trust, as customers feel that the brand is not only responsive but anticipatory of their needs. Proactivity, especially paired with transparency, lessens any doubt and anxiety customers may feel and shows them their experience is top of mind.

Emotional Moments of Delight

Sometimes, it's the unexpected gestures that leave the most lasting impressions. Small moments of delight, such as a surprise discount, a handwritten thank-you note, or a thoughtful gift, can turn routine interactions into memorable experiences. These thoughtful gestures don't have to be grand to make an impact—they simply need to show that the brand is attentive and appreciative. These moments of delight create emotional connections that customers are likely to remember and talk about, adding a layer of personal warmth that is often missing in today's service offerings.

Transparency and Accountability

Transparency is key to building trust. When brands communicate openly about challenges, admit mistakes, and take ownership of resolving issues, they demonstrate accountability and respect for their customers. This openness shows customers that the brand is committed to honesty and improvement, which builds trust and emotional loyalty. Accountability fosters a sense of security, as customers know the brand will always strive to provide the best possible experience and be upfront when things don't go as planned.

Ensuring Psychological Safety

Psychological safety, in the context of customers and their relationship with brands, refers to creating an environment where customers feel confident and comfortable enough to provide honest feedback without fear of being ignored, dismissed, or judged.[3] It is the assurance that their opinions, whether positive or critical, will be respected, valued, and acted upon constructively.

This concept is rooted in trust and respect. Customers are more likely to share their genuine thoughts and experiences when they believe that the brand will listen empathetically, respond appropriately, and use the feedback to improve products, services, or customer interactions. A psychologically safe environment for customers fosters open communication, strengthens brand loyalty, and encourages a collaborative relationship where both parties work toward shared goals of better experiences and outcomes.

Creating psychological safety for customers is a critical, though often overlooked, element in developing a strong, lasting customer–brand relationship. While psychological safety is often discussed in the context of employee culture, applying it to the customer experience (CX) brings immense value. A psychologically safe environment encourages customers to openly share their honest experiences, knowing that they'll be heard, respected, and supported without fear of judgment or negative consequences. This builds trust and establishes a dynamic where customers feel empowered, knowing their feedback has the potential to shape the experience for the better.

Here's how brands can cultivate psychological safety for customers.

Establishing Trust Through Consistency

Consistency in how customers are treated across all touchpoints is foundational to psychological safety. Customers' expectations are largely informed by past experiences, and when interactions are consistently positive, supportive, and empathetic, they come to trust that the brand values and respects them. If customers are met with empathy and understanding, whether they're sharing a positive review or a complaint, they feel safe knowing they'll be treated fairly each time. On the other hand, inconsistency breeds apprehension, leading customers to hesitate when sharing feedback, unsure if it will be welcomed or disregarded. When customers trust that the brand's response will be consistent, they are more likely to engage openly and confidently.

Eli Weiss, VP of Retention Advocacy at Yotpo and former Senior Director of Customer Experience and Retention at Jones Road Beauty, identifies this mismatch between customer experience and their expectations when there is disconnect between what the customer wants and the presentation and messaging that the brand is conveying. "Most terrible customer experiences boil down to one thing: a mismatch between expectations and reality. Think about it—when you order an inflatable pool flamingo from AliExpress and it takes three weeks to arrive, no one's shocked. That's expected. But if your Gucci shoes take an extra two days to arrive, suddenly it's a big deal. Why? Because our expectations are set by how a brand positions itself—through pricing, marketing, and the language used on their site."

Creating a Space for Honest Feedback

Psychological safety in CX requires actively inviting customers to share their honest opinions, without fear of repercussions. This goes beyond simply providing a feedback form—it means fostering an environment where customers know that every piece of feedback, whether praise or criticism, is welcomed and respected. Customers need assurance that their insights are valued and will be used constructively to enhance the experience. Brands can reinforce this by making feedback channels easily accessible, acknowledging all feedback promptly, and expressing appreciation for the customer's input. When customers feel assured that they can be candid without fear of retaliation, they're more likely to share valuable insights that can drive genuine improvement.

Acting on Feedback Transparently

Psychological safety for customers doesn't stop at gathering feedback; it requires brands to show that customer input drives real, visible change. When brands act on customer feedback and transparently communicate those changes, customers feel respected and valued as active participants in shaping the brand experience. This transparency can be as simple as sharing updates on product improvements, announcing policy changes based on customer suggestions, or highlighting customer-inspired innovations in newsletters or on social media. When customers see the tangible impact of their feedback, it reinforces that their voice matters, encouraging ongoing engagement and trust.

Responding with Empathy and Respect

How a brand responds to customer feedback—especially negative feedback—directly affects the customer's sense of psychological safety. A response that is empathetic, respectful, and focused on resolution signals to the customer that their experience is valued, and that their feedback is taken seriously. Whether a customer is frustrated, disappointed, or simply offering suggestions, empathetic listening and a commitment to finding solutions help customers feel comfortable sharing their experiences. Importantly, when representatives approach every interaction with respect, customers understand that they can speak up without fear of judgment or defensiveness from the brand. This respect builds a foundation of mutual understanding and open communication, further reinforcing psychological safety.

Building Customer Empowerment

Empowerment is a key component of psychological safety, as it reinforces that customers have influence and agency in their interactions with the brand. When customers feel empowered to make choices—whether by selecting products that align with their values, choosing between service options, or having the autonomy to resolve minor issues themselves—they experience a heightened sense of control and security. Empowering customers also means providing clear, accessible information about policies, procedures, and support options, allowing them to navigate their experience confidently. When customers know they have options and the brand supports their autonomy, they feel psychologically safe, as they understand they have a voice in the relationship.

Adopting a "No Punishment" Approach to Feedback

A crucial aspect of psychological safety is ensuring customers feel safe from retaliation or punitive responses, especially when they express dissatisfaction. When customers fear that sharing negative feedback could lead to ignored emails, poor service, or exclusion from future promotions, it silences their voice and damages trust. Adopting a "no punishment" approach means that every piece of feedback is seen as valuable, no matter the tone or sentiment. By training customer service teams to handle all feedback constructively and reframing complaints as opportunities for growth, brands demonstrate that they value transparency over perfection, building a culture of openness that customers can trust.

Communicating a Customer-Centric Culture

Finally, a brand's commitment to psychological safety should be clearly communicated in its values and policies. When customers see that the brand emphasizes customer satisfaction, transparency, and continuous improvement, it establishes a sense of security that encourages them to share their authentic experiences. This communication can be reinforced in customer touchpoints—like emails, websites, and social media—where the brand expresses its dedication to customer well-being and partnership. When a brand openly states that customer feedback is integral to its mission, customers feel they are part of a collaborative relationship rather than simply consumers.

The Role of Psychological Safety in Strengthening Brand Loyalty

Creating psychological safety for customers has a profound impact on brand loyalty and advocacy. When customers know they are in a safe environment, they're more likely to express themselves honestly, return for future interactions, and recommend the brand to others. Psychological safety fosters trust, strengthens emotional engagement, and transforms customer feedback into a valuable resource for continuous improvement. Over time, this safety creates an environment where customers feel not just heard but actively involved in the brand's growth, leading to a deeper, more committed relationship differentiator that sustains loyalty and drives lasting brand affinity.

KEY TAKEAWAYS

- **Transforming customer service with emotional connection:** Customer service that prioritizes emotional connection and empathy fosters brand affinity, moving beyond simple issue resolution.

- **Empathy and active listening as loyalty foundations:** Empathy and active listening make customers feel valued and respected, strengthening trust and laying a foundation for long-term loyalty.

- **Personalized and timely engagement:** Tailored interactions and prompt responses demonstrate commitment to customers' unique needs, reinforcing reliability and care.

- **Building lasting connections:** Combining empathy, personalization, and timeliness creates a trusted partnership, turning customers into loyal advocates.

- **Empowering and training teams for empathy:** Empathy training and empowering representatives to make customer-centered decisions enable more authentic, meaningful interactions.

- **Recognizing and reinforcing empathy:** Acknowledging empathetic actions promotes a service culture centered on compassion and respect.

- **Proactive communication and moments of delight:** Proactively anticipating customer needs and offering thoughtful gestures strengthen emotional bonds and make interactions memorable.

- **Creating psychological safety:** Consistency, openness to feedback, and respect create a safe environment where customers feel valued and free to share openly.

- **Transparency and customer-centric culture:** Transparent use of customer feedback and a commitment to customer-first values build trust, engaging customers in the brand's growth.

Notes

1 L. Lehnert and C. Kuehnl. Empathy at the heart of customer experience: A holistic framework for understanding and enhancing consumer empathy through the lens of customer experience, *Psychology and Marketing*, 2024, 42, 332–58. onlinelibrary.wiley.com/doi/10.1002/mar.22130 (archived at https://perma.cc/CYY9-R3SC)

2 O. S. Itani, E. A. Goad, and F. Jaramillo. Building customer relationships while achieving sales performance results: Is listening the holy grail of sales? *Journal of Business Research*, 2019. www.sciencedirect.com/science/article/abs/pii/ S0148296319303017 (archived at https://perma.cc/FR57-A2QC)

3 A. Gallo. What is psychological safety? *Harvard Business Review*, February, 2023. hbr.org/2023/02/what-is-psychological-safety (archived at perma.cc/ 4NRY-L2YL)

5

Personalization and Engagement

How Data and Creativity Create Core Memories

Personalization offers a way to make a scalable experience feel more intimate for consumers.

People want to feel special. It doesn't matter how much money they spend or if it's for a special occasion. There is an inherent need for people to have a personalized experience not only to create more value add for the consumer, but it also helps consumer decision-making.

For creative executive and former LEGO Creative Director James Gregson, personalization resolves the problem of trying to talk to everyone with the same message. "I'm increasingly frustrated by this 'We know our audience better than anyone' handwaving that a lot of brands seemingly celebrate. I'm not always sure they do. Not unless they've done the deep, analytical work of understanding your audience's nuanced needs, behaviors, and motivations. Bring back the focus groups, I say! And not every few years. Every year. Because the idea that one message can resonate with everyone fundamentally misunderstands how people engage with brands. Your audiences are complex, layered, and often contradictory. Success comes from embracing and addressing these nuances, not glossing over them."

Personalization as a Driver of Engagement

Personalization involves tailoring experiences, messages, and offerings to individual customer preferences, behaviors, and needs. This bespoke approach significantly enhances customer engagement by making the interaction more relevant and meaningful. Studies show that personalized experiences lead to higher customer satisfaction, increased loyalty, and greater lifetime value. In a study by the University of Texas on personalization and consumer behavior, personalization is not only preferred for online experiences, but it aids the consumer in multiple ways.[1] One key benefit is the elimination of information overload. If a brand only offers you products and services tailored to your past experience or needs, it's harder to become overwhelmed during the purchasing experience.

Creating Memorable Brand Experiences

Creating memorable brand experiences goes beyond transactions; it's about crafting moments that resonate with customers on a deeply personal level. When personalization is done effectively, it transforms ordinary interactions into remarkable experiences that customers recall fondly and share with others. These core memories become part of how customers identify with the brand, influencing future behaviors and preferences. We'll do a deeper dive on core memories later in this chapter. Here are some key elements to consider when creating unforgettable brand experiences.

Going Beyond the Transaction

Personalization that resonates with customers treats each interaction as a chance to engage them meaningfully. Simple touches like addressing customers by name, remembering past interactions, and tailoring recommendations to their preferences make each experience feel customized and unique. When customers feel acknowledged and valued as individuals, it fosters a positive association with the brand, making each interaction more than just a transaction. The goal is to create a sense of connection, where the brand feels like it's part of the customer's journey rather than simply a provider of products or services.

Curating Surprise and Delight

Incorporating elements of surprise and delight can turn an everyday transaction into a memorable experience. When brands go out of their way to make a customer feel appreciated, it builds goodwill and reinforces a positive emotional connection. These moments of delight make customers feel special and valued, which strengthens their loyalty and often leads to word-of-mouth advocacy. The element of surprise makes the experience more memorable, as it breaks from the expected, everyday brand interaction.

Leveraging Storytelling for Deeper Impact

Storytelling is a powerful tool for creating memorable experiences that align with customers' values. By sharing stories about the brand's mission, its people, or how customers have benefited from the brand, companies can foster a deeper emotional connection. Storytelling allows customers to see themselves as part of the brand's narrative, making their interactions feel more meaningful. When customers resonate with a brand's story, they're more likely to remember their experience, feel aligned with its purpose, and integrate the brand into their own identity.

Creating Experiences That Reflect Customer Values

Today's consumers are increasingly values-driven, choosing brands that reflect their own beliefs and principles. By understanding what matters to customers—whether it's sustainability, inclusivity, or innovation—brands can create experiences that align with these values. This could mean offering eco-friendly packaging, supporting charitable causes, or celebrating customer diversity through personalized content. When customers see their values reflected in their brand experience, it creates a stronger emotional connection and reinforces their decision to stay loyal.

According to entrepreneur and strategist Adrienne Sheares, values are crucial to connection and can lead to emotional connection faltering if there is a misalignment. "If a brand's values don't align with their actions, that's a recipe for disaster. Values are not just platitudes. They must represent the company. Trust erodes when that doesn't align, and customer affinity falls apart.

"The lack of alignment of brand values is not a PR issue—it's a company-wide issue.

"The best way to avoid poor alignment is to break down silos and have a 360 view of your brand—including a SWOT analysis. Leaders need to ask: Do our actions routinely fit with our brand values? Look at the weaknesses in everything from products and services to company culture. What doesn't align? How can we fix that?"

Consistent and Meaningful Interactions Across Touchpoints

For a brand experience to be memorable, it must be consistently meaningful across all touchpoints, whether in-store, online, or through customer service. A seamless experience, where each interaction builds on the last, helps customers feel that the brand is genuinely invested in understanding and serving them. Consistency across touchpoints reinforces the brand's commitment to personalization and leaves a lasting impression of care and attentiveness.

For Marketing and SEO Strategist Holly Miller Anderson, getting this right is a major struggle for brands. "*This* is the million-dollar question. In my opinion, I think no brand is getting this right 100 percent of the time but not for lack of trying. It has more to do with the reality of how the world works. Being able to respond and adapt, at scale, to aspects like the speed of technology, your internal tech stack, or the pace of consumer demand in social media. In particular, for sports where athletes wear a particular look or shoe—that can create instant demand. Is that product also available for purchase on your site? Or on Amazon (product-related searches start there, y'all)? Consumers will buy it at the price point and convenience that matters to them. Especially in real-time events, it's a function of planning for product availability and search demand and those are challenging, moving targets to try and control.

"I think more brands, especially since the global pandemic, are working to level up offering buying online and picking up in store or better aligning their in-store catalogue with what's reflected in their app. We're trying to be as fast as Amazon and as ubiquitous as the Starbucks or CVS on every corner, and that's really hard to do because consumer demand is in a state of constant flux."

Celebrating Customer Milestones

Celebrating important milestones—like birthdays, anniversaries with the brand, or product usage achievements—can make customers feel acknowledged and appreciated. Personalized messages or small rewards for these milestones reinforce that the brand values the relationship. These celebratory gestures create memorable moments that deepen the emotional bond between the customer and the brand.

Encouraging Shared Experiences

Creating opportunities for customers to share their brand experiences with friends, family, or a wider community can amplify the memorability of those interactions. Brands can encourage this by offering referral programs, incentives for social sharing, or collaborative events where customers can participate together. When customers share their experiences, it strengthens their connection to the brand and creates new memories around it. These shared experiences foster a sense of pride and belonging, making the brand a part of customers' social lives.

Investing in Long-Term Relationship Building

Memorable experiences are not just single events but part of an ongoing relationship. By continuously engaging customers in meaningful ways, brands can create a series of positive memories that deepen over time. Long-term engagement can include loyalty programs that reward consistent support, personalized follow-ups after purchases, or exclusive access to new products. These ongoing interactions show that the brand values the customer beyond one purchase, encouraging a stronger emotional connection that makes the brand experience a memorable and integral part of the customer's life.

The Power of Simplicity and Convenience

Sometimes, memorable experiences are built through simplicity and ease. Ensuring a smooth, convenient, and frictionless experience can be as impactful as any grand gesture. When brands streamline the customer journey—by minimizing wait times, providing easy access to customer support, or simplifying the checkout process—it creates a positive, stress-free experience that customers are likely to remember. A seamless, hassle-free interaction is memorable because it respects the customer's time and effort, creating a lasting impression of the brand's attentiveness.

REAL-WORLD EXAMPLE
Netflix[2]

Netflix uses sophisticated algorithms to analyze viewing habits and preferences, delivering personalized content recommendations. This customization not only enhances the user experience but also keeps viewers engaged and loyal to the platform.

REAL-WORLD EXAMPLE
Spotify[3]

Spotify's personalized playlists, such as Daylists and Daily Mix, are designed based on individual listening habits and preferences. This deep level of personalization enriches the user experience, creating a strong emotional connection with its users. This all culminates in the ultimate personalized experience, Spotify Wrapped, with users excited to learn about their listening habits for the year in sharable content that goes viral every year.

The Intersection of Data and Creativity

Personalization doesn't just happen. There is a level of customer intelligence (read: data) that you need to have in order to do this.

While data provides insights into customer preferences and behaviors, creativity brings these insights to life through compelling and authentic experiences. Balancing data and creativity involves using data to inform and guide creative strategies without losing the human touch that makes personalization feel genuine.

As creative executive and former LEGO Creative Director James Gregson shares, "The tension between authenticity and creativity has been fundamental to advertising since its inception. But we've overcorrected in a way. The term 'authenticity' has lost meaning because we spent decades prioritizing short-term sales over brand building. Now we're scrambling to build the trust we should have been nurturing all along. I believe the real challenge isn't balancing authenticity and creativity—it's remembering that meaningful brand building requires long-term commitment."

The Role of Technology

Technology forms the backbone of personalization by enabling brands to gather, analyze, and interpret vast amounts of customer data. Advanced algorithms, machine learning, and AI help brands understand individual customer needs, preferences, and behaviors in unprecedented detail. Customer relationship management (CRM) systems consolidate customer data from various touchpoints, providing a comprehensive view of each customer's journey. These tools ensure that personalized experiences are not just guesses but are grounded in accurate, data-driven insights.

Combining Data Insights With Storytelling

Data gives brands powerful insights into customer preferences, habits, and values, but these insights come alive through creative execution. Instead of simply recommending a product based on past purchases, brands can use storytelling to add emotional depth to those recommendations. This storytelling approach goes beyond products, aligning with the customer's values and fostering an emotional bond.

Dynamic, Contextual Personalization

Dynamic personalization allows brands to adjust content based on real-time data, creating interactions that are not only relevant but also immediate. A creative approach to personalization might involve dynamically adjusting the website experience to feature customer testimonials for that product or offering a small incentive, like free shipping, alongside a message that speaks to the product's benefits. This contextual, real-time approach makes customers feel noticed and understood, increasing the likelihood of engagement.

A/B Testing for Creative Optimization

A/B testing allows brands to optimize the creative aspects of personalized content, ensuring that it resonates as effectively as possible with different customer segments. Testing various elements—such as the tone of voice, imagery, layout, or call-to-action phrasing—provides valuable feedback on what engages each segment best. This iterative, data-backed approach keeps creative personalization fresh and aligned with customer expectations.

Personalized Offers and Incentives

Using data to tailor offers, discounts, or rewards specific to individual preferences makes personalization both meaningful and actionable. Creative incentives make offers feel more thoughtful and relevant, turning routine purchases into memorable experiences that acknowledge and reward the customer's loyalty and preferences.

Creating Memorable Customer Milestones

Personalizing moments that recognize customer milestones or achievements creates lasting memories. By celebrating a customer's anniversary with the brand, acknowledging their progress on a fitness journey, or simply thanking them for a significant purchase milestone, brands can use creativity to make customers feel appreciated. Celebrating these moments makes customers feel connected and valued, creating positive associations that enhance brand loyalty.

Integrating Personalization With Offline Experiences

Bringing personalization into offline experiences—such as in-store visits, events, or product packaging—adds an extra layer of memorability. A brand might send an email with personalized product recommendations, then have those items set aside for the customer in-store, creating a seamless online-to-offline experience. Another approach could be adding personalized notes or packaging for online orders, reinforcing the personal touch. These physical elements amplify the impact of digital personalization, creating a more comprehensive experience that resonates with customers on multiple levels.

When brands thoughtfully integrate these two components, they move beyond merely anticipating needs to crafting experiences that customers find genuinely memorable and meaningful. This powerful blend of creativity and data fosters deeper emotional connections, turning routine interactions into memorable brand moments that customers cherish and remember.

Best Practices for Meaningful Personalization

For meaningful personalization to resonate with customers, follow best practices that build trust, relevance, and a seamless experience. Here's how each of these principles can enhance personalization efforts.

Transparency

Transparency about data usage is the cornerstone of customer trust, especially as customers grow more aware of data privacy. Being upfront about how and why customer data is collected, stored, and used can turn potential concerns into a trust-building opportunity. Clear communication about data collection (e.g., asking customers to opt in or offering options to manage their data preferences) helps customers feel secure and respected. Transparency can also go a step further by showing customers the value they receive from their data, such as tailored product recommendations or customized loyalty rewards. When brands openly communicate their intentions, customers are more likely to view personalized experiences positively and feel comfortable engaging on a deeper level.

Relevance

Personalization is only meaningful when it aligns with the customer's current interests, preferences, and circumstances. This means brands should go beyond basic data like name or purchase history to consider real-time needs, seasonal preferences, and contextual factors. Brands can use data signals such as browsing history, previous purchases, or local events to create experiences that resonate. Relevance can also be enhanced by adapting to changing customer behavior; as preferences evolve, the personalization approach should adjust accordingly to avoid outdated or irrelevant recommendations.

By delivering timely and pertinent messages, brands can show they understand and anticipate their customers' needs.

Consistency

Consistency is vital for creating a cohesive customer experience. When personalization efforts are not aligned across channels—such as website, email, social media, and in-store—it can lead to confusion and dilute the impact of personalized engagement. A unified brand voice across all touchpoints reassures customers that the brand recognizes them, no matter where they interact. Consistent messaging and experiences help reinforce the personalized relationship, making each interaction feel authentic and reliable. Consistency also strengthens brand identity, helping customers feel connected to the brand in a unified way across all channels.

How do you build that consistency muscle for customers? According to CX professional Alison Bukowski, "Simply put: Invest in a strong customer-facing organization. Organizations must have a chief customer officer (CCO) that oversees functions dedicated to customer success, customer experience/engagement, customer marketing, customer education, and customer support. The whole is stronger than the sum of its parts and with all primary customer-facing business units under one umbrella, that strategy can be developed cohesively and executed seamlessly. In addition, a strong leader in the CCO role is imperative to success; customer experience is the job of the entire organization—we hear it often, but rarely is it properly executed. Executive support is essential. Customer-centric culture is kind of a throw-away phrase at this point. Communication-centric or collaboration-centric culture would be more appropriate—without complete buy-in across the organization that the customer experience is what drives new business, retails and expands existing business, and creates customer advocates, you're going to continue going in circles."

Adaptability and Responsiveness

Customers' needs and preferences are dynamic, so personalization efforts must be flexible and responsive. Brands that can quickly adapt to shifts in behavior, seasonality, or external events create a more relevant and engaging experience. Adaptability also includes responding to customer feedback—brands that modify their approach based on feedback are better positioned to meet evolving expectations. By staying responsive, brands demonstrate a commitment to understanding and meeting customer needs over time.

When executed well, personalization becomes more than just a marketing tool; it transforms into a meaningful dialogue that reinforces loyalty and creates lasting, positive impressions.

Getting the Best From Customer Data

Data is abundant, but customer loyalty can still feel elusive. The true power lies not in the amount of data a brand collects, but in how effectively it uses it. By analyzing the right data points—transactional, behavioral, and feedback—brands can enhance customer experiences, anticipate needs, and build lasting relationships.

Transactional data provides insights into purchasing behavior, revealing what customers buy, how often, and where. A customer's purchase history helps brands tailor product recommendations, while spending patterns like average transaction value (ATV) and customer lifetime value (CLV) offer valuable insights into what types of promotions or products are likely to resonate with different customer segments. Channel preferences, such as whether a customer prefers shopping online, in-store, or via mobile, allow brands to design seamless, omnichannel experiences that meet customers wherever they engage the most. By leveraging this data, brands can personalize offers, predict future buying behavior with predictive analytics, and design targeted loyalty programs to reward repeat customers.

Behavioral data tracks customer engagement and actions beyond the point of purchase. It helps brands understand how customers interact with their digital and physical spaces. By analyzing website navigation patterns, brands can identify which products customers are most interested in. Tracking click-through rates (CTR) on emails or advertisements reveals what content resonates with customers, and the amount of time spent on a site or app signals how engaged a customer is. Cart abandonment rates show where customers experience friction during the purchase process, while social media interactions such as likes, shares, and comments provide insight into the content and topics that spark customer interest. With this data, brands can deliver highly personalized content, refine their messaging, and retarget customers who may have shown interest but did not complete a purchase, enhancing overall engagement.

Feedback data, often more qualitative, gives brands direct insight into customer satisfaction and pain points. Surveys such as net promoter score offer structured feedback on customer experiences, while customer reviews and ratings provide unfiltered opinions about a product or service. Customer service interactions are another rich source of information, revealing recurring issues or areas where the customer experience falls short. By closely analyzing this feedback, brands can identify gaps in the customer experience, address recurring issues, and drive product or service improvements. Taking action based on feedback not only improves the overall experience but also demonstrates to customers that their opinions are valued, building trust and loyalty.

To truly harness the potential of all this data, brands must integrate transactional, behavioral, and feedback data to create comprehensive customer profiles. This integration allows brands to segment customers based on different factors such as purchase history, engagement, and preferences, enabling them to deliver more targeted marketing and personalized experiences. With the help of predictive personalization, powered by advanced data analytics, brands can anticipate future customer behaviors based on past patterns, offering relevant recommendations and personalized promotions. Analyzing the full customer journey—using both behavioral and feedback data—lets brands identify pain points and friction areas, allowing them to improve the customer experience at key touchpoints and strengthen their connection with customers, ultimately fostering long-term loyalty.

By strategically analyzing and integrating transactional, behavioral, and feedback data, brands can go beyond just collecting information. They can use these insights to craft personalized experiences that enhance customer satisfaction, drive retention, and support sustainable growth.

Analyzing Data for Personalization

Analyzing customer data is key to creating a personalized, seamless experience that resonates with individual preferences and needs. By leveraging data analytics, brands can gain a deeper understanding of their customers, anticipate their needs, and tailor interactions in ways that feel meaningful. There are several strategies to focus on, along with additional approaches to consider.

Segmentation

Segmenting customers by shared characteristics, behaviors, or preferences enables brands to personalize marketing efforts, product recommendations, and engagement strategies. Effective segmentation can be based on demographic information (age, location, income), behavioral data (purchasing habits, website interactions), or psychographic factors (values, interests, lifestyle choices).

Predictive Analytics

Using historical data to predict future behaviors allows brands to anticipate and meet customer needs before they arise. Predictive analytics can inform everything from product recommendations and content suggestions to customer support needs and proactive outreach.

Machine Learning and AI

AI and machine learning algorithms can process vast amounts of data to identify hidden patterns, trends, and customer preferences that might otherwise go unnoticed. These insights can inform hyper-personalized marketing strategies, such as individualized product recommendations, targeted messaging, and dynamic pricing models. Machine learning models can also analyze customer sentiment in real time across touchpoints, allowing brands to quickly adjust their approach if a customer shows signs of dissatisfaction.

Real-Time Personalization

Real-time personalization allows brands to tailor interactions as they happen, creating a highly responsive and dynamic customer experience. By continuously adapting to the customer's current journey, real-time personalization enhances relevance and engagement, increasing the likelihood of conversion and satisfaction.

Voice of the Customer Analytics

VoC programs capture direct feedback from customers across various channels, including surveys, reviews, and social media. By analyzing this data, brands gain valuable insights into customer sentiment, preferences, and pain points, allowing them to make meaningful improvements to products, services, and overall experiences. VoC analytics not only helps in identifying trends but also empowers brands to respond to specific issues or requests, building trust and loyalty through responsiveness and transparency.

Eli Weiss, current VP of Retention Advocacy at Yotpo and former Senior Director of Customer Experience and Retention at Jones Road Beauty, saw the power of this first-hand. "Understanding customer feedback goes way beyond just reacting when someone says they hate your face moisturizer and deciding to change the formula. It's also about understanding what a customer's actions—or lack thereof—are telling you.

"For instance, at Jones Road Beauty, we noticed that if a customer took our quiz and marked their skin type as 'oily,' but then bought a product for dry skin and didn't buy anything again, that's on us. It wasn't that they didn't like the brand; it was likely because the product didn't match their needs.

"Using that insight, we could follow up in a personalized, thoughtful way, suggesting a product better suited for their skin type. It's about showing customers that you're paying attention and you care about their experience."

Customer Journey Mapping

Customer journey mapping involves visualizing the entire customer experience across multiple touchpoints, from initial brand awareness to post-purchase support. By analyzing data at each stage of the journey, brands can identify areas for improvement, streamline processes, and enhance interactions. Mapping the customer journey provides a holistic view of the customer experience, highlighting moments where personalization can be applied to create a more seamless and satisfying journey.

Churn Prediction and Retention Analytics

Identifying at-risk customers early on allows brands to intervene and potentially prevent churn. By analyzing factors such as purchase frequency, interaction history, and customer feedback, brands can develop models to predict when a customer is likely to leave. With these insights, brands can deploy retention strategies like offering incentives, personalized outreach, or tailored support to re-engage customers before they make the decision to churn. Retention analytics not only improves customer lifetime value but also signals a brand's commitment to maintaining a positive relationship with its customers.

Omnichannel Integration

Integrating data across all customer interaction channels—online, in-store, mobile, and customer service—provides a complete view of each customer's journey. Omnichannel data integration helps brands deliver a unified experience, allowing for consistent, personalized engagement across platforms.

Data Privacy and Ethical Use of Data

While gathering and analyzing customer data can vastly improve personalization, the ethical handling of this data is just as important. Misusing customer data—such as using it without permission, selling it to third parties, or failing to protect it securely—can erode trust and undo the benefits of personalization. Customers need transparency about how their data will be used, with options to control or opt out of data-sharing practices.

Creating Core Memories

The ultimate goal of personalization is to create core memories—positive, lasting impressions that influence future customer behaviors and loyalty. This can be achieved through consistent, authentic, and emotionally engaging experiences that make customers feel valued and understood.

In *Inside Out*, Pixar personifies "core memories" as glowing orbs that represent pivotal, emotionally charged moments in a character's life, defining their personality and shaping their identity. In the film, each of these core memories plays a crucial role in building different "islands" of personality, such as Family Island, Friendship Island, and Honesty Island. These core memories, often connected to experiences of joy, sadness, fear, or other strong emotions, influence the character Riley's behavior, preferences, and interactions. Pixar's storytelling emphasizes how certain experiences, especially ones tied to intense emotions, can remain vivid and impactful, forming a foundation for who Riley is and how she views the world around her.

In psychology, the closest concept to Pixar's core memories is known as autobiographical memory—a category of long-lasting, significant memories that form our personal narratives.[4] Autobiographical memories are central to our self-identity, allowing us to remember who we are and where we come from, and they play a powerful role in our ability to connect emotionally with others.[5] These memories tend to be vivid and emotionally rich, often encompassing events that reflect personal growth, relationships, and achievements. Unlike simple factual recall, autobiographical memories contain emotional resonance, situational context, and personal meaning, which explains why they are more likely to be remembered over time.

Brands that aim to create meaningful connections with customers can aspire to become part of their autobiographical memories. When a brand experience feels highly personalized, authentic, and emotionally engaging, it has the potential to leave a lasting, positive impression. These types of experiences, such as celebrating a milestone purchase, surprising a loyal customer, or resolving an issue in a memorable way, can create "core memory" moments for customers. By tapping into the elements that make autobiographical memories powerful—emotional depth, personal relevance, and positive associations—brands can foster deeper loyalty, encouraging customers to recall these moments fondly and feel an ongoing, meaningful connection.

In essence, while "core memories" may be a fictional construct, the concept has real-life parallels in how meaningful customer experiences can shape loyalty and brand affinity, aiming to achieve a place in the emotional fabric of customers' lives.

KEY TAKEAWAYS

- **Scalable personalization:** Effective personalization can make large-scale customer interactions feel intimate, meeting the inherent desire for individuals to feel recognized and valued.

- **Enhanced engagement:** Personalized interactions that reflect customer preferences lead to higher engagement, satisfaction, loyalty, and lifetime value, simplifying decision-making by reducing information overload.

- **Creating memorable experiences:** Memorable brand experiences, or "core memories," arise from personalized, emotionally engaging interactions. These experiences foster positive associations, shaping how customers view and connect with the brand long term.

- **Beyond transactions:** Each customer interaction should aim to build connection and engagement, with simple touches (such as personalized greetings or tailored recommendations) transforming transactions into valuable experiences.

- **Surprise and delight:** Small, unexpected gestures—such as personalized thank-you notes or exclusive discounts—strengthen positive emotional connections, making customers feel appreciated and enhancing loyalty.

- **Storytelling:** Storytelling aligned with a customer's values and experiences deepens emotional engagement, helping customers relate to the brand's mission and feel part of its journey.

- **Reflecting customer values:** Brands that align experiences with customer values (e.g., sustainability or inclusivity) strengthen loyalty, as customers feel their personal beliefs are understood and represented.

- **Consistency across channels:** To build trust and reinforce relationships, personalization should be seamless across all brand touchpoints (e.g., online, in-store), ensuring a cohesive experience and unified brand identity.

- **Community and belonging:** Building a community around shared values and interests transforms customers into advocates, fostering loyalty and a sense of connection to the brand.

- **Empathy and responsiveness:** Addressing customer needs with empathy, understanding, and adaptability ensures that personalized experiences remain respectful and valuable, responding to changing preferences and feedback.

- **Data and creativity balance:** Integrating data insights with creative storytelling enables brands to deliver experiences that are both relevant and engaging, creating memorable, personalized interactions that feel genuine.

Notes

1 L. F. Bright. Consumer control and customization in online environments: An investigation into the psychology of consumer choice and its impact on media enjoyment, attitude, and behavioral intention, University of Texas Repository, 2008. https://repositories.lib.utexas.edu/items/c955109d-6d45-4846-9c62-3061cdee9be2 (archived at https://perma.cc/JE7L-RJJ8)

2 Netflix. How Netflix's recommendations system works, Netflix Help Center, 2025. help.netflix.com/en/node/100639 (archived at https://perma.cc/8M66-H3CC)

3 Spotify. How Spotify uses design to make personalization features delightful, Spotify Newsroom, October 18, 2023. newsroom.spotify.com/2023-10-18/how-spotify-uses-design-to-make-personalization-features-delightful/ (archived at perma.cc/WXN5-9VNQ)

4 American Psychological Association (APA). Autobiographical memory, APA Dictionary of Psychology, 2023. dictionary.apa.org/autobiographical-memory (archived at perma.cc/97VR-AK5R)

5 T. E. A. Waters. Relations between the functions of autobiographical memory and psychological wellbeing, Memory, 2013, 22(3), 265–75. pubmed.ncbi.nlm.nih.gov/23537126/ (archived at https://perma.cc/5FDF-6TZX)

6

Building Loyalty at Scale

What Great *Looks Like*

Fostering meaningful connections with customers isn't a one-size-fits-all tactic. The strongest brands understand that loyalty is cultivated through authentic, thoughtful interactions that resonate in different situations, especially during life's challenges and moments of vulnerability. Whether showing empathy in action during personal hardships, transforming a crisis into a triumph, tapping into cultural touchpoints, or making small gestures that leave a big impact, brands have countless opportunities to foster connection and affinity.

This chapter explores these diverse approaches, showcasing how brands can authentically show up for their customers, build loyalty, and turn ordinary moments into extraordinary ones—even when the circumstances are far from ideal. These brands and moments showcase the difference between creating a good enough customer experience versus moments customers can't stop talking about.

Implementing a Great vs. Good CX Approach

REAL-WORLD EXAMPLES
Empathy in Action: Chewy

Chewy exemplifies how a brand can treat customers like family, approaching each interaction with deep empathy and care for their pets as cherished members of the household. This philosophy is at the core of Chewy's customer service, which goes beyond transactional exchanges to build genuine emotional connections with pet owners. One of the most heartwarming examples of this is how Chewy responds to the loss of a pet. Instead of viewing it as a simple account update or product cancellation, the company offers comfort and support akin to what a close friend or family member might provide. Customers often receive condolence flowers and handwritten sympathy cards, letting them know that Chewy truly understands the pain of such a loss. They even allow customers to memorialize their pet profiles instead of deleting them, ensuring the memory of their beloved companion remains honored.

Chewy's thoughtful gestures extend to delightful surprises that strengthen the bond with their customers. Many pet owners have been touched to receive hand-painted portraits of their pets as unexpected gifts, turning moments of interaction with the company into cherished memories. During the holiday season, the company invites pets to "write" letters to "Chewy Claus," making the experience festive and inclusive while also donating to charities for each letter submitted. These gestures show that Chewy doesn't just see pets as animals but as integral family members deserving of celebration and care.

Chewy's compassion is also evident in its customer-centric policies. For instance, when customers seek to return items, especially after the loss of a pet, the company often issues a full refund and suggests donating the products to local shelters. This approach transforms a potentially mundane or difficult interaction into an opportunity for generosity and community support. Additionally, Chewy's 24/7 customer support ensures that pet owners always have someone to turn to for help, no matter the time of day or night.

As customer experience expert Dan Gingiss states, Chewy acts as a customer-centered company, because even when the customer is calling to cancel, they are still looking to provide value for them. "I would argue that a company like Chewy probably wouldn't immediately go to 'Let's cut the customer service team', right? Would be easy for them to cut the condolence cards and the flowers after a pet dies? That'd be a simple cut, a budget cut, right?

"And yet they understand that that's one of the things that connects their customers and is a great retention tool. This is fascinating because, in theory, when a pet dies that means that they've just lost a customer. But Chewy knows that almost every pet owner is going to get another pet eventually. And if they can, on the way out the door, have that customer still smiling, then when they inevitably get another pet, they're right back shopping with Chewy again."

Through these actions, Chewy demonstrates that their commitment to customers is not just about sales but also about fostering meaningful, family-like relationships. By treating every pet as a beloved family member and every customer with genuine care, Chewy has set a benchmark for empathetic, relationship-driven customer service. They don't see these interactions as a time when they lost a customer, but instead a time when they were able to show up for their customers when they needed compassion most.

Taking Action to Make Things Right: Sephora

Sephora's popularity is more than just its selection of products and locations. When there is criticism, they take action to make things right. Digital strategist and comms pro Adrienne Sheares highlights how they responded to racial backlash. "Before the murder of George Floyd in 2020, which prompted many brands to reevaluate their racial biases, Sephora was already facing backlash for racial insensitivity. In 2019, music superstar SZA called out the brand for discrimination after being racially profiled by a sales associate. Sephora responded by closing stores for company-wide anti-bias training and took further action in 2020. While many companies made feel-good statements or posted black squares on social media, Sephora went beyond and became one of the first to sign the 15 percent pledge—a commitment to dedicate at least 15 percent of shelf space to Black-owned businesses.

"Since then, Sephora has significantly invested in Black-owned brands, getting them on their shelves and in front of their customers. The 15 percent pledge is a clear, measurable goal on which they update their stakeholders.

"What's admirable about Sephora is that it has taken a long-term approach. They've commissioned studies around racial bias in retail, created a short film, *Black Beauty is Beauty*, and highlighted stories of Black entrepreneurs in the beauty industry. It's a 360 approach—that goes beyond statements and one-time action."

Showing Up Consistently and Authentically: Bookshop.org

As Plot's Head of Marketing, Christina Le shares, "Their Threads account, in particular, is like reading the inner monologue of a funny, bookish friend (super relatable and effortlessly on point). What's cool about it is that they manage to stay true to their mission of supporting independent bookstores while also tapping into what's happening culturally. They're not just chasing trends but they're making it all feel personal and intentional.

"What really stands out, though, is how they engage with their audience. The person behind the account is super active in the comments, and I feel like when you grow past a certain amount of followers, it's very easy to fall off this but they seem to be replying in a way that feels natural and conversational even today. It's clear they're not just speaking *at* their audience. They're part of the community. This kind of back-and-forth builds a strong relationship and makes people want to stick around, which honestly explains how they've grown so fast."

Tapping Into Culture: McDonald's

McDonald's has established itself as more than just a fast-food chain, by tapping into cultural moments that resonate deeply with its customers. Through celebrity collaborations and partnerships with niche communities like anime fans, the brand has positioned itself as a participant in the cultural passions of its audience. These efforts transform McDonald's from a transactional brand into a meaningful part of its customers' lives, building deeper emotional connections and relevance.

Celebrity collaborations, such as meals with Travis Scott, BTS, and Cardi B, turn simple menu items into cultural events.[1] The BTS Meal, for example, combined personalized food offerings with exclusive branded merchandise, creating a shared global experience that celebrated fandom. Similarly, partnerships with anime properties, like the "WcDonald's" concept or *Jujutsu Kaisen*, allowed McDonald's to engage with dedicated subcultures by offering unique packaging, limited-edition products, and immersive content.[2] These moments build loyalty by aligning the brand with what customers love.

Cultural integration isn't just a marketing tactic; it's a strategy for fostering emotional resonance. Consumers, especially younger generations, value authenticity and want to engage with brands that reflect their interests. By embedding itself in music, entertainment, and anime fandoms, McDonald's strengthens its emotional ties and generates excitement that extends across social media, creating organic buzz and advocacy.

Creating Connection Through Personalization: Spotify

Spotify has redefined how brands can use customer data to create deeply personal and culturally impactful experiences. Spotify Wrapped, the annual campaign that compiles a user's listening habits into a vibrant, shareable story, exemplifies this approach. By analyzing individual trends—such as top artists, favorite genres, and total minutes streamed—Spotify turns raw data into a celebration of each user's unique musical identity. This innovative use of personalization transforms Wrapped into a cultural phenomenon that dominates social media every December.

Wrapped isn't just a year-end recap—it's a tool for self-expression. By highlighting listening habits, Spotify allows users to signal who they are through their musical tastes. For many, music reflects emotions, milestones, and moments, and Wrapped becomes a snapshot of their year. Sharing Wrapped results on social media lets users tell their story, sparking conversations over shared favorites, unexpected surprises, and personal discoveries. It's a digital badge of identity that users proudly share, signaling their individuality and building connections with others who resonate with their taste.

This campaign also fosters emotional engagement, as it validates users' preferences and makes them feel seen. Wrapped's playful, creative format turns data into a celebration of personal taste, reinforcing Spotify's role as a platform that understands its users on a deeper level. It transforms listening from a passive activity into a defining part of self-expression. Customers don't just use Spotify; they see it as a cultural companion that amplifies their identity.

Leading With Purpose: Patagonia

Patagonia exemplifies what it means to be a brand with a purpose, leading with a mission that transcends profits and aligns deeply with its values. Founded by Yvon Chouinard, the outdoor apparel company has long been a pioneer in environmental advocacy, embedding sustainability into every facet of its business. In 2022, Patagonia took its commitment to the planet a step further with an unprecedented move: Chouinard transferred ownership of the company, valued at approximately $3 billion, to a trust and nonprofit organization dedicated to fighting climate change.[3] This bold action ensured that all of Patagonia's profits—around $100 million annually—would go toward protecting the environment and addressing climate issues.

This decision was not only groundbreaking but also a testament to Patagonia's ethos as a company that genuinely lives its purpose. While many brands leverage environmental messaging as a marketing tool, Patagonia's actions prove its authenticity and depth of commitment. From its use of sustainable materials and ethical supply chains to its repair-and-reuse programs, Patagonia consistently aligns its business practices with its environmental mission. The company's transparency and refusal to compromise its values have earned it the trust and loyalty of purpose-driven consumers.

For customers, Patagonia is more than a brand; it's a movement they can feel proud to support. By addressing global challenges head-on and prioritizing the health of the planet over profits, Patagonia resonates with individuals who seek to make a positive impact through their purchases. At a time when consumers increasingly demand accountability from companies, Patagonia's unwavering focus on purpose stands as a model for how brands can build enduring relationships through authenticity and action.

Small Gestures, Big Impact: Costco

Costco has built unwavering customer loyalty by prioritizing value over profits, exemplified by its decision to keep the price of its iconic hot dog and soda combo at $1.50 since 1985. Despite rising inflation and increased costs, Costco refuses to raise the price, reinforcing its commitment to customers rather than inflating profits. This decision is more than a pricing strategy—it's a symbol of Costco's dedication to delivering consistent value and earning trust. By resisting the pressure to adjust prices, the company demonstrates that it values long-term relationships with its customers over short-term financial gains. This approach cements Costco's reputation as a retailer that genuinely cares about its customers.

The perception that brands prioritize profits over people has created a widening gap between businesses and their customers. Costco's deliberate choice to hold the line on pricing feels refreshingly different—like a statement of solidarity rather than a sales tactic. For consumers, this choice resonates deeply, especially those striving to provide for their families in the face of economic uncertainty. It transforms Costco from a mere retailer into a trusted ally, reinforcing the idea that the company values their well-being over inflating its bottom line.

By prioritizing affordability in even small ways, Costco fosters a sense of loyalty and goodwill, making shoppers feel seen and supported. This relationship goes beyond transactions, positioning Costco as a partner in their customers' efforts to stretch every dollar and care for their households.

Nailing an Experience: Pop-Tarts and the Pop-Tarts Bowl

The Pop-Tarts Bowl showcased how "experience" marketing can ignite excitement, drive participation, and turn fans into loyal customers. By transforming a typical sponsorship into a lively, immersive spectacle, Pop-Tarts made the event more than a game—it became a celebration of the brand.[4] From sprinkle-covered sidelines to foil-wrapped goalposts and a one-of-a-kind trophy—a functional toaster embedded in a football atop a Stanley Cup-inspired base—every detail reflected the brand's fun, quirky personality.

Pop-Tarts didn't just entertain; they actively involved fans. The interactive mascot "sacrifice," complete with voting and dramatic flair, pulled audiences into the action and created a shared moment of humor and excitement. Online, custom GIFs and playful social content kept the energy alive, turning casual viewers into passionate participants. These moments made fans smile and, more importantly, crave Pop-Tarts.

On-site, Pop-Tarts amplified the fun with food trucks, art installations, and thoughtful fan experiences like guides and schedules to ensure everyone could join in. By connecting fans to the brand through humor and interactivity, Pop-Tarts turned their Bowl into more than an event—it was an irresistible invitation to buy into the brand's world, sprinkles and all.

The Pop-Tarts Bowl proved that experiential marketing doesn't just entertain—it builds excitement, engages fans, and drives sales. By leaning into their playful identity and executing with creativity, Pop-Tarts left audiences laughing, participating, and heading to the store for their next box.

What Needs to Stay Human and What Needs to be Automated

Automation and technology have become indispensable in enhancing efficiency and scalability in customer experience. With the ability to manage vast amounts of data, automate repetitive tasks, and provide immediate responses, technological solutions can significantly improve various aspects of CX. However, there are intrinsic elements of customer experience that necessitate a human touch—especially when it comes to empathy, nuanced understanding, and emotional connections.

Balancing technology with the human touch is just as much an art as it is a science. Done well, it provides the efficiency that leadership wants with the compassion and thoughtfulness that customers need. Done poorly and they act against each other and result in automated services that don't really solve the problem and humans who don't have enough time and resources to effectively help the customer either.

Brands should offer customers the option to choose their preferred mode of interaction, effectively allowing them to "pick their own adventure." This approach respects individual preferences for either a human touch or a quicker, more convenient automated approach. For routine inquiries or tasks, such as checking order status, updating personal information, or accessing general information, automated responses and self-service portals can provide prompt and efficient solutions. However, for more complex issues, feedback, or personalized services, giving customers the option to speak with a human representative can significantly enhance their experience.

Empathy and the Human Element

Despite the efficiency offered by automation, there are aspects of customer experience where human empathy is irreplaceable. Situations involving complex problem-solving, emotional support, or nuanced customer disputes require a level of understanding and sensitivity that only human agents can provide. Customers who are dealing with emotionally charged issues or who seek detailed explanations often prefer human interaction over automated systems. This human touch helps in building emotional connections, demonstrating genuine care, and fostering a sense of trust and loyalty.

Best Practices for Integrating Automation and Human Touch in CX

As CX professional Alison Bukowski suggests, build with the customer in mind. "Customer-centricity has to be involved in every decision a company makes. I think the first question to ask is: How will this technology enhance a customer's experience with our product, service or brand? Will it directly touch the customer and what is that interaction like? If it's an internal technology or tool, will it improve efficiency to free up resources to focus on the overall customer experience? Some may say that technology cannot enhance an emotional connection between a brand and its customer—but what's really true is that technology cannot create an emotional connection, but it can indeed enhance it. If simplifying a process makes something easier for a customer, that emotional connection is enhanced. If technology allows a customer to do something more easily, remotely, with fewer clicks, it's enhancing that connection. What we often overlook is no amount of technology is going to create that emotional connection; that starts with the humans behind the brand."

Optimizing customer support requires a clear distinction between tasks best suited for automation and those that need human touch. Routine inquiries like order tracking and frequently asked questions (FAQs) can be efficiently handled by automation, ensuring quick resolutions. More complex and emotionally sensitive issues, such as disputes or highly personalized concerns, should be addressed by human agents who can provide empathy and nuanced solutions. Effective task segmentation enhances both efficiency and customer satisfaction.

Even in automated interactions, personalization improves the experience. Using customer data, brands can tailor responses by incorporating names, recent purchases, or preferences. For example, a shipping confirmation email referencing the specific item ordered or recommending complementary products makes the interaction feel more thoughtful and engaging.

Automation should never be a barrier to human support. Customers should have clear, easy ways to escalate issues when needed, whether through a help button in an app, a visible contact number, or a chatbot option to connect with a live agent. Providing these choices ensures customers feel in control and can access the level of support they need without frustration.

To maintain high-quality service, brands must regularly assess automated systems through customer feedback and performance data. Identifying overly generic responses or inefficient resolution paths allows for continuous improvement. Ensuring a smooth transition between automated tools and human agents also prevents customer frustration and maintains consistency.

A human-centered approach to design further enhances the experience, making interactions intuitive and seamless across all touchpoints, from website navigation to issue resolution. By prioritizing customer needs, brands can remove friction, improve satisfaction, and foster loyalty.

Striking the right balance between automation and human support is key to exceptional service. Automation drives efficiency by managing routine tasks, while human agents deliver personalized, empathetic interactions where they matter most. Offering customers the choice of how they engage ensures a seamless blend of technology and human connection, leading to a more satisfying experience.

Successful Tactics and Initiatives for Building Loyalty

Brands that go beyond transactional interactions to genuinely connect with their customers can achieve remarkable loyalty and advocacy. This approach is exemplified by Chewy, whose commitment to exceptional customer care has set a high standard in the industry. Inspired by their strategies, here are detailed explanations and actionable tips on how businesses can enhance their customer relations by embedding empathy into their brand DNA, celebrating customer milestones, leveraging personal touches, and cultivating long-term relationships. These steps not only deepen customer connections but also transform how customers perceive and interact with a brand over time.

Embed Empathy in Brand DNA

Empathy allows businesses to move beyond transactions and understand customers as individuals. By prioritizing genuine connection, brands build trust, enhance personalization, resolve conflicts effectively, and foster long-term loyalty.

When employees actively listen and acknowledge customer concerns, they create meaningful relationships that drive retention. Personalized interactions, tailored to a customer's emotions and needs, feel more thoughtful and impactful than generic responses. Empathy also plays a key role in conflict resolution—validating frustrations can de-escalate tensions and turn negative experiences into positive ones, strengthening customer trust.

For empathy to thrive, it must extend beyond customer-facing roles. Leaders set the tone by modeling empathy toward employees and customers, ensuring it shapes company culture and decision-making. How employees are treated directly impacts how they show up for customers—when they feel valued, supported, and equipped with the time and resources to do their jobs well, they can deliver better experiences. On the other hand, when companies cut frontline workers, they remove a critical layer of direct customer interaction, which can erode service quality and weaken customer relationships.

Open communication within teams fosters a supportive environment, enabling employees to extend the same care to customers. Additionally, non-customer-facing teams should understand how their work impacts the overall experience, aligning every department around a unified, customer-centric approach.

By embedding empathy at every level and ensuring employees have the support they need, businesses create deeper connections, improve customer satisfaction, and build lasting loyalty.

Actionable Tips for Improving Customer Experience Through Empathy

Develop training programs that focus on emotional intelligence and active listening skills. Employees should be able to recognize emotional cues—both verbal and non-verbal—and respond in a way that shows genuine understanding. These programs can include:

SCENARIO-BASED LEARNING

Using role-playing exercises allows employees to practice responding to a range of customer emotions, including frustration, confusion, or excitement. By simulating real-life customer interactions, staff can refine their communication styles and problem-solving approaches, ensuring they adapt to the emotional states of different customers. These exercises provide a safe environment for employees to build confidence and develop the skills necessary to navigate complex or emotionally charged situations, ultimately enhancing their ability to deliver empathetic and effective service.

EMOTIONAL INTELLIGENCE ASSESSMENTS

Incorporating emotional intelligence assessments into employee development programs helps staff understand their current level of empathy and emotional awareness. These tools provide valuable insights into how employees perceive and respond to emotional cues, enabling targeted growth and improvement. Regularly integrating these assessments into performance evaluations ensures that emotional intelligence remains a focus for continuous learning, empowering employees to build stronger connections with customers and colleagues over time.

Feedback Systems

Implementing robust feedback mechanisms ensures that customers have a platform to express how they felt during their interaction with the brand. Here's how feedback can drive continuous improvement:

SENTIMENT ANALYSIS

This goes beyond capturing what customers say by uncovering how they feel about their interactions with a brand. By analyzing the tone and emotion behind customer feedback, these tools provide valuable insights into areas where empathy might be falling short or where teams are performing exceptionally well. By tracking emotional responses, sentiment analysis helps brands refine their approach and deliver more empathetic and effective service.

CLOSED-LOOP FEEDBACK

Collecting customer feedback is only the first step; acting on it is what drives real improvement. A closed-loop feedback system ensures that insights are shared across relevant teams and that concrete steps are taken to address gaps in empathetic service. For example, if customers frequently express frustration about a specific process, teams can collaborate to identify solutions and implement changes. This approach not only resolves immediate issues but also fosters continuous refinement of customer experience strategies, ensuring that feedback leads to meaningful and lasting improvements.

Customer Journey Mapping With Empathy Lenses

Map out the customer journey while actively considering the emotions customers may experience at each touchpoint. By visualizing the emotional highs and lows throughout the customer's interaction with the brand, companies can identify where additional empathetic support is needed, whether that's in pre-purchase decision-making, post-sale follow-ups, or during problem resolution.

Acknowledging and celebrating customer milestones fosters a deeper emotional connection between the customer and the brand. Such celebrations show customers that a brand values their personal experiences and is attentive to their life events. They act as bright spots in the customer's journey.

What steps can you take?

LEVERAGE CRM TOOLS

CRM tools are invaluable for maintaining detailed records of important customer milestones, such as anniversaries, birthdays, or other significant events. By using CRM software, brands can organize and track this information systematically, ensuring no opportunity to recognize and celebrate these moments is missed. These tools not only help businesses stay organized but also enable them to personalize their approach to customer interactions, fostering a sense of appreciation and connection.

CREATE CUSTOMIZED OUTREACH INITIATIVES
Using the insights from CRM tools, brands can develop highly customized outreach initiatives that resonate with customers on a personal level. For example, sending personalized emails, thoughtful messages, or even physical cards and gifts on special occasions shows customers that they are valued as individuals, not just as transactions. This level of attentiveness strengthens emotional bonds, enhances loyalty, and demonstrates a brand's commitment to building meaningful relationships with its audience. Thoughtful gestures tailored to important dates leave a lasting impression and encourage customers to feel more connected to the brand.

HANDWRITTEN NOTES
Including handwritten thank-you notes in customer packages can leave a lasting impression, particularly for first-time or high-value purchases. This small but thoughtful gesture demonstrates genuine appreciation and adds a personal touch to the customer experience. It shows customers that the brand values their business and takes the time to go beyond automated interactions, creating a deeper emotional connection.

PERSONALIZED RECOMMENDATIONS
Using data analysis to provide personalized recommendations is a powerful way to enhance the customer experience. By leveraging insights about individual preferences and past purchases, brands can suggest products or services that align with each customer's unique needs. This tailored approach not only makes interactions more relevant but also reinforces that the brand understands and values its customers, encouraging repeat business and loyalty.

Cultivate Long-Term Relationships

Building long-term relationships with customers entails a consistent commitment to their satisfaction and success, seeing them as partners rather than transactions.

What steps can you take?

LOYALTY PROGRAMS

Establishing comprehensive loyalty programs is a proven way to encourage repeat business while making customers feel valued. These programs reward customers for their continued engagement with the brand, offering incentives such as discounts, exclusive access, or special perks. By recognizing and appreciating their loyalty, brands can strengthen emotional connections and motivate customers to remain engaged, fostering a deeper, long-term relationship.

REGULAR CHECK-INS

Proactively scheduling regular check-ins with customers, especially after significant purchases or services, demonstrates a commitment to their satisfaction. These touchpoints provide an opportunity to address any potential issues before they escalate and to ensure the customer is happy with their experience. Regular follow-ups not only improve customer satisfaction but also show that the brand values their input and cares about maintaining a positive relationship.

COMMUNITY BUILDING

Creating spaces for customers to connect with the brand and with each other fosters a strong sense of community and belonging. Whether through forums, special events, or online groups, these initiatives encourage meaningful interactions that extend beyond transactions. A thriving community not only deepens loyalty but also transforms customers into advocates, strengthening the overall connection with the brand. By nurturing these relationships, brands can build a supportive network that reinforces trust and long-term engagement.

Customer Engagement and Delight

Brand affinity and loyalty are not just about delivering great products but also about how brands engage and delight their customers consistently.

Maslow's Hierarchy of Needs posits that human behavior is motivated by needs ranging from the fulfillment of the most basic physiological necessities to the more complex psychological needs for esteem and self-actualization.[5] This model can be mirrored in brand loyalty, where basic customer expectations must first be met before more nuanced and emotionally driven engagements can become loyalty.

Expanding on Maslow's foundational concept, I've crafted a version illustrating the Hierarchy of Customer Delight (Figure 6.1), which suggests a layered approach to engaging customers. At its base, the model insists on product reliability and functional customer support—akin to Maslow's physiological and safety needs. It then ascends to encompass responsive communication and personalized experiences fostering belonging, and culminates in shared values and emotional resonance, paralleling Maslow's esteem and self-actualization stages.

Effective customer engagement requires a diverse, multichannel approach wherein interactions aren't limited to transactions or service issues but extend to regular and meaningful communication. Brands that "show up" not just when there's a glaring need or during promotional periods but consistently across the customer lifecycle, lay a strong foundation for trust and affinity.

As Tristan Lombard, developer and engineering community builder and consultant, shares, empathy doesn't work in a vacuum. "Get your teams more comfortable in front of the camera and send short videos to your customers. I know this doesn't always scale, but it's important in an async world for others to see you. And the same goes for those building customer champion programs. I am an introvert moonlighting as an extrovert, but how am I supposed to get my sweet nerdy devs and engineers in front of cameras and advocating for the value of our products if I cannot post in the community and on social media? In addition, brands need to step up and acknowledge the events going on in the world. This is hard when it feels like everything is in a spiral, but being a beacon of light, understanding the pains of customers, and modeling what empathy looks like can really help humanize brands and make customers feel empowered to lift others too. For example, think about anti-trans laws being passed and companies staying silent. Remember that per Forbes, LGBTQIA+ global purchasing power this year sits at $3.9 trillion and will only continue to grow.[6] In addition, 78 percent surveyed say they will switch or consider switching companies based on their stance on these issues."

Empowerment Through Knowledge

Brands that empower their customers with knowledge, be it through informative content, user-friendly tools, or responsive customer education, enable them to make informed choices. This not only boosts the customer's confidence in their decisions but also in the brand facilitating those decisions.

FIGURE 6.1 The Hierarchy of Customer Delight (an adaptation of Maslow's Hierarchy of Needs)

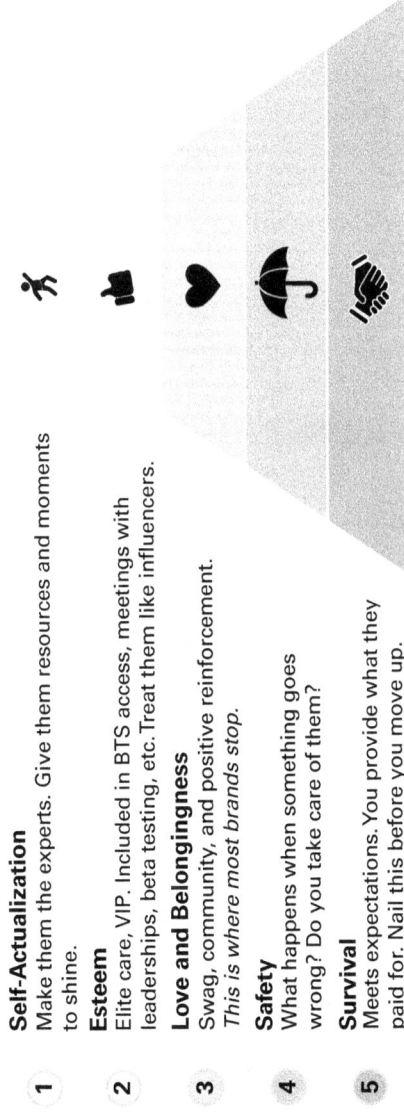

1 Self-Actualization
Make them the experts. Give them resources and moments to shine.

2 Esteem
Elite care, VIP. Included in BTS access, meetings with leaderships, beta testing, etc. Treat them like influencers.

3 Love and Belongingness
Swag, community, and positive reinforcement. *This is where most brands stop.*

4 Safety
What happens when something goes wrong? Do you take care of them?

5 Survival
Meets expectations. You provide what they paid for. Nail this before you move up.

SOURCE Adapted from: A. H. Maslow. A theory of human motivation, *Psychological Review*, 1943, 50(4), 370–96. psycnet.apa.org/record/1943-03751-001

The virtuous cycle of engagement, characterized by deliberation and empathy, adapts Maslow's psychological theories into actionable customer service strategies that go beyond mere satisfaction to true delight and loyalty. Through genuine engagement that respects both foundational and higher-level needs, brands can cultivate a loyal customer base that not only believes in the product but also in the ethos of the brand itself.

Ultimately, true brand affinity and loyalty are achieved not just by meeting needs but by anticipating them, delighting consistently across every interaction, and fostering a culture of safety, transparency, and shared values. This not only ensures a robust customer–brand relationship but also transforms customers into passionate advocates and stewards of the brand's ongoing legacy.

KEY TAKEAWAYS

- **The little things matter:** A personalized touch, handwritten note, or empathetic gesture can leave lasting impressions.

- **CX is about anticipation:** The best brands think ahead, understanding customer needs before customers even voice them.

- **Be human, always:** In an era of digital transactions, maintaining a human connection remains vital.

- **Every interaction is an opportunity:** From product delivery to post-sale support, each touchpoint shapes the customer relationship.

Notes

1   J. Wiklund. Case study: Celebrity-backed limited time offerings boost McDonald's revenue, The Food Institute, August 4, 2021. foodinstitute.com/focus/case-study-celebrity-backed-limited-time-offerings-boost-mcdonalds-revenue/ (archived at perma.cc/AW2S-YMYK)

2   S. Rudge. McDonald's WcDonald's: A masterclass in engagement, Food Chain Magazine, 2024. foodchainmagazine.com/news/mcdonalds-wcdonalds-a-masterclass-in-engagement/ (archived at perma.cc/T4VC-BXFG)

3   K. Trafecante. Patagonia ownership, CNN Business, September 14, 2022. www.cnn.com/2022/09/14/business/patagonia-ownership/index.html (archived at perma.cc/8RSB-NHH6)

4 C. Garnett. Are you not entertained? Pop-Tarts once again brings spectacle to bowl games, Campaign Live, 2024. www.campaignlive.com/article/not-entertained-pop-tarts-once-again-brings-spectacle-bowl-games/1900912 (archived at perma.cc/NP66-2C2B)

5 A. H. Maslow. A theory of human motivation, *Psychological Review*, 1943, 50(4), 370–96. psycnet.apa.org/record/1943-03751-001 (archived at https://perma.cc/M3SB-LH2D)

6 C. Murray. Companies blasted for supporting Pride last year—like Nike and Target—appear to pull back in 2024, Forbes, June 5, 2024. www.forbes.com/sites/conormurray/2024/06/05/companies-blasted-for-supporting-pride-last-year-like-nike-and-target-appear-to-pull-back-in-2024 (archived at perma.cc/QMU7-TMA7)

7

What Does Success Look Like?

The Metrics That Matter

You can do incredible work but, let's be honest, you need the data to show you are successful. Leadership doesn't want to hear that you "run on vibes."

Understanding and tracking the right metrics is key to evaluating success. This chapter focuses on the critical metrics companies should track, the balance between qualitative and quantitative metrics, and the role of real-time data and analytics in driving strategic decisions and improvements.

Critical Metrics for Evaluating Customer Relationship Strategies

When it comes to assessing the success of customer relationship strategies, several key performance indicators stand out. These metrics provide insightful data that helps organizations measure and enhance their customer relationship efforts. Here are some of the critical metrics:

- Customer lifetime value: CLV measures the total revenue a business can reasonably expect from a single customer account throughout the business relationship. It's a critical metric because it helps companies understand the long-term value of their customers and allocate resources efficiently.

- Net promoter score: NPS gauges customer loyalty by asking customers how likely they are to recommend a company's product or service to others. It is a strong indicator of customer satisfaction and potential for growth.

- Customer retention rate: CRR indicates the percentage of customers a company retains over a specific period. High retention rates generally signify strong customer loyalty and successful relationship management.

- First contact resolution: FCR measures the percentage of customer service inquiries resolved during the first contact. It's a critical metric for assessing the efficiency and effectiveness of customer support.

- Customer effort score: CES measures the effort required by customers to interact with a company, resolve issues, make a purchase, or utilize a service. It is typically measured by asking customers to rate the ease of their experience on a scale, such as "How easy was it to get your issue resolved today?"

- Continuous improvement/continuous delivery (or deployment) health: CI/CD health refers to the overall effectiveness, efficiency, and reliability of a company's continuous improvement/continuous delivery (deployment) practices. In the context of customer relationship strategies, CI/CD health is a critical metric that can directly influence customer satisfaction, product quality, and delivery speed.

Tristan Lombard sees CI/CD health as a core KPI to monitor. "People will say NPS, but that's just a comfort blanket for C-suite and those beholden to board and investors. Risk of churn has always been it for me. No question. And that can vary depending on your organization. For my field, it has most likely been reflected in their CI/CD health score and the time to deployment."

Balancing Qualitative and Quantitative Metrics

Quantitative and qualitative metrics, when combined, offer a comprehensive view of customer relationships that is greater than the sum of its parts. Quantitative data such as sales figures, retention rates, and lifetime value metrics provide concrete evidence of business performance. They answer the question "What is happening?"

Meanwhile, qualitative metrics like customer satisfaction (CSAT) and engagement offer deeper insights into the emotional and experiential aspects of customer interactions. Qualitative answers the question, "Why is it happening?"

CSAT measures how satisfied customers are with a company's products or services. This feedback is invaluable as it highlights areas that require enhancement and can serve as an early warning system for potential issues that could affect customer loyalty.

While your revenue numbers might be decreasing or your customer churn numbers might be increasing, those numbers alone can't explain why it's happening. You need qualitative data to provide that so you can then take action to right the ship and save your revenue and customer relationships.

Understanding Customer Metrics

When it comes to measuring customer experience, several key metrics provide insight into how customers interact with a brand, their satisfaction, and their potential value over time. Understanding these metrics and their components can guide businesses in making data-driven decisions to improve customer relationships and overall business performance.

Customer Lifetime Value

CLV is one of the most critical metrics in assessing the long-term profitability of a customer. CLV is a projection of the total revenue a customer is expected to generate throughout their relationship with a company. This metric is broken down into several key components, each contributing to the overall calculation of CLV.

Average purchase value is the first key component of CLV. It is calculated by dividing the total revenue by the number of purchases over a specific period. This provides insight into how much a customer spends on average, giving a foundation for future revenue predictions. The higher the average purchase value, the more lucrative the customer relationship is.

Another important component is purchase frequency, which reflects how often a customer buys from the business within a given timeframe. This is determined by dividing the number of purchases by the number of unique customers over the same period. High purchase frequency indicates a loyal customer base, which is essential for predicting sustained revenue streams.

Customer lifespan helps estimate the duration of the relationship between the customer and the business. By calculating the average number of years a customer continues to make purchases, companies can estimate how long they can expect to benefit from each customer relationship, which is vital for projecting total lifetime value.

Finally, gross margin is crucial for understanding profitability. It is calculated by subtracting the cost of goods sold (COGS) from total revenue, then dividing the result by total revenue. This component ensures that businesses focus not just on revenue but on the actual profit generated by each customer, allowing companies to prioritize customers who contribute most to the bottom line.

CLV is essential for effective resource allocation because it helps identify which customer segments are most valuable and worth additional investment. It also informs marketing strategies, enabling targeted campaigns focused on high-value customers, and aids in product development by guiding priorities based on the needs and preferences of these customers. Monitoring metrics like revenue per customer, churn rate, and customer acquisition cost (CAC) ensures a sustainable balance between customer acquisition and retention.

Net Promoter Score

NPS is another pivotal metric that provides insight into customer satisfaction and loyalty. It categorizes customers into three groups: promoters, passives, and detractors, based on how likely they are to recommend the company to others.

Promoters are customers who score the business 9 or 10 on a scale of 0–10, indicating high satisfaction and a strong likelihood to advocate for the brand. They are the drivers of positive word-of-mouth, which can lead to new customer acquisition and repeat business. In contrast, passives score 7–8. While they are generally satisfied, they are not enthusiastic enough to promote the business and are more susceptible to switching to competitors if they find a better offer. Detractors, who score 0–6, are dissatisfied and pose a risk to the company's reputation. They may spread negative feedback and actively discourage potential customers from engaging with the brand.

It's easy to fall into a trap here, though. Many companies will immediately engage with the lower scores as those customers are the highest churn risk, and they might even reach out to the top scores to get customer stories and testimonials. The trap is completely ignoring the middle scores. Those customers are the next to churn or the next to become brand advocates, but if you ignore them they will feel ignored and only slip further into dissatisfaction.

The overall NPS is calculated by subtracting the percentage of detractors from the percentage of promoters. A higher NPS indicates strong customer loyalty and satisfaction. Response rate is another critical metric, as it shows how many customers are willing to provide feedback. Additionally, tracking follow-up actions based on NPS results can reveal how effectively businesses respond to customer concerns and whether these actions improve satisfaction.

To improve NPS, businesses can implement a customer feedback loop, ensuring that feedback is addressed swiftly. Employee training enhances customer service interactions, and product improvements based on customer feedback can further boost satisfaction.

Customer Retention Rate

Customer retention rate measures how well a company retains its existing customers over a specific period. Retention is crucial for maintaining a stable customer base and reducing churn. To calculate retention, businesses first identify the existing customers at the start of a period, which serves as a baseline. They also track new customers acquired during the period to differentiate between retained and newly acquired customers. Finally, the customers remaining at the end of the period represents the net number of customers after accounting for churn and new acquisitions.

Retention is highly correlated with cost efficiency because retaining an existing customer is generally less costly than acquiring a new one. A high retention rate also indicates strong customer loyalty, suggesting that customers are satisfied and willing to continue their relationship with the company.

Key metrics to monitor in relation to retention include the churn rate, which is inversely related to retention and offers insight into customer loss. The repeat purchase rate reveals how frequently customers return to make additional purchases, and customer interaction frequency shows how often they engage with the brand. Businesses can improve retention by implementing loyalty programs, providing personalized communication, and enhancing customer support to resolve issues quickly and effectively.

First Contact Resolution

FCR measures the efficiency of a company's customer support by tracking the percentage of customer issues that are resolved during the first interaction. A high FCR rate reflects operational efficiency and customer satisfaction, as it demonstrates that the company can address issues without the need for multiple interactions. Conversely, a high number of follow-up requests suggests inefficiencies or resource constraints within the support team.

FCR is closely tied to customer satisfaction, because customers appreciate fast and effective issue resolution. It also impacts operational efficiency, as resolving issues on the first contact reduces the workload on support teams, allowing them to handle more inquiries.

Key metrics to monitor include the FCR rate, average handling time (AHT) for resolving issues, and CSAT specifically for first-contact interactions. Strategies to improve FCR involve investing in training programs to equip support staff with the necessary skills, developing a comprehensive knowledge base for quick issue resolution, and empowering teams to resolve issues without escalations.

Customer Effort Score

CES measures how easy it is for customers to interact with a business or resolve their issues. Ease of resolution is a key component, and a lower effort score indicates a smoother experience for the customer, which directly impacts their satisfaction and loyalty. Interaction simplicity refers to how straightforward it is for customers to navigate the company's processes. Complex or frustrating interactions can lead to dissatisfaction and increased churn.

A low CES often correlates with higher customer satisfaction and serves as a strong loyalty indicator because customers who experience effortless interactions are more likely to return and recommend the business to others. Metrics to monitor include the CES score, correlation with CSAT, and resolution time, as faster resolutions typically lead to lower effort for the customer.

To improve CES, businesses can focus on simplifying processes, such as streamlining customer support workflows, and integrating systems to reduce redundant information requests. Proactive support is also critical, as anticipating and addressing common customer issues before they arise reduces the overall effort required by the customer. Identify where there is friction throughout the customer journey and see what you can lessen or remove.

Continuous Improvement/Continuous Delivery (or Deployment) Health

In the context of customer experience, the health of a company's CI/CD processes plays a significant role in maintaining product quality and stability. Process efficiency is a critical component, measured by metrics such as build and deployment frequency and cycle time—the time it takes from code commit to deployment. A shorter cycle time reflects a more agile and responsive CI/CD pipeline.

Automation and testing are essential for maintaining a high-quality CI/CD process. Test automation coverage tracks how much of the codebase is covered by automated tests, with higher coverage reducing the likelihood of bugs or errors. The build success rate measures the percentage of successful builds, indicating stability and reliability in the deployment process.

Quality and stability are further evaluated through metrics like the incidence rate (post-deployment incidents or failures) and rollback frequency (how often releases need to be rolled back). A low incidence rate and fewer rollbacks signal a well-functioning CI/CD system.

Monitoring these metrics helps companies maintain customer trust and satisfaction by ensuring the rapid, reliable delivery of new features and fixes.

Strategies to improve CI/CD health include investing in automation, continuously monitoring for areas of improvement, and fostering cross-functional collaboration between development, operations, and customer-facing teams to align product updates with customer needs.

Social Brand Sentiment

CX and customer support (CS) have access to a lot of the metrics we've mentioned above, but with siloed companies these teams are not necessarily collaborating with the social team and getting access to the social listening and sentiment data that is visible to potential customers who are scrolling online. This data must be visible and added to the CX 360-view to understand their customers from a holistic and omnichannel approach.

How is the brand perceived as a singular brand? In comparison to competitors? Do you have active advocates who recommend you when someone asks for brands to consider for their problem(s)?

CSAT Strategies for B2B and B2C

Business-to-business (B2B) and business-to-consumer (B2C) refer to two different types of commercial relationships and approaches. In B2B, companies sell products or services directly to other businesses, typically focusing on building long-term relationships, offering personalized support, and addressing specific organizational needs. B2B transactions are often more complex, involving multiple decision-makers, longer sales cycles, and customized solutions. B2C, on the other hand, involves businesses selling directly to individual consumers, where the focus is on meeting immediate needs, enhancing user experience, and driving brand loyalty. B2C sales are generally faster and more transaction-based, often leveraging broad marketing strategies and emotional appeals to attract a larger customer base. While B2B emphasizes value, efficiency, and return on investment (ROI) for businesses, B2C aims at convenience, personalization, and satisfying the personal preferences of consumers.

For B2B, deploy CSAT surveys following key milestones in the customer journey, such as post-implementation or after support interactions. Given the often complex nature of B2B relationships, these surveys should include open-ended questions that allow clients to provide feedback on specific aspects of their experience.

For B2C, integrate CSAT surveys into various points of the consumer journey, especially after purchase and customer support interactions. For B2C markets, quick and simple rating scales (like star ratings or emoji scales) can increase response rates and provide fast, actionable data.

One of the most effective ways to improve customer experience is by gathering and acting on feedback in a timely and meaningful manner. The key to leveraging feedback lies not only in collecting it but also in taking swift and targeted actions to address concerns. Here are two crucial tactics that can significantly enhance customer relationships and satisfaction:

REAL-TIME FEEDBACK

Implementing real-time feedback tools is a powerful tactic for capturing customer sentiment during or immediately after service delivery. The immediacy of real-time feedback allows businesses to gauge customer reactions at the most critical touchpoints when emotions are still fresh and unfiltered. This provides a more authentic and accurate reflection of the customer's experience compared to feedback gathered long after the interaction has occurred. Real-time feedback can be collected through various channels, such as in-app surveys, text message prompts, or feedback widgets embedded on websites or within customer service portals. By acting on this immediate feedback, companies can address minor issues before they escalate into larger problems, reinforcing the customer's sense of being heard and valued. Additionally, this approach helps businesses quickly identify trends or recurring issues that can be addressed proactively.

FOLLOW-UP ACTIONS ON FEEDBACK

While collecting feedback is crucial, the true value lies in the follow-up actions taken in response to that feedback, particularly when it comes to addressing negative responses. When customers take the time to voice their dissatisfaction, it presents a unique opportunity for businesses to turn a negative experience into a positive one by showing that they care about the customer's concerns. Prompt follow-up actions not only help resolve the specific issue but also demonstrate the company's commitment to customer satisfaction, which can lead to improved brand perception and loyalty. This proactive approach can often transform unhappy customers into loyal advocates. Moreover, consistently following up on feedback—whether positive or negative—sends a message to customers that their opinions matter and are integral to the company's continuous improvement efforts.

Together, real-time feedback and thoughtful follow-up actions form a dynamic feedback loop that fosters stronger customer relationships. By addressing issues swiftly and showing a genuine commitment to resolving concerns, businesses can enhance their reputation, boost customer loyalty, and ultimately improve their overall customer experience.

Customer Engagement

Customer engagement tracks how actively customers interact with a brand across various channels, such as social media, newsletters, or website visits. High levels of engagement typically indicate a strong emotional connection, which can predict long-term loyalty and advocacy.

STRATEGIES FOR B2B AND B2C

For B2B, focus on creating value-driven content, such as whitepapers, webinars, and case studies, that resonates with business clients. Engaging B2B clients often involves providing solutions to their business problems through thought leadership and industry insights.

For B2C, leverage interactive content, contests, and personalized communication via emails or social media to boost engagement. Consumer brands can benefit significantly from creating vibrant community spaces where customers can interact with the brand and each other.

TACTICS

To maximize customer engagement and satisfaction, businesses need to employ a range of tactics that integrate data-driven insights with strategic actions. One key approach is the segmentation of customer audiences based on data. By analyzing customer demographics, behaviors, and preferences, companies can create tailored engagement strategies that resonate with different types of customers. Personalized content and targeted messaging not only improve the relevance of communication but also increase the likelihood of engagement across diverse customer segments. The effectiveness of these strategies can be further amplified by using engagement metrics tools such as Google Analytics, CRM systems, or specialized engagement platforms. These tools enable businesses to measure customer interactions with precision, allowing for iterative optimization of engagement tactics based on real-time data.

Integrating Metrics for a Holistic View

A comprehensive understanding of customer behavior requires integrating various data points into a unified view. Dashboard integration plays a crucial role in this, as it allows businesses to combine both qualitative and quantitative metrics on a single platform. These integrated dashboards offer a complete picture of customer health and overall business performance, enabling decision-makers to identify trends and patterns quickly. To deepen this analysis, businesses can also perform data correlation analysis, which helps to reveal relationships between qualitative factors—such as customer satisfaction—and quantitative outcomes, like churn rates or average order value. Understanding these correlations allows companies to predict how improvements in customer experience might impact revenue and long-term loyalty.

Strategic Decision-Making

The integration of both qualitative and quantitative insights can significantly enhance strategic decision-making across product development and marketing efforts. These combined insights ensure that product or service development is aligned with actual customer preferences and behaviors. Additionally, aligning strategies between marketing and customer service is essential for maintaining consistency in customer experience. By sharing data-driven insights across departments, companies can ensure that both teams understand the key factors influencing customer satisfaction and overall business outcomes, resulting in more cohesive and effective strategies.

Data-Driven Decision-Making

Real-time data and analytics are transforming how businesses in both B2B and B2C sectors enhance customer relationships and drive loyalty. These tools offer a multitude of opportunities for companies to act swiftly, make informed decisions, and tailor experiences to meet the evolving needs of their customers. Here is an expanded view on how real-time analytics can be turned into actionable strategies that benefit both B2B and B2C brands.

Immediate Insights Into Customer Behavior

Real-time behavior tracking lets businesses quickly adapt to changes in customer preferences and market dynamics. For B2B enterprises, where sales cycles are longer and transactions are typically larger, understanding client needs as they evolve can lead to better service and product alignment. For B2C companies, quick adaptations to consumer behavior can greatly enhance the customer journey and increase retention rates.

TOOLS AND TACTICS

For B2B, use analytics tools to track client interaction across digital platforms like LinkedIn or industry-specific forums to adjust marketing and sales strategies accordingly.

For B2C, implement real-time tracking on e-commerce platforms to monitor changes in consumer behavior, adjusting marketing tactics and inventory in response to emerging trends.

Proactive Issue Resolution

Identifying and addressing issues before they become problematic is crucial. B2B relationships often hinge on trust and reliability; resolving issues swiftly can strengthen these aspects. For B2C brands, quickly resolving issues prevents negative reviews and enhances customer satisfaction, directly impacting loyalty.

TOOLS AND TACTICS

For B2B, set up systems to alert account managers about service disruptions or delays in project timelines, allowing for immediate client communication and problem-solving.

For B2C, use real-time data to monitor customer satisfaction across helpdesk inquiries and social media. Automated tools can alert teams to spikes in complaint volumes, triggering fast responses.

Personalized Interactions

Both B2B and B2C sectors can benefit enormously from personalizing interactions based on the analysis of real-time data.

TOOLS AND TACTICS

For B2B, leverage CRM systems to create client profiles that update in real time with information from interactions, email exchanges, and social media engagements. Use this data to tailor communications, proposals, and product demonstrations to specific client needs and preferences.

For B2C, use customer data from past purchases and online behavior to offer personalized product recommendations, discounts, and content, thereby enhancing the shopping experience and increasing sales conversions.

Dynamic Loyalty Programs

Tailoring loyalty programs based on customer engagement and purchase behavior ensures that rewards remain relevant and effective at fostering loyalty.

TOOLS AND TACTICS

For B2B, implement tiered loyalty programs that reward long-term clients with exclusive benefits such as access to beta products, extended warranties, or customizable service packages.

For B2C, use customer purchase data to offer personalized rewards programs, which could include points systems, special birthday rewards, or early access to new products.

Predictive Analytics

Predictive analytics can forecast future buying patterns based on real-time data, enabling companies to better prepare and customize their approaches.

TOOLS AND TACTICS

For B2B, use predictive models to identify potential upsell or cross-sell opportunities and to assess customer risk profiles.

For B2C, predict consumer trends and likely purchases, dynamically adjusting marketing campaigns and stock levels to align with predicted demands.

Summary

By harnessing the power of real-time data and analytics, both B2B and B2C brands can transform their approach to customer relationships. B2B companies can strengthen their client partnerships through personalized and proactive engagements while B2C brands can enhance the consumer experience through immediacy and personalization. This strategic use of data not only improves customer satisfaction but also drives loyalty, setting the foundation for sustained business success in all market sectors.

KEY TAKEAWAYS

- **Measuring customer success begins with the right metrics:** Effective customer relationship management relies on tracking the right metrics, which provide insights into both immediate performance and long-term success.

- **Customer lifetime value for strategic focus:** CLV reveals the total revenue potential from a customer, helping businesses allocate resources effectively by identifying high-value customer segments.

- **Net promoter score as a loyalty indicator:** NPS assesses customer satisfaction and likelihood to recommend, categorizing customers as promoters, passives, or detractors, offering a clear measure of brand sentiment.

- **Customer retention rate reflects loyalty:** A high retention rate shows strong customer relationships, reducing the need for constant acquisition efforts and highlighting areas that strengthen loyalty.

- **First contact resolution measures service efficiency:** FCR indicates how effectively support teams address issues on the first try, impacting customer satisfaction and operational efficiency.

- **Customer effort score enhances experience tracking:** CES evaluates how easy it is for customers to interact with the brand, emphasizing simplicity in resolving issues and a smooth customer journey.

- **Continuous improvement/continuous delivery (or deployment) health reflects product reliability and quality:** CI/CD health metrics ensure that development cycles are efficient and stable, directly influencing customer satisfaction by providing a reliable product experience.

- **Balancing qualitative and quantitative insights:** Combining quantitative metrics (sales, retention) with qualitative data (customer satisfaction, engagement) offers a complete understanding of customer relationships, answering both "what" and "why."

- **Customer feedback drives improvement:** Real-time and post-interaction feedback helps brands act quickly to resolve issues and adapt services based on real customer experiences.

- **Proactive follow-up strengthens customer trust:** Addressing feedback promptly shows commitment to customer satisfaction, helping to retain customers and foster positive brand perception.

- **Dashboard integration for unified insights:** A centralized dashboard that combines different metrics provides a holistic view, supporting swift decision-making based on both customer health and business performance.

- **Data-driven personalization enhances engagement:** Real-time data enables tailored interactions for both B2B and B2C, from personalized recommendations to targeted loyalty programs, driving deeper customer connections.

- **Predictive analytics anticipate customer needs:** Leveraging predictive models helps businesses forecast behaviors and preferences, allowing for proactive adjustments in marketing and inventory.

- **Strategic loyalty programs based on data:** By analyzing engagement, brands can craft dynamic loyalty programs that resonate with customers, increasing retention and satisfaction.

- **Feedback loops lead to continuous improvement:** Regular, thoughtful follow-up on feedback fosters stronger relationships, builds trust, and helps businesses remain agile and responsive to evolving customer needs.

8

The Storytellers

Creating Content That Captivates

Storytelling has long been a core part of human communication. In marketing and content creation, storytelling helps brands build emotional connections with their customers by engaging them on a deeper level. This chapter explores the power of storytelling, effective examples, essential elements of compelling narratives, authenticity in brand storytelling, and the role of various content formats in captivating audiences.

The Power of Storytelling for Building Emotional Connections

Storytelling in marketing is about more than just conveying information; it's about creating a narrative that resonates emotionally with the audience. Stories can evoke a wide range of emotions, helping to establish a personal connection between the brand and the customer. By integrating storytelling into marketing strategies, brands can make their messages more memorable, relatable, and impactful.

It's a powerful tool for engagement and for inspiring emotion that fosters preferred behaviors, whether that be purchasing, engaging, sharing, or following along with future content.

According to Ted Harrison, former Head of Production at Twitter/X and current CEO and Founder of neuemotion, "Humans have been telling stories for north of 30,000 years. For the longest time, history itself was only passed through the verbal recounting of tales of ancestors passed from one generation to the next. If there were a Periodic Table of Human Elements, storytelling might very well be the third one listed on the chart after water and fire. Telling stories activates the human imagination in a way that moves people to grief, joy, and every advertiser's favorite word: action. It's a built-in mechanism for human bonding."

Elements of a Compelling Brand Story That Resonates

Brands seeking to create connection and emotional resonance with their audience tend to incorporate storytelling into their brand messaging. Storytelling can not only encourage an emotional response but can also be significantly more memorable. That emotional resonance not only means that the viewer is more likely to do an action because of that emotion, but they are also more likely to recall it later. That makes storytelling a must for companies who want to stay in the hearts and minds of their audience.

By tapping into fundamental human experiences, storytelling becomes a vital strategy for brands aiming to cultivate connection and brand recall. Compelling brand stories share several key elements that make them emotionally resonant and impactful.

Authenticity

Authenticity forms the bedrock of effective storytelling. Consumers are drawn to stories that feel genuine and honest. Authentic stories build trust and credibility by aligning the brand's message with its core values and mission.

It's important not to get lost in the idea of storytelling as simply a tactic. Ted Harrison finds that "everyone gets caught up in the romanticism of storytelling itself when it comes to using it in their marketing efforts: storytelling for the sake of saying they told a story. Anyone who paid any attention at all in their literature studies knows that the best works were never about telling stories, but rather the human experience. Brands that dig deeply into the humanity and lived experiences of their audiences tell the best stories that achieve their objectives while simultaneously not sucking the soul out of telling one. This is the difference between storytelling as a tactic vs. storytelling as connection. Brands must be human first, always."

Determining the brand's personality is a crucial step in starting the storytelling process from an authentic perspective. According to Vikki Ross, a copy writing, brand, and tone-of-voice expert and consultant, "A brand needs a personality. It informs who they are, why they do what they do, what they say and how they say it. And all of that helps their audience get to know them and decide if they like them and want to spend time and money with them.

"Think about all the products that exist in the world. So many are so similar, so it's the brand that the product comes from that people buy into. Sure, the product probably comes first, but it's the brand that will keep people coming back to that product. It's the brand that makes people feel something. Confident, excited, invited, inspired, motivated, powerful, sophisticated…"

Emotional Appeal

Emotions are quite literally the heart of storytelling. Stories that evoke happiness, nostalgia, inspiration, or even sadness are more likely to be remembered and cherished by audiences. Emotional appeal can turn a mundane marketing message into a powerful narrative that leaves a lasting impact. By tapping into universal emotions, brands create stories that resonate on a personal level, making their message more memorable and influential.

Clear Message

A compelling brand story conveys a clear and consistent message that aligns with the brand's mission and vision. This clarity ensures that the story is easily understood and relatable, allowing the audience to connect with the brand's purpose. A well-defined message provides cohesion and direction to the narrative, making it more effective in communicating the brand's values. Apple's storytelling consistently revolves around themes of innovation and simplicity, clearly conveying their mission to "think different."[1]

Having a clear message and then sharing it consistently makes it stick. A cohesive message that aligns with the brand's core values and vision reinforces trustworthiness and reliability. This means that the tone, style, and substance of the brand's stories should be uniform whether communicated via social media, email newsletters, advertisements, or in-person interactions.

Consistency helps build a recognizable and dependable brand image. Patagonia exemplifies this by consistently communicating its dedication to environmentalism across all its channels, ensuring their message resonates and remains credible.

Relatable Characters

Characters bring a story to life and incorporating relatable characters can significantly enhance a brand's storytelling efforts. These characters can be customers, employees, or even fictional personas that embody the brand's values. By showcasing characters that the audience can identify with, brands create a personal connection that humanizes their message. Nike's use of real athletes that their customers love makes their campaigns more memorable and easier to root for. These characters personify the brand's ethos of perseverance and determination. Something and someone to aspire to.

Highlighting real customer stories adds a significant layer of authenticity. User-generated content and testimonials are powerful tools to provide genuine and impactful narratives. Customers sharing their personal experiences with a brand can evoke a strong emotional response from others who see these stories as credible and relatable. Encouraging customers to share their stories not only democratizes the brand's narrative but also fosters a community of engaged advocates.

Influencing Consumer Behavior Through Storytelling

Storytelling is not just about captivating the audience; it also serves as a strategic tool to influence consumer behavior. By weaving narratives that reflect the aspirations, challenges, and values of their target audience, brands can guide consumers toward desired actions. Stories create a context in which the brand's products or services become the solution to the audience's needs and desires.

Showing what happens behind the curtains can humanize a brand and make it more approachable. Sharing behind-the-scenes content about how products are made, who makes them, or insights into the company culture can cultivate a sense of transparency and trust. This content can take the form of video documentaries, photo essays, or blog posts that go into the daily workings of the brand.

Creating a Community Through Shared Stories

Effective storytelling can also foster a sense of community among customers. When consumers see their own stories reflected in a brand's narrative, it creates a feeling of belonging and solidarity. This communal bond can be strengthened through interactive storytelling methods, such as user-generated content, where customers share their experiences with the brand.

Authentic storytelling can also include the positive impact a brand has on society. By highlighting real-life stories of how the brand's efforts in social responsibility, sustainability, or community service have made a tangible difference, brands can build a powerful, emotionally resonant narrative. These stories should focus on real people and communities benefiting from the brand's initiatives, avoiding any semblance of self-promotion.

Continuous Engagement and Active Listening

Engaging continuously with your audience and actively listening to their feedback can enhance storytelling authenticity. By responding to comments, participating in discussions, and adapting based on customer feedback, brands show they value their customers' voices. This engagement should not be a one-time activity but an ongoing process that helps refine the brand's narrative to better reflect the needs and desires of the audience.

Copywriting and branding consultant Vikki Ross sees this engagement as an invitation from the brands. "It's up to brands to invite people in, and to make them feel welcome. To give them something to believe in, and to add value to their lives. If brands are interrupting people on screens in their homes and in their hands, in the pages of their favorite publications, on radios in their cars, and on billboards in their cities, their first objective should be to do so with respect. Brands can't expect to attract attention without earning that attention. And that takes time. Time to write their story, and time to find the right way to tell it."

The Appeal of Nostalgia

Nostalgia has a unique role in storytelling by drawing on positive memories and emotions from the past, helping brands build deeper connections with potential customers. When a story, product, or brand message evokes nostalgia, it can transport customers to comforting, joyful, or simpler times, often tied to meaningful life stages. This emotional recall creates a bond because people naturally trust and feel reassured by experiences that remind them of fond memories.

In brand storytelling, nostalgia makes customers feel understood on a personal level, fostering loyalty and familiarity. Through nostalgic elements in products, packaging, or advertisements, brands create a bridge between the customer's past and present, enhancing relevance and authenticity. This connection often translates into "stickiness"—customers feel compelled to stay with the brand because it taps into a sense of identity, belonging, or comfort. The brand essentially piggybacks off of the positive sentiment someone has around their memories or childhood.

Nostalgia also strengthens brand recall and can inspire word-of-mouth advocacy, as customers are inclined to share products and experiences that resonate with their past. By rooting the brand in these shared cultural or personal memories, nostalgia-driven storytelling reinforces loyalty, encouraging customers to return not only for the product or service but for the familiar, meaningful experience the brand consistently delivers.

The Role of Different Content Formats in Storytelling

While storytelling is important, there are different ways to craft and share those stories. Each content format has unique strengths, offering distinct ways to connect with audiences emotionally and deliver meaningful narratives.

Video is one of the most powerful storytelling tools because of its ability to combine visuals, audio, and motion. It can evoke emotions quickly and capture attention in ways that other formats cannot. Videos are particularly effective for sharing compelling stories on social media platforms, where dynamic and visually engaging content performs well. Whether it's a short emotional clip, a product demonstration, or a behind-the-scenes glimpse into the brand, video content can create an immediate and lasting impact. This is specifically important for brands who know their audience is made up of visual learners.

Podcasts offer a platform for in-depth storytelling and conversations. Unlike videos or social posts, podcasts give brands the opportunity to delve into complex topics or narratives in a conversational and accessible format. They are ideal for sharing brand stories, expert insights, or interviews that engage listeners over longer periods. Podcasts also foster a sense of intimacy, as listeners often tune in during personal moments, like commuting or exercising, making the content feel more direct and personal. This is specifically helpful for brands who know their audience is made up of auditory learners.

Blog posts are well-suited for detailed storytelling that requires context and depth. They are perfect for explaining complex narratives, sharing brand history, or diving into technical subjects that require more elaboration. In addition to their storytelling power, blog posts can be optimized for search engines, making them an effective tool for attracting organic traffic and introducing new audiences to the brand. They provide a platform for educational content, thought leadership, and evergreen stories that can continue to engage readers over time.

Social media excels in delivering bite-sized storytelling that is quick, engaging, and highly shareable. Platforms like Instagram, Twitter/X, and TikTok are perfect for sharing snapshots of a brand's narrative in creative, concise formats. Posts, reels, and stories can capture attention with short, visually compelling content, while live sessions add an interactive element, allowing real-time engagement with the audience. Social media's immediacy and versatility make it an essential format for connecting with diverse customer segments.

Vikki Ross has witnessed first-hand how social media has changed the game for brands and customer connection. "Their brand personality is in full effect over on social media. More than in any of their other marketing channels. Anyone can see they're big on entertainment—they're fans. They don't just tell their audience what's on the platform—any brand can announce details and cast or creator information—they show they're watching with them. They talk about things only fellow fans know. Customers feel like they're sharing an experience with the brand that provides it. Non-customers feel like they might be missing out."

Each content format contributes uniquely to storytelling, and brands can maximize their impact by leveraging these strengths strategically. Whether it's through emotionally charged videos, thought-provoking podcasts, detailed blog posts, or snappy social media updates, selecting the right format for the right audience ensures that the story not only resonates but inspires action.

Exercises to Build Storytelling Skills for Marketing and Engagement

Storytelling is the oldest form of communication, but its relevance in today's marketing and engagement strategies has never been stronger. Brands that use storytelling effectively don't just sell products—they create experiences, foster trust, and build loyalty. A *Harvard Business Review* study found that stories are 22 times more memorable than facts alone, highlighting their power in cutting through the noise of crowded marketplaces.[2]

But where should a brand begin? Whether you're a startup or an established business, the following frameworks offer timeless methods for crafting narratives that connect. Here's how they work—and how to make them work for you.

Five Frameworks for Storytelling and How to Use Them

THE HERO'S JOURNEY[3]
The Hero's Journey, popularized by Joseph Campbell, positions the customer as the hero and the brand as the guide.

To implement the Hero's Journey framework in your storytelling, start by identifying the hero—your customer. Consider their primary struggle or desire, as this will form the emotional core of your narrative. What is it that they truly want to achieve, and what is standing in their way?

Next, define the challenges they face. These obstacles are the tension in your story, the barriers that prevent the hero from reaching their goal.

Understanding these challenges helps you craft a narrative that feels authentic and relatable to your audience.

Once the challenges are clear, position your brand as the guide. This is where your expertise and tools come into play. What do you offer that makes the customer's journey easier or more achievable? By framing your brand as the mentor, you empower the hero to take action.

Finally, illustrate the transformation that occurs when your customer engages with your brand. How does their life improve? Paint a vivid picture of the success or resolution they achieve, showing the tangible and emotional benefits of choosing your brand as their ally.

EXAMPLE

Nike's "Just Do It" campaigns often depict ordinary people overcoming extraordinary odds, with Nike products acting as their trusted guide.[4] While it highlights top athletes, Nike understands that by wearing Nike, anyone can be and feel like an athlete.

THE GOLDEN CIRCLE[5]

Simon Sinek's Golden Circle starts with the "Why"—your brand's purpose—before moving to the "How" (your methods) and the "What" (your products or services). It's a framework rooted in values and purpose, ensuring your storytelling feels authentic and emotionally resonant.

To implement the Golden Circle framework, begin by identifying your "Why." This is the core of your brand's purpose, the driving force behind everything you do beyond profit. Reflect on questions like: What motivates us? Why do we exist as a brand? Defining your "Why" creates a strong foundation for your storytelling, ensuring your message resonates on a deeper emotional level with your audience.

Once your "Why" is clear, move on to clarifying your "How." This step focuses on what makes your approach or process unique. Consider the elements that set you apart from competitors, whether it's innovation, craftsmanship, or a customer-centric philosophy. Understanding your "How" allows you to communicate the distinct value you bring to your customers.

Finally, outline your "What"—the tangible products or services you offer. Ensure that what you provide aligns with your "Why" and reinforces your purpose. This alignment between your offerings and your mission not only strengthens your story but also creates consistency and authenticity in every interaction with your audience.

> **EXAMPLE**
>
> Apple's marketing consistently starts with its "Why"—challenging the status quo through innovation.[6] This foundational purpose offers consistency through all its campaigns, from iPhone launches to sustainability initiatives.

STORYBRAND FRAMEWORK[7]

Donald Miller's StoryBrand framework simplifies storytelling by casting your customer as the protagonist and your brand as the guide. The framework emphasizes clarity: define the customer's problem, offer a clear plan, and show what success looks like.

To implement the StoryBrand framework, start by identifying the problem your customer is facing. Focus on the specific pain points that your brand is solving. What challenges or frustrations are your customers experiencing, and how do these issues impact their lives? By clearly defining the problem, you create a relatable and compelling starting point for your story.

Once the problem is identified, offer a plan that provides a clear and simple path forward. This plan should outline actionable steps your customers can take to engage with your brand and solve their problem. Think of this as a roadmap that removes uncertainty and builds confidence in your ability to guide them toward a solution.

Finally, paint a vivid picture of success. Show how their life will improve after they engage with your brand. What tangible or emotional benefits will they experience? By illustrating the positive outcomes, you give your customers a clear vision of the transformation they can achieve, making your story both inspiring and actionable.

THE PIXAR STORY SPINE FRAMEWORK[8]

Pixar's storytelling framework distills complex narratives into a simple sequence: "Once upon a time… Every day… One day… Because of that… Until finally…" This structure is ideal for brands looking to tell concise and impactful stories.

To implement the Pixar Story Spine framework, begin by setting the scene with "Once upon a time…" This opening establishes the context of your customer's world before your brand entered the picture. Think about what their life looked like at that moment—what challenges they faced, what unmet needs existed, and what routines defined their experience. This step isn't just about describing their situation; it's about understanding the underlying causes of their struggles and the emotional landscape of their daily lives.

Next, introduce the catalyst for change with "One day…" This pivotal moment builds tension and highlights what triggered the customer's need to seek a solution. Was it a sudden challenge, a gradual realization, or an external event that disrupted their status quo? Here, it's crucial to examine the cause-and-effect relationship between the problem and the customer's decision to act. By understanding this turning point, you can frame your brand as the natural and timely answer to their need.

Finally, bring the story to resolution with "Until finally…" This is where you show how your brand transformed the situation, resolving the customer's challenges and creating a better outcome. What was the result of their engagement with your brand, and how did it improve their life? Focus on the emotional and practical effects of this transformation, illustrating the cause-and-effect relationship between your intervention and their success. By connecting the dots, you create a narrative that is both compelling and deeply satisfying.

THE THREE ACT STRUCTURE[9]

Borrowed from classic storytelling, the three act structure is straightforward but powerful: the setup (introduce the problem), the conflict (the struggle), and the resolution (the solution). It's flexible enough to use in everything from brand videos to email campaigns.

To implement the three act structure in your storytelling, begin by defining the setup. This is where you establish the foundation of your story by identifying the problem your brand is solving. Think about the challenges your customers face and how these issues affect their lives. The setup is not just about stating the problem but understanding its root cause and why it matters to your audience. This sets the stage for your narrative and hooks your audience with a relatable starting point.

Next, delve into the conflict, which forms the emotional core of your story. Explore the stakes that make the problem urgent and pressing for your customers. What happens if the issue isn't addressed? What are the potential consequences or missed opportunities? Highlighting these stakes creates tension and a sense of importance, encouraging your audience to engage with the story and seek a resolution.

Finally, resolve the story with a meaningful solution. Show how your brand steps in to address the problem and deliver a transformative outcome. Focus on the tangible and emotional benefits of your solution, illustrating how it alleviates the conflict and improves your customer's life. By connecting the resolution to the initial problem and conflict, you create a cohesive and compelling narrative that resonates with your audience.

EXAMPLE

Volvo's emotional EX90 ad uses this structure, beginning with a woman telling her partner that she's pregnant and this will be their first child (setup). In the background there are cars driving around while the woman is walking around her city.[10] At the same time, her partner is speaking to his mother with the good news, daydreaming about having a daughter and watching her grow up. The woman grabs take-out food and goes to cross the street, just as a Volvo driver is about to hit her (conflict), but the woman is safe, because of course the Volvo was able to stop in time (resolution). It cuts to black with a statement saying: "Sometimes the moments that never happen matter the most." It ends with the man in the hospital, outside the room where his child has just been born. The woman is safe and the life they want to build with their child can happen. It's a powerful story about safety and what can change in the blink of an eye.

Exercises to Build Storytelling Skills

Building storytelling into your marketing and engagement strategies requires intentional effort. Start with empathy mapping to understand what your customers think, feel, see, and do. From there, conduct internal interviews to uncover narratives within your company—milestones, challenges, or customer success stories that reflect your brand values. User-generated content is another goldmine for authentic storytelling; ask customers to share their stories through testimonials or social media.

For a more structured approach, create content pillars—key themes that align with your brand's mission. Storyboarding can then help you visually map these ideas, ensuring they flow naturally across your marketing and engagement strategies. Finally, use role-playing to step into your customer's shoes and experience their journey. This will help you identify pain points and opportunities to engage more meaningfully.

A PROCESS FOR BRANDS TO IMPLEMENT STORYTELLING

To create compelling and effective storytelling for your brand, start by auditing your brand identity. Revisit your mission, values, and purpose to ensure they are clear and well-defined. These foundational insights should guide your storytelling efforts, providing a consistent and authentic voice for your narratives.

Next, invest time in understanding your audience. Use tools such as surveys, focus groups, and data analytics to build detailed customer personas. Go a step further by incorporating empathy mapping, which helps you uncover emotional triggers and understand your audience's thoughts, feelings, and experiences. This understanding is crucial for crafting stories that truly resonate. Collaborate across teams who you know are customer-facing. What can they share about your customers' story that will help craft your narrative?

Once you have a clear sense of your audience and identity, choose a storytelling framework that aligns with your brand's voice and goals. Whether it's the Hero's Journey, the Golden Circle, or another approach, select a structure that fits naturally with your audience's journey and addresses their specific pain points. This alignment ensures that your stories feel both relevant and impactful.

With your framework in place, begin crafting and testing narratives. Develop stories that reflect your chosen structure and test them in small campaigns or with focus groups to gauge their emotional resonance and clarity. Feedback from these tests will help you refine your approach and ensure your stories connect with your audience.

Storytelling doesn't stop with the story itself—it must integrate seamlessly across all channels. Ensure your narrative is consistent at every touchpoint, from social media campaigns to customer service interactions. Consistency builds trust and reinforces your brand's identity across platforms.

Finally, measure and refine your efforts. Use metrics such as engagement rates, customer feedback, and conversions to evaluate the success of your storytelling. Pay attention to what resonates most with your audience and adjust your approach accordingly. Storytelling is an iterative process, and continuous refinement will help you deliver narratives that captivate and inspire.

Storytelling is both an art and a science, but when done right it's transformative. It builds bridges between brands and customers, making every interaction more meaningful. Whether you're crafting a marketing campaign or improving customer engagement, the frameworks and processes outlined here provide a clear roadmap for success. Start small, iterate often, and don't forget: the most powerful stories are the ones where your customers see themselves as the hero.

KEY TAKEAWAYS

- **The power of storytelling:** Storytelling in marketing is crucial for building emotional connections. It goes beyond conveying information to create memorable, relatable, and impactful narratives that resonate with the audience on an emotional level.

- **Act like a fan:** Brands can join the conversation and keep the audience engaged by being part of the discussion, not just prompting it.

- **Key elements of a compelling brand story:** Effective storytelling involves clear structure and emotional resonance. The Pixar Story Spine offers a template: "Once upon a time... And every day... But one day... Because of that... Until finally... And ever since that day..."

- **Authenticity:** Authenticity is essential to connection through storytelling. Consumers are drawn to genuine and honest stories that align with a brand's core values and mission, building trust and loyalty.

- **Emotional appeal:** Emotional appeal is critical in storytelling. Stories that evoke emotions like happiness, nostalgia, inspiration, or even sadness are more likely to be remembered and cherished, creating profound connections with the audience.

- **Clear message:** A compelling brand story must convey a clear and consistent message that aligns with the brand's mission and vision. This clarity ensures that the audience understands and relates to the brand's purpose.

- **Relatable characters:** Characters are central to any story. By incorporating relatable characters—whether customers, employees, or fictional personas—brands can personify their values and create a personal connection with the audience. Consumers want to be able to see themselves with the brand. Is your audience represented in your storytelling and marketing?

- **Influencing consumer behavior:** Storytelling can guide consumer actions by reflecting their aspirations and challenges, positioning the brand's products or services as solutions. This approach can significantly impact purchasing decisions, brand loyalty, and advocacy.

- **Creating a community:** Storytelling fosters a sense of community by highlighting shared experiences and values. Interactive methods like user-generated content can strengthen this communal bond, building a community of loyal advocates.

- **Different content formats:** Leveraging various content formats is key for delivering emotionally resonant stories.

Notes

1   R. Siltanen. The real story behind Apple's "Think Different" campaign, *Forbes*, December 14, 2011. www.forbes.com/sites/onmarketing/2011/12/14/the-real-story-behind-apples-think-different-campaign/ (archived at https://perma.cc/YS2F-8M6H)

2   P. J. Zak. Why your brain loves good storytelling, *Harvard Business Review*, October 2014. hbr.org/2014/10/why-your-brain-loves-good-storytelling (archived at perma.cc/DWC3-M3K3)

3   Joseph Campbell Foundation. Joseph Campbell: The hero's journey, Joseph Campbell Foundation. www.jcf.org/learn/joseph-campbell-heros-journey (archived at perma.cc/V9NE-P7FZ)

4   D. Wieden. 02: Nike (1987) – Just Do It, *Creative Review*, n.d. www. creativereview.co.uk/just-do-it-slogan (archived at https://perma.cc/242J-7DC4)

5   S. Sinek. Golden Circle, Simon Sinek Official Website. simonsinek.com/golden-circle/ (archived at perma.cc/P2P7-8A4T)

6   D. Chaffey. Golden Circle model: Simon Sinek's theory of value proposition "start with why," Smart Insights, January 21, 2024. www.smartinsights.com/digital-marketing-strategy/online-value-proposition/start-with-why-creating-a-value-proposition-with-the-golden-circle-model/ (archived at perma.cc/K2Y6-R89K)

7   StoryBrand Official Website. storybrand.com/ (archived at perma.cc/9HH3-UH4H)

8   Improv Encyclopedia. Story spine, 2024. improvencyclopedia.org/games/Story_Spine.html (archived at perma.cc/GBP8-5399)

9   Arc Studio. The three-act structure in screenwriting, March 9, 2022. www.arcstudiopro.com/blog/three-act-structure-in-screenwriting (archived at perma.cc/D6LC-UAWQ)

10 A. Houston. Ad of the day: Emotive Volvo ad tells personal story around safety, The Drum, November 22, 2024. www.thedrum.com/news/2024/11/22/ad-the-day-emotive-volvo-ad-tells-personal-story-around-safety (archived at perma.cc/D667-S24Q)

9

Putting It All Together

The Customer Experience Blueprint

When it comes to creating an exhaustive and thoughtful customer experience, you need to realize it takes a village. It encompasses all the members of your team that create or work on anything the customer sees or engages with.

You need a holistic approach that spans the entire customer lifecycle. Often, we see customer experience discussed as something wholly owned by the customer success and support teams. That couldn't be further from the truth. While customer success and support can be, and usually are, the frontline defense for a company when there is a problem or concern, that is only a part of the full customer experience.

The customer doesn't just magically become loyal in moments where they talk to a brand to get help. It just feels like a more dire need in that moment, but the customer experience is the byproduct of all these micro moments, where brands have the opportunity to show up for their audience and eventually their customers. This experience is a spectrum of social media, advertising, personal experience, references, reviews, employee engagement, PR, and so much more.

Customer Journey Mapping and Game Theory

The biggest disconnect between brands and customers, when it comes to CX, is that brands think about the destination and customers see and feel the journey.

A customer making it to the next part of the customer journey doesn't necessarily mean that they had a great time and are enjoying the process. The milestones along the way don't tell the whole story.

While the brand can see whether the customer transitions through the journey and converts, the customer is feeling every piece of friction or delight.

In order to really understand what you customer is experiencing, you need to put yourself in their shoes and see all the things that make up those micro moments along their journey. You need to do customer journey mapping.

One small caveat here. Customer journey mapping won't solve all your problems if you still only see the journey as milestones. It isn't and won't be some linear path with predictable moments. You need to account for other variables. You need to account for some people getting lost along the way and needing to be found (and wanting to be found) by the brand so they can get back on track.

As we build out a customer journey and all the major behavior milestones, we need to do a little game theory. Customer journey mapping is the process of visualizing the entire customer experience across touchpoints, from the first interaction with a brand to the post-purchase phase. It helps businesses understand key moments that matter to customers and identify opportunities for improving the overall experience. Game theory, a mathematical framework used to anticipate decision-making and strategic interactions, can be applied to customer journey mapping to better understand customer behavior and nudge them toward desired outcomes.

Mapping out all of these different variations turns a linear and simple 2D interpretation of the customer's journey into a vibrant, messy, and web-like structure that actually is more realistic to how us messy humans engage with brands.

If it's not a little messy, it isn't human.

By leveraging game theory principles, businesses can predict customer responses at various stages of their journey and craft strategies that influence positive actions at each milestone. This approach allows for creating a customer journey map that not only reacts to customer behavior but also shapes it proactively.

In game theory, each decision point is viewed as a strategic interaction, where both the customer and the business make choices that influence future outcomes.[1] The customer journey can be broken down into a series of stages, or milestones, where decisions are made based on perceived benefits, risks, and incentives. At each milestone, the company can design actions that nudge the customer toward the next desired outcome, using psychological, emotional, or rational triggers.

Each milestone in the customer journey can be treated like a game, where the customer faces choices (to continue engaging, to purchase, or to disengage), and the company's goal is to nudge them toward a favorable decision. It's easy to get preoccupied with only nudging and influencing customers into the next part of the customer journey, instead of focusing on the entire journey as an experience in itself.

As we look at the customer journey, we can break it down into these segments:

Awareness → Consideration → Onboarding → Engagement → Feedback → Retention → Advocacy

Awareness: Capturing Attention in a Red Ocean

In the awareness stage, customers are becoming familiar with a brand or product. This phase is a zero-sum game, where multiple brands are competing for the same finite resource: customer attention. Understanding how customers make decisions about which brand to engage with is critical, especially when they are inundated with choices.

Businesses need to ask questions like, "What are my competitors offering?" and "What factors influence the customer's initial interest?" These questions help identify not only the value proposition customers are looking for but also the friction points that prevent them from engaging with your brand. The key to optimizing this phase is reducing the effort required for customers to notice and interact with your content. This can be achieved through clear messaging, targeted ads, or social proof that showcases the value your product offers. Ultimately, businesses should aim to create a low-risk entry point, such as a free trial or introductory offer, to encourage engagement.

Consideration: Earning Trust and Standing Out

During the consideration stage, customers are evaluating their options and deciding whether to engage further with your product or service. This stage is a prisoner's dilemma: both the customer and the business benefit from mutual trust and cooperation, but trust can be hard to establish without transparency and clear value communication. Just like in the prisoner's dilemma, the brand and consumer are both better off if they trust each other instead of "ratting each other out."

Here, businesses need to explore questions like, "What information do customers need to feel confident?" and "How do I reduce perceived risk?" Asking these questions is necessary because the decision to engage further often hinges on whether customers believe the brand is trustworthy and will deliver on its promises. The challenge is to provide enough information to build confidence without overwhelming the customer. By offering detailed product comparisons, customer testimonials, and guarantees (such as free returns), businesses can optimize this stage by reducing perceived risk and making it easier for customers to choose their brand.

Onboarding: Delivering Immediate Value

The onboarding stage is a sequential game, where the first interactions with the product influence whether the customer continues using it or churns. At this critical juncture, businesses must focus on delivering immediate value to customers—what game theory would term a "quick win." The quicker a customer realizes the product's benefits, the more likely they are to continue using it.

Key questions to ask at this stage include, "What is the quickest way for the customer to realize value?" and "How can I personalize the onboarding experience?" These questions help businesses focus on eliminating friction and providing the right guidance to ensure the customer feels confident and supported. Optimizing the onboarding process requires simplifying steps, providing easy-to-follow instructions, and offering personalized resources or tutorials that align with the customer's specific needs. This reduces the likelihood of early churn and builds a solid foundation for long-term engagement.

Engagement: Fostering Continued Interaction

The engagement stage can be seen as a repeated game, where the customer's continued interaction with your product or service determines their long-term loyalty. Here, the focus is on maintaining and increasing customer engagement by reinforcing the value of your product over time.

Questions like, "What motivates customers to stay engaged?" and "How can I use data to personalize engagement?" are essential at this stage. Understanding what keeps customers coming back allows businesses to design personalized experiences that enhance the value of the product. Optimization strategies might include leveraging behavioral triggers like in-app notifications, personalized emails, or loyalty rewards to encourage regular use. Additionally, businesses can use customer data to predict when a customer might disengage and proactively introduce features, updates, or offers that reignite their interest. By continually providing value and rein-forcing positive experiences, businesses can build habits of use that lead to long-term loyalty.

Feedback: Gathering Insights to Drive Improvement

In the feedback stage, the goal is to encourage customers to share their thoughts and experiences, which can then be used to improve the product and overall experience. This stage can be modeled as a coordination game, where both the business and customer benefit from honest, actionable feedback.

Asking the right questions such as "How can I make it easy for customers to provide feedback?" and "What are the most actionable insights I can gather?" helps optimize this stage by removing barriers to participation and ensuring the feedback is meaningful. Customers are more likely to provide feedback if the process is simple, and they feel that their input will lead to real improvements. Offering incentives for feedback (e.g., discounts or entries into giveaways) and showing customers how their feedback leads to positive changes creates a feedback loop that fosters a sense of partnership between the customer and the business.

According to Alison Bukowski, VP of Customer Experience at Point of Reference, "Customer feedback and engagement are the identity of an organization, or should be. Too often we see organizations treating customer engagement activities such as NPS and CSAT surveys as checkboxes in their directionless journey to customer-centricity. And if not this, the other greatest offender is failing to create a feedback loop, embedded in the DNA of a customer journey map (assuming this exists—another challenge area for many). A feedback loop should be built almost like a project plan; it deserves the same time, care, and consideration. When will we reach out to customers? Why are we reaching out? What are we going to say? Does the message need to be tailored based on persona? Industry? Geography? Cultural considerations? What happens once we receive the feedback? Who is collecting it and collating it? How will the information be shared? And with whom? What are the next steps and takeaways? And most importantly, how will we communicate the action taken on the feedback from customers?"

Retention: Reducing Churn and Encouraging Loyalty

The retention stage is similar to an iterated game, where customers continually assess the value, they receive from your product versus alternatives. At this stage, the goal is to prevent churn by addressing potential dissatisfaction early and providing incentives for loyalty.

Businesses need to ask questions like, "What are the primary reasons customers churn?" and "How can I provide ongoing value?" These questions help identify early warning signs of disengagement, such as declining usage patterns or support requests, allowing businesses to take proactive steps to retain customers. Optimizing this phase involves monitoring customer health metrics, offering personalized retention strategies (e.g., exclusive discounts, loyalty rewards), and continuously delivering value through product improvements or new features. By demonstrating that staying with your brand is more beneficial than switching, businesses can cultivate long-term loyalty and reduce churn.

Advocacy: Turning Customers Into Advocates

In the advocacy stage, the goal is to transform loyal customers into brand advocates who actively promote your product or service to others. This phase can be modeled as a repeated cooperation game, where both the customer and the business benefit from mutual reinforcement—customers gain social capital or rewards by sharing their positive experiences, while the brand gains new customers through authentic, word-of-mouth referrals.

The customer advocacy stage is crucial because it not only helps retain loyal customers but also amplifies brand growth by leveraging the power of social proof. In game theory terms, businesses must provide continuous incentives and value, ensuring that the "payoff" for the customer (both emotional and tangible) exceeds the cost of advocating for the brand. To optimize this stage, businesses need to carefully design mechanisms that encourage advocacy while maintaining authenticity.

Empathy Mapping

As customers move through different stages of their journey—from awareness to consideration, purchase, onboarding, and retention—their thoughts, feelings, and actions evolve. Applying empathy maps to each stage of the customer journey reveals deeper insights into how customers perceive value, where their frustrations lie, and what emotional needs arise at key moments.[2]

These insights enable teams to proactively address concerns, build stronger emotional connections, and ultimately deliver a more satisfying, engaging, and loyal customer experience. There's often a disparity between what customers say and what they truly feel. This disconnect can arise due to various reasons, such as:

Social Desirability Bias[3]

When providing feedback, customers may sometimes express what they believe is socially acceptable rather than their genuine feelings. This phenomenon, known as social desirability bias, can result in customers downplaying negative experiences or withholding criticism to avoid seeming overly harsh. For instance, during surveys or interviews, a dissatisfied customer might avoid stating their true feelings about a brand to maintain a positive impression. This bias can skew feedback and make it difficult for brands to accurately gauge customer satisfaction or pinpoint areas for improvement.

Cognitive Dissonance[4]

This occurs when customers hold conflicting beliefs or attitudes about a brand, often rationalizing their feelings to maintain loyalty despite negative experiences. For example, a customer might claim to love a brand but feel deeply frustrated with its customer service. Instead of openly addressing this frustration, they might suppress or justify it to reconcile their emotional connection to the brand with the reality of their dissatisfaction. Understanding cognitive dissonance helps brands uncover hidden dissatisfaction and work toward resolving issues that customers may not readily express.

Unconscious Motivations

Customers are not always fully aware of the deeper motivations driving their behavior and preferences. While they may articulate surface-level wants, such as "I want a good deal," their underlying emotional needs could be more complex, such as a desire to feel smart or validated in their purchasing decisions. These unconscious motivations often shape how customers perceive and interact with a brand, even if they cannot explicitly identify them. Recognizing and addressing these deeper needs allows brands to connect with customers on a more meaningful and emotional level.

Contextual Influences

Customer feedback can be heavily influenced by the context in which it is given, with feelings often shifting based on the surrounding environment. A customer might report satisfaction when asked about a service in a positive or neutral setting, but their true frustrations may emerge in moments of stress or conflict, such as during a service failure. These contextual influences highlight the importance of capturing feedback across different scenarios and understanding how external factors can impact customer sentiment. This approach ensures that brands gain a more accurate and comprehensive view of the customer experience.

Deceptive Patterns

As we break down how to guide customers through the various stages of their journey, it's essential to address deceptive patterns. Deceptive patterns, also known as dark patterns, are design tactics that manipulate users into actions they might not otherwise take, such as unintended purchases or unwelcome subscriptions.[5] While these methods may yield short-term gains, they often erode trust and damage long-term customer relationships.

Employing deceptive patterns can lead to immediate conversions, but at the cost of user satisfaction and brand integrity. When customers realize they've been misled, they may feel frustrated or betrayed, which can result in negative reviews, increased churn rates, and a tarnished reputation. In an era where consumers are increasingly aware of manipulative design practices, transparency and honesty are paramount.

Prioritizing ethical design not only fosters trust but also encourages genuine engagement and loyalty. By creating user experiences that respect autonomy and provide clear, honest information, brands can build stronger, more sustainable relationships with their customers. Avoiding deceptive patterns is not just a matter of ethics; it's a strategic decision that benefits both the user and the business in the long run.

The Blueprint

Creating a truly effective customer journey map involves both understanding the emotional needs of customers and anticipating their decision-making behaviors (see Table 9.1). By combining empathy mapping (which helps uncover what customers are thinking, feeling, and experiencing) with game theory (which predicts and guides decision-making behaviors), businesses can craft a seamless and satisfying customer experience that turns prospects into loyal advocates. Additionally, a key aspect of this process is engaging in regular self-assessment, asking critical questions to evaluate where your CX currently stands and how it can be improved (see Figure 9.1).

We also need to make sure that we don't fall into the trap of only thinking about the customers' behavior. Brands and their teams' behavior is just as important in terms of fostering these relationships and nudging them through the journey.

FIGURE 9.1 CX flywheel

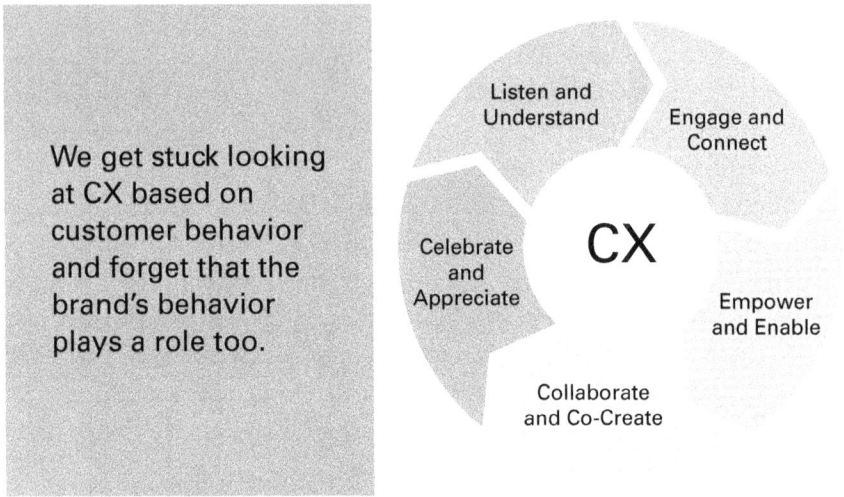

Community Intelligence: Connecting All the Dots

In Chapter 3, we discussed the power of social listening. While social moni-toring tracks mentions, tags, and direct interactions, and social listening dives deeper into analyzing trends, sentiment, and broader conversations, community intelligence takes it a step further. It's the comprehensive process of pulling together insights from *every* touchpoint—social media, surveys, engagement metrics, customer feedback, and more. Community intelligence isn't just about hearing what people are saying online or analyz-ing how they feel about a specific campaign; it's about understanding the full spectrum of your audience's behaviors, emotions, and needs across multiple channels. This big-picture view allows brands to move beyond reactive strategies and build proactive, emotionally connected relationships with their communities.

Where social listening might highlight patterns in online conversations—such as a recurring complaint about a product feature or an unexpected positive response to a campaign—community intelligence stitches that information together with data from other sources. Maybe the same frustra-tion is surfacing in post-purchase surveys or support tickets, or perhaps engagement metrics show a decline in product-related content interactions. By combining these different data streams, community intelligence gives brands a more holistic understanding of what their audience cares about and why. It's not just isolated feedback—it's a 360-degree view of your community's relationship with your brand.

The real value of community intelligence lies in what you *do* with it. This deeper understanding allows brands to make informed decisions that resonate on an emotional level. It could be tweaking a product feature based on feedback trends, reshaping messaging to align with customer values, or even rethinking a brand's larger mission to reflect what the community truly wants. For example, if social listening reveals growing interest in sustainability, and survey data confirms customers are prioritizing eco-friendly products, a brand might invest in greener practices. When customers see their input reflected in meaningful changes, it fosters a sense of ownership and loyalty, turning them into active participants in the brand's journey.

Ultimately, community intelligence creates an ongoing, dynamic feedback loop that extends beyond any single platform or touchpoint. It's not just about listening—it's about integrating insights from across your entire ecosystem to build deeper, more authentic connections. By leveraging this intelligence, brands don't just respond to their communities—they evolve with them, creating relationships rooted in trust, empathy, and shared values. This is the foundation of transforming customer–brand interactions from transactional to truly transformative.

This blueprint breaks down each phase of the customer journey—awareness, consideration, onboarding, engagement, retention, and advocacy—and outlines the important questions businesses should ask to reflect on their current efforts, identify areas for improvement, and optimize the journey using both empathy mapping and game theory. It's time to take that customer intelligence and build with it.

Awareness: Capturing Attention Through Emotion and Clarity

In the awareness stage, your brand has the opportunity to make a first impression. Customers are flooded with options, so the challenge here is to cut through the noise and create an immediate emotional connection.

Use empathy mapping to assess the emotional state of your audience at the moment they encounter your brand. Are they frustrated with current solutions, or curious about new ones? Then apply game theory to position your brand as a low-risk, high-value option, offering clear, concise messaging that addresses their pain points right away.

KEY QUESTIONS

- What does a bad, good, and great customer experience look like at this stage?
- How effectively are we grabbing attention and making an emotional connection?

Consideration: Building Trust and Minimizing Risk

The consideration stage is about solidifying interest and building trust. Customers are now comparing your brand against others and need to minimize risk before making a decision.

Here, empathy mapping helps you understand unspoken fears (e.g., wasting time or money). Meanwhile, game theory guides you to reduce perceived risks by offering incentives like free trials or satisfaction guarantees. The key is to eliminate hesitation while reinforcing that choosing your brand is a rational and emotionally sound decision.

KEY QUESTIONS

- What does a bad, good, and great experience look like when customers are deciding whether to engage with your brand?
- Are we truly making customers feel confident and comfortable choosing us?

Onboarding: Delivering Immediate Value

In the onboarding stage, you need to turn that initial decision into satisfaction by delivering immediate value. This is a critical moment where customers either confirm they made the right choice or start doubting it.

Use empathy maps to get a sense of whether customers feel overwhelmed, excited, or confused as they start using your product. Then, from a game theory perspective, focus on delivering "quick wins" that reinforce their choice, guiding them toward early successes with your product.

KEY QUESTIONS

- What does bad, good, and great onboarding look like? How quickly are we getting customers to see value?
- Are we giving customers immediate value and helping them see quick results?

Engagement: Sustaining Interest and Deepening Loyalty

The engagement stage is where the long-term relationship is built. Sustaining interest requires ongoing value delivery, but, more importantly, fostering emotional connection and loyalty.

Empathy maps can identify what motivates customers to keep using your product or what could lead to disengagement. Use game theory to reward consistent use and foster emotional attachment through personalization, exclusive offers, or community engagement.

KEY QUESTIONS

- What does a bad, good, and great experience look like for ongoing engagement?
- Are we consistently providing reasons for customers to stay engaged?

Feedback: Harnessing the Voice of the Customer

Feedback is a cornerstone of the customer journey map, offering invaluable insights into how customers perceive and interact with a brand. This section captures the voice of the customer—their thoughts, feelings, and suggestions at various touchpoints—and serves as a critical tool for brands to refine their strategies, improve experiences, and foster loyalty. By integrating feedback effectively, businesses can ensure they stay aligned with their customers' evolving needs and expectations.

KEY QUESTIONS

- Is there a pattern of feedback (positive, neutral, or negative)?
- What action can and should be taken based on the feedback received?

Retention: Preventing Churn and Building Long-Term Loyalty

Retention is about maintaining the relationship over time. At this stage, customers expect continued value but also need reasons to stay loyal.

Here, empathy mapping helps you assess whether long-term customers feel satisfied or taken for granted. Game theory suggests anticipating churn risks and addressing them proactively through personalized retention efforts like special offers or exclusive services.

KEY QUESTIONS

- What does bad, good, and great retention look like?
- Are we retaining customers by addressing their evolving needs and preventing churn?

Advocacy: Turning Satisfied Customers Into Advocates

Finally, advocacy is where satisfied customers become passionate brand advocates, spreading the word and reinforcing your brand's value through their networks.

Use empathy maps to understand what drives advocacy—whether it's a sense of pride, community, or value. Game theory can then guide you to create win-win advocacy programs, offering incentives like referral rewards or recognition that motivate customers to share their positive experiences.

KEY QUESTIONS

- What does a bad, good, and great advocacy experience look like?
- Are we effectively converting satisfied customers into active advocates?

What Does "Great" Look Like?

It's important not just to build out the full customer journey but also to thoughtfully realize that "good enough" isn't the goal. It's not enough to do just enough for customers not to churn. That level of care doesn't create love and affinity. It simply means they won't leave until someone offers something better or cheaper. It's only a matter of time before they churn because they aren't truly being taken care of.

The goal is to build a customer journey that not only meets the rational expectations of your customers but also addresses their emotional needs—leading to a seamless, rewarding experience from start to finish. Think about how you can nudge (persuade/gently push) the consumer through this stage. What steps are you taking to make them want to take the desired action? By aligning both the emotional and rational elements of the journey, you can create a holistic customer experience that transforms potential buyers into lifelong advocates, driving loyalty, satisfaction, and organic growth.

TABLE 9.1 Customer journey map

	AWARENESS	CONSIDERATION	ONBOARDING	ENGAGEMENT	FEEDBACK	RETENTION	ADVOCACY
PAIN POINTS							
TOUCHPOINTS							
DECISION OPTIONS							
EMPATHY							
NUDGES							
KPIS							

KEY TAKEAWAYS

- **Holistic customer experience:** CX goes beyond support; it's shaped by all brand interactions, from marketing to PR and employee engagement.

- **Journey mapping and game theory:** Visualize key milestones and use game theory to predict customer behavior, nudging them toward desired actions with strategic incentives.

- **Awareness:** Capture attention with clear, emotional messaging. Use low-risk entry points to reduce friction and guide first interactions.

- **Consideration:** Build trust and reduce perceived risks with clear comparisons and guarantees. Address hidden fears with empathy.

- **Onboarding:** Deliver immediate value to reassure customers. Simplify steps to avoid overwhelm and focus on quick wins.

- **Engagement:** Sustain interest through personalized triggers and regular value. Foster emotional connections to deepen loyalty.

- **Retention:** Prevent churn with early intervention and personalized offers. Continuously monitor customer satisfaction and needs.

- **Advocacy:** Turn loyal customers into advocates with referral programs and incentives, understanding what drives them to share.

- **Self-assessment:** Regularly evaluate performance at each stage, asking what bad, good, and great CX looks like, and adjust accordingly.

- **Emotional and rational alignment:** Meet both emotional and rational customer needs to create a lasting, impactful journey that drives advocacy.

Notes

1 D. Ross. Game theory, Stanford Encyclopedia of Philosophy, 2023. plato. stanford.edu/entries/game-theory/ (archived at perma.cc/KQB8-872Q)

2 B. Kitch. Empathy mapping, Mural, 2023. www.mural.co/blog/empathy-mapping (archived at perma.cc/E4LA-ZWRR)

3 M. F. King and G. C. Bruner. Social desirability bias: A neglected aspect of validity testing, *Psychology & Marketing*, 2000, 17(2), 79–103. onlinelibrary. wiley.com/doi/abs/10.1002/(SICI)1520-6793(200002)17:2%3C79::AID-MAR2%3E3.0.CO;2-0 (archived at https://perma.cc/S2FT-5YCB)

4 B. P. George and M. Edward. Cognitive dissonance and purchase involvement in the consumer behavior context. *IUP Journal of Marketing Management*, 2009, 8 (3/4), 7. www.proquest.com/openview/ee438efa00194db02f0352592403d392/1 (archived at https://perma.cc/XPA5-43JL)

5 Deceptive Patterns. www.deceptive.design (archived at perma.cc/B8PL-Z55C)

PART TWO

Building a Community Step-By-Step

10

Building a Sense of Community

You can't build a house of trust, without a foundation of time.

TRISTAN LOMBARD

Building a strong sense of community is crucial for brands aiming to establish scalable and lasting relationships with their customers. Creating and nurturing customer communities fosters a sense of belonging and connection, which can significantly enhance brand loyalty and retention. While Part One discussed all the elements that influence the customer experience and work to build customer–brand relationships, all of those elements can feel siloed in larger organizations. Silos divide teams and make it difficult to have the optimal customer experience because it feels impossible to align when each department/team doesn't understand what the others are doing. Enter community, the silo killer. Community is the ultimate solution for silos as it creates an inclusive space for external (customers) and internal (brand employees and leadership) members to come together to work and connect.

Let's bring it all together and build this community/silo killer step-by-step.

This chapter focuses on the importance of community building, offers successful examples, examines effective strategies for nurturing communities, and explores the role of online platforms and social media in this endeavor.

> Community is relationships at scale.

Creating a sense of community around a brand helps to establish strong, scalable relationships with customers.

Max Pete, Community Lead at Origin and former Community Engagement Program Manager at Square, sees the power of communities as a core way to create bonds and build trust. "When brands create a community, they're not just selling stuff, they're also making a space where their customers feel like they're a part of something bigger. Brands that nail this create loyal customers who stick around not just for the product, but for the relationships and the sense of community they've built."

Building a community is about creating a space where customers feel valued and connected. It's crucial for brands that want to establish deep, scalable relationships.

The Loss of Third Places

The "third place" refers to a space where you could come together beyond the first place (home) and the second place (school/work). Coined by Ray Oldenburg, an American sociologist, third places such as cafes, parks, community centers, and local pubs have historically served as vital hubs for social interaction, fostering a sense of community and belonging.[1] However, the advent of digital technology, urban development, and, more recently, the global Covid-19 pandemic has led to the erosion of these essential social spaces.

The decline of third places has left a noticeable gap in modern society, one that digital connections alone cannot fully replace. These spaces were more than just physical locations. They were environments where people from different walks of life could gather, share ideas, and build relationships in a natural and informal way. Without them, many individuals feel increasingly disconnected, longing for the sense of community these places once provided.

Urban development has only deepened this issue, as many shared spaces have been replaced by commercialized areas or eliminated entirely. Independent coffee shops and pubs are closing, replaced by large chains, while parks and public squares are being crowded out by private developments. The global Covid-19 pandemic further accelerated this shift, leading to the closure of gathering spots and pushing people into online spaces to maintain their social lives. While these virtual spaces serve a purpose, they lack the depth of interaction that physical third places provided—the kind of connection that comes from simply being present with others in a shared environment.

Brands have an opportunity to step in and fill the void left by traditional third places. By designing spaces that encourage connection and interaction, brands can reintroduce the sense of belonging that people crave. This might include creating welcoming physical spaces like pop-up stores, branded cafes, or community-focused events. On the digital front, brands can foster connection through well-designed platforms, such as hosting online events, workshops, or spaces where people with shared interests can come together.

For this strategy to succeed, brands need to focus on authenticity and inclusivity. They should consider questions like: What do people need to feel part of a community? How can we create spaces where real interactions happen, rather than surface-level engagement? By stepping into this role, brands can not only strengthen their bond with customers but also help rebuild the sense of connection and belonging that third places once offered so naturally.

The Impact of Belonging on Brand Loyalty and Customer Retention

A strong sense of belonging within a customer community is a powerful driver of brand loyalty and customer retention. When customers feel emotionally connected to a community associated with a brand, their relationship with the brand evolves from a mere transactional interaction to a meaningful, personal connection. This emotional bond significantly enhances brand loyalty and has far-reaching impacts on customer retention and advocacy. Here's how fostering a sense of belonging can transform your brand.

Increased Customer Retention

Belonging to a community strengthens emotional ties with the brand, which in turn reduces churn rates. When customers identify with a community, they find a sense of purpose and connection that goes beyond the product or service itself. This emotional investment makes them less likely to switch to competitors, as they would be leaving behind a valuable support network and sense of identity.

For instance, Apple has successfully created a loyal customer base by fostering a strong community through its Apple Store events and online forums. Apple users often feel a part of an exclusive community with shared values and experiences, enhancing their emotional ties to the brand and reducing the likelihood of defection.

Enhancement of Customer Advocacy

Loyal community members often evolve into brand advocates. These individuals don't just passively consume products; they actively promote the brand to others, attract new customers, and defend the brand against criticism. This organic advocacy is rooted in their personal, positive experiences and deep emotional connection with the community.

For example, LEGO's community of fans (the LEGO Ideas platform) allows users to submit ideas for new sets, which are then voted on by the community. This sense of involvement and acknowledgment turns customers into passionate advocates who promote the brand enthusiastically.

Higher Engagement Levels

Community members who feel a strong sense of belonging are more likely to engage in brand-related activities, such as participating in discussions, attending events, and providing valuable feedback. This higher level of engagement contributes to a vibrant community environment where ideas and experiences are freely shared, further enriching the community and the brand experience.

How Belonging Fosters Loyalty

Belonging catalyzes loyalty by deepening customers' emotional connection to the brand. When customers feel they are part of a community, their interactions with the brand transcend typical consumer-brand relationships. They start identifying with the brand's values and mission, which aligns with their personal beliefs and experiences.

EMOTIONAL INVESTMENT
When customers see a brand fostering a genuine community, they become emotionally invested. This investment makes them more likely to stick with the brand through ups and downs, as they feel a personal stake in its success.

SHARED EXPERIENCES
Communities provide a space for shared experiences, where customers can connect over common interests and challenges. This shared experience creates a bond among community members and, by extension, between the members and the brand.

IDENTITY AND BELONGING

When customers find a community that resonates with them, it becomes part of their identity. This sense of belonging ensures that the brand is not just a choice but a part of who they are, leading to unwavering loyalty.

Leveraging Community for Brand Loyalty

To build a vibrant and engaged community around your brand, it's essential to create spaces where customers can interact, share stories, and connect with both the brand and each other. This can be done by developing forums, social media groups, or branded online communities that facilitate these interactions. These spaces act as platforms for customers to discuss their experiences, seek advice, and build relationships, enhancing their overall engagement with the brand.

Encouraging user-generated content is another powerful way to foster deeper connections. When customers feel comfortable sharing their own content related to the brand—such as reviews, photos, or stories—it strengthens their sense of belonging. Recognizing and rewarding these contributions can further solidify their loyalty, as it shows that their input is valued and appreciated by the brand.

Hosting events and challenges, both online and offline, also provides excellent opportunities for community participation. Webinars, virtual challenges, or in-person events allow customers to actively engage with the brand in meaningful ways, creating shared experiences that build stronger ties within the community.

Maintaining an active feedback loop is crucial for nurturing a healthy community. By encouraging feedback and actively listening to community members, brands can demonstrate that customer voices truly matter. Implementing changes based on these suggestions reinforces the idea that the brand is responsive and dedicated to its customers' needs.

Lastly, celebrating community members by highlighting their stories and successes through the brand's communication channels fosters a sense of appreciation and loyalty. Showcasing individual stories not only boosts the morale of those featured but also inspires other community members to stay engaged, knowing their contributions are valued.

In essence, a strong sense of belonging within a customer community transforms the customer–brand relationship from transactional to emotional. This transformation leads to increased customer retention, enhanced advocacy, and higher engagement levels. Brands that successfully create and nurture these communities will not only benefit from loyal customers but also from passionate advocates who drive organic growth and reinforce the brand's market position.

REAL-WORLD EXAMPLE
Figma and Notion

Figma and Notion are highly customizable and collaborative tools used to bring their customers' imaginations to life, whether through the visuals of Figma or the organization and spaces in Notion. For Max Pete, Community Lead at Origin and former Community Engagement Program Manager at Square, Figma and Notion nail this. "Both of these are great products on their own but have seen massive growth because of the awesome community that they've built around their product. From meetups to giving their customers a way to earn revenue from utilizing their platform, these communities are really paving the way for how to be member first."

REAL-WORLD EXAMPLE
LEGO

LEGO's "customer first" strategy enables them to engage dynamically with their fan community. By tracking mentions, hashtags, and discussions, LEGO identifies well-received products and themes. They frequently showcase user-generated content and collaborate with influencers to craft campaigns that resonate with their audience. This practice of active engagement and fan celebration fosters a strong sense of community and brand loyalty.[2]

How Do You Build a Community That Offers a Sense of Belonging?

The "build it and they will come" sentiment only works in baseball movies. It doesn't work when it comes to community. Whether you are building your first community or are a seasoned professional, you need to create and build with purpose. One of the first questions you need to answer is, "Who is the community for?" This creates the cornerstone on which you answer all the other questions, as the needs, desired behaviors, and impact metrics will be dictated by these people.

Instead of immediately playing with community platforms and dreaming of what to call your community, you need to start with the basics and determine your ideal community member profile. Similarly to the traditional ideal customer profile that you'll see in marketing and business plans, you need to determine your target audience and deep dive into understanding them and their needs.

Demographics

When you're gearing up to build a community, understanding your target demographics is necessary for its future success. As community professional Marjorie Anderson states, knowing your desired member audience is valuable. "I think there's a lot of value in understanding who your community members are and what is important to them. This requires some research at the outset. It's not just how they want to interact with a brand, but good user research also helps you understand what makes people human—what keeps them up at night or brings them joy. Things they find funny or that cause them stress. In business we call it 'customer pain points' but it's really understanding who they are as humans and then delivering messaging that helps connect to them as such. But don't overdo it. Using weird slang or colloquialisms just to seem like you 'get' people is weird. Spend time really understanding members and how you can be helpful to them... then deliver on it. Not just for the sake of building your brand but because it's just the right thing to do. Otherwise, they'll feel used and will see right through it and, at the early stages, that will cause you to lose people before you gain their trust."

Let's dive into why asking questions about demographics matters, and how this shapes the future of your community.

Personas

Who is this community meant for? Understanding who your community is meant for helps you create a clear picture of your ideal member. Are they professionals, hobbyists, students, or enthusiasts of a particular field? Knowing this guides all your future decisions—from content creation to event planning—ensuring everything aligns with their interests and needs.

Psychographics

Understanding your members' hobbies, interests, values, and personality traits allows you to tailor activities, discussions, and content that genuinely engage them. Aligning with their interests keeps them coming back, while fostering an environment that resonates with their values creates a sense of authenticity and belonging. Recognizing common personality traits helps you communicate more effectively, whether members prefer written exchanges or live interactions. Additionally, knowing their preferred media consumption—whether books, movies, or online content—ensures you deliver material in ways they enjoy, enriching their overall experience.

Pain Points

Understanding the challenges and difficulties your community members face allows you to create a supportive and empathetic environment. Whether they struggle with professional hurdles, daily stresses, or unmet needs, your community can provide solutions and relief. Recognizing sources of stress or dissatisfaction helps tailor activities and resources that offer comfort and support. Additionally, identifying unmet needs or desires enables your community to fill gaps that others don't, making it an indispensable part of their lives.

Motivations

What is their carrot? Understanding your members' goals and aspirations allows you to support them in meaningful ways, whether they seek career growth, new skills, or personal fulfillment. Recognizing what motivates their engagement—whether networking, learning, or fun—helps you design activities that boost participation. Identifying key incentives, such as recognition, exclusive access, or rewards, enables you to create effective engagement strategies. Lastly, knowing the positive outcomes they seek—whether personal growth, connections, or achievements—ensures your community meets their expectations, driving satisfaction and long-term retention.

Skills and Expertise

Understanding the skills and expertise of your community members allows you to leverage their strengths for peer-to-peer learning, collaboration, and other initiatives. Highlighting areas where they excel not only enhances the community's value but also provides experts with a platform to share their knowledge, fostering respect and appreciation. Encouraging members to contribute based on their skills creates a dynamic environment where everyone has something valuable to offer. Additionally, recognizing areas where they seek growth helps you provide tailored educational content and opportunities, keeping them engaged and invested in their development.

Communication Preferences

Understanding your members' preferred communication channels—whether email, social media, or forums—ensures your messages reach them effectively. Knowing their preferred frequency of communication helps strike the right balance between engagement and overwhelm. Matching the tone of communication, whether formal, informal, or casual, makes messages more relatable and engaging. Catering to content format preferences, whether visual, written, or a mix, enhances content consumption and enjoyment. Lastly, recognizing whether members favor real-time discussions or asynchronous communication allows you to structure interactions in ways that maximize participation and convenience.

Community Engagement History

Understanding members' past experiences with online or offline communities helps create an environment that builds on what they enjoyed while avoiding past pitfalls. Recognizing notable contributions or achievements can identify potential leaders and active participants who drive engagement. Knowing their preferred level of involvement—whether as observers, active participants, or leaders—allows for roles that match their interests. Lastly, learning why they joined or left previous communities provides insights into what to emphasize or avoid, ensuring a more fulfilling and lasting community experience.

Future Expectations

Understanding members' future expectations helps in planning and delivering value to keep the community relevant. Knowing how they envision their roles—whether as leaders, contributors, or learners—fosters growth opportunities. Identifying desired features or activities ensures future enhancements align with their interests, keeping engagement high and satisfaction strong.

Feedback and Improvement

Understanding how members prefer to provide feedback ensures you gather valuable insights in a way that feels natural and comfortable for them.

Identifying areas they believe need improvement helps implement meaningful changes that enhance their experience. Directly asking what would make their experience more satisfying ensures you address their needs effectively, fostering a happy and engaged community.

Cultural Needs

Recognizing cultural nuances fosters an inclusive and respectful community where everyone feels welcome. Gathering additional relevant insights allows for a more personalized experience, deepening your understanding of members' needs and preferences.

Seeing a theme in all of these parts? Understanding. You must deeply and empathetically understand the people you are building the community for. They can tell when you get them, or you don't.

Desired Community Member Behaviors

You've determined who you want the community to be for and have hopefully done careful research and social listening to understand their needs, pain points, and desired experience. Now, what would you want them to do if they joined the community?

Obviously there will be some members who will be less engaged. You may label these members as lurkers or learners: members who are in the community but do not post or directly engage with others in the community. There is a natural tendency to see lurkers as a bad thing, but this way of thinking can make it easier to fall into the trap of seeing these community member relationships as transactional.

Lurkers in a community represent a significant and often underappreciated source of potential. While they might not be actively posting or engaging in discussions, they bring value simply by observing, consuming, and sharing interest in the content. Lurkers are often in the early stages of engagement; they're learning the community culture, forming connections with its content, and building trust. Rather than viewing them as inactive members, it's more accurate to see them as thoughtful participants who are preparing for future involvement.

Creating an environment that gently encourages lurkers to engage can unlock this potential. By fostering a welcoming atmosphere with low-pressure opportunities for participation, communities make it easier for lurkers to take that first step. Small gestures, such as quick polls, simple questions, or visible success stories within the community, show lurkers that engagement is positive and accessible. For many, the choice to participate comes down to feeling safe and valued—knowing that their contributions, however small, will be respected and appreciated.

When communities invest in inclusivity and provide clear pathways for lurkers to engage, they're nurturing a reserve of untapped insights, perspectives, and support. Over time, lurkers who feel welcomed and understood often transition into active contributors, bringing fresh energy and ideas to the community. In this way, lurkers are not passive but rather are vital members who represent future growth and depth, making their journey from observation to engagement a key focus for any thriving community.

When considering what behaviors you want members to exhibit once they join the community, also remember to think about their experience as they join, return, and engage. Is there friction when it comes to doing any of these behaviors? Is there a way to incentivize these behaviors or make them easier to do?

When you're building a community, understanding the behaviors you want to encourage is crucial for its long-term success. Here, we'll break down each key area and explain why these questions matter and how they can shape a thriving, engaged community.

Participation

Understanding how often members prefer to engage helps set expectations and maintain a steady flow of activity. A balance between frequent participation and member availability ensures discussions and events feel dynamic without overwhelming participants.

Clarifying what types of contributions add value—such as thoughtful discussions, resource sharing, or event participation—helps members understand how they can meaningfully contribute. When members see the impact of their involvement, they are more likely to stay engaged.

Identifying key moments for increased participation, like special events or initiatives, allows for strategic planning that maximizes engagement. Creating excitement around these moments encourages members to show up and contribute when it matters most.

Recognizing and rewarding participation, whether through shout-outs, badges, or exclusive opportunities, fosters a culture of appreciation. When members feel valued, they are more likely to stay active and invested in the community.

Collaboration

Encouraging collaborative projects strengthens community bonds by fostering teamwork and a shared sense of purpose. Planning structured initiatives ensures meaningful engagement and provides opportunities for members to contribute in impactful ways.

Selecting the right tools and platforms for collaboration enhances efficiency and participation. Whether it's communication apps, project management tools, or shared workspaces, having seamless systems in place makes working together more effective.

Facilitating connections between members through networking events, collaboration forums, or directories helps spark meaningful partnerships. When members can easily find and connect with like-minded collaborators, the community becomes more dynamic and interconnected.

Recognizing and rewarding successful collaborations through incentives like awards, public acknowledgments, or exclusive opportunities encourages continued participation.

Knowledge Sharing

Encouraging members to share their expertise fosters a culture of learning and collaboration. Providing structured ways to share knowledge—such as tutorials, articles, or webinars—ensures valuable insights are accessible to all.

Establishing dedicated channels for resource sharing, like forums, libraries, or regular knowledge-sharing sessions, makes it easy for members to contribute and benefit from each other's expertise. These mechanisms enhance the community's value and create an environment of continuous learning and support.

Positive Communication

Establishing clear communication guidelines fosters respectful and constructive interactions, creating a welcoming space where members feel safe to express themselves. Clear expectations help prevent conflicts and set a positive tone for engagement.

Having a structured approach to conflict resolution ensures that issues are handled fairly and promptly, reinforcing the community's commitment to harmony and member well-being.

Encouraging considerate language and tone promotes inclusivity and respect, ensuring that all members feel valued and heard.

Actively promoting inclusivity and diversity in communication strengthens the sense of belonging for all members. Using inclusive language, celebrating diverse perspectives, and ensuring representation in discussions contribute to a more equitable and engaging community.

Problem-Solving

Ensuring the community has clear processes for addressing challenges reassures members that their concerns will be handled effectively. A structured approach fosters a proactive and resilient environment where issues can be resolved efficiently.

Having designated channels for reporting problems streamlines issue resolution and keeps the community running smoothly. Clear communication around these processes helps maintain transparency and trust.

Providing problem-solving resources—such as expert access, troubleshooting guides, or peer support—empowers members to tackle challenges confidently. Equipping the community with the right tools fosters self-sufficiency and collaboration.

Celebrating successful problem-solving efforts reinforces a culture of resilience and innovation. Recognizing these achievements encourages members to engage actively in finding solutions and supporting one another.

Mentorship

Establishing a formal mentorship program provides structured support for newcomers while fostering knowledge-sharing and growth within the community. It helps integrate new members and ensures they have guidance from experienced peers.

Creating clear pathways for experienced members to offer mentorship encourages active participation and strengthens community bonds. Providing designated spaces or programs for mentorship enhances accessibility and engagement.

Offering resources such as training materials, guidelines, or regular check-ins ensures both mentors and mentees have the tools they need to succeed. Structured support helps make mentorship effective and rewarding.

Recognizing and appreciating mentorship efforts motivates experienced members to contribute and reinforces a culture of learning. Public acknowledgment, rewards, or special roles can further encourage participation, enriching the community experience.

Determining Desired Behaviors

Establishing clear and concise community guidelines sets expectations for behavior and fosters a respectful, organized environment. Well-defined rules provide a foundation for positive interactions and help prevent misunderstandings.

Outlining expected behaviors ensures all members are aware of community standards, promoting a culture of respect and inclusivity. Clear guidelines contribute to maintaining a welcoming and supportive space for everyone.

Feedback Mechanisms

Collecting feedback from community members is essential for continuous improvement. Surveys, feedback forms, and discussions provide valuable insights that help shape a better experience for everyone.

Regular opportunities for feedback ensure that community needs and concerns are consistently addressed. A proactive approach allows for timely adjustments, fostering a responsive and evolving community.

Recognition and Rewards

Recognizing and rewarding positive behaviors encourages members to contribute in meaningful ways, reinforcing a strong and supportive community culture. Acknowledgment can range from public recognition to tangible rewards that motivate continued engagement.

Implementing systems like badges, awards, or other forms of recognition provides clear incentives for participation. These initiatives foster appreciation, inspire excellence, and create a sense of achievement within the community.

Community Leaders' Example

Community leaders play a crucial role in setting the standard for behavior. By actively participating, collaborating, and sharing knowledge, they inspire others and help cultivate a positive and engaged culture.

When leaders are visibly involved, it encourages members to follow their example. Their contributions elevate discussions, foster meaningful interactions, and reinforce a strong, supportive community environment.

Training and Resources

Providing training sessions and resources helps members understand and adopt behaviors that strengthen the community. Workshops, online courses, or written guides can offer valuable insights and set clear expectations.

Ensuring these resources are easily accessible encourages ongoing learning and deeper engagement. When members can conveniently access guidance, they are better equipped to contribute meaningfully and positively to the community.

Communication and Reinforcement

Clearly communicating desired behaviors ensures that all members understand expectations. This can be done through onboarding materials, regular updates, and announcements that reinforce community values.

Ongoing reinforcement via newsletters, announcements, or community updates helps keep these behaviors top of mind. Consistently reminding members of expectations fosters a positive and engaged community culture over time.

Habit/Growth Loops

One major trap that community builders fall into is they hyper-focus on the joining and onboarding phase of the community and forget that making someone convert and join a community is difficult but making them return repeatedly is significantly more difficult.

This is where habit loops come in. In the previous section we discussed the desired behaviors we want community members to exhibit. Obviously, one of those would be to return to the community regularly and engage. What types of habit loops can we set up so that members join and then have the community top of mind, so they remember and want to return?

To illustrate the importance of habit loops, consider the following examples of how they can be applied within a community.

Participation in Discussions

To encourage regular participation in discussions, you can start by setting up triggers like email notifications about new discussions or relevant topics, and weekly digests highlighting popular discussions. These notifications serve to draw members back to the community by keeping them informed about ongoing conversations. The action here involves members clicking on the notification to view the discussion and posting a comment or response. This active engagement increases their investment in the community.

To keep things exciting, you can offer variable rewards such as positive feedback from other community members, recognition through badges or leaderboard standings, and access to exclusive content or resources. These rewards make participation more rewarding and encourage members to keep coming back. Further investment is achieved as members accumulate reputation points or badges and subscribe to specific discussion categories for personalized updates. This ongoing investment deepens their connection to the community.

Collaboration on Projects

For collaborative projects or community initiatives, begin with triggers like announcing new collaborative projects and providing regular updates on ongoing projects. These keep members informed and invite them to express interest in joining. The action here involves members collaborating with team members on project tasks. This teamwork fosters a sense of unity and purpose, which is needed for deep engagement.

Successful collaboration can be rewarded with the recognition of project contributions, access to project-specific resources or insights, and even the successful completion of the project itself. These variable rewards highlight the value of collaborative efforts and motivate members to participate. When members invest time and effort in project tasks and accumulate project-related achievements or badges, their sense of accomplishment and connection to the community grows.

Knowledge Sharing

Knowledge-sharing events, such as webinars or workshops, can be effective habit loops as well. Start by announcing upcoming events and making recommendations based on members' interests and expertise. These announcements serve as triggers to pique their interest. The action involves members registering for and actively participating in these events by asking questions or sharing insights. Active participation helps members feel like integral parts of a knowledgeable and engaged group.

Rewards such as access to event recordings or additional resources, recognition as knowledgeable participants, and networking opportunities with industry experts serve as powerful incentives. These rewards motivate continued participation and make members feel valued for their contributions. Investment grows as members spend time attending events and contributing to discussions or Q&A sessions, further cementing their engagement in the community.

Positive Feedback and Recognition

Positive feedback and recognition are also key components of habit loops. Triggers can be system-generated notifications of positive feedback received and public recognition for achievements or contributions. These notifications make members aware of their positive impact quickly. The subsequent action involves members responding to the positive feedback and showcasing received badges or achievements on their profiles. This fosters a sense of pride and accomplishment.

Variable rewards such as increased visibility within the community, opportunities for leadership roles, and exclusive access to community events keep members motivated to maintain positive behavior. The continued active participation and contributions that result from this positive feedback loop further strengthen the community.

Implementation Considerations

When implementing habit loops, monitoring and analytics are essential. Use analytics tools to track member engagement and identify areas for improvement regularly. Analyze the data to gauge the effectiveness of your habit loops and make necessary adjustments. Establishing mechanisms for collecting feedback on habit loops ensures you stay aligned with members' preferences and needs. This might include regular surveys or open discussions.

Communication plays a crucial role as well. Clearly communicate the benefits of participating in each habit loop and keep members updated on new opportunities and rewards. Effective communication keeps members informed and excited about ongoing and new activities. Active involvement from community leaders is also vital. Ensure leaders participate in and encourage habit loops, setting an example by demonstrating desired behaviors. Their engagement can inspire the rest of the community to follow suit, creating a more dynamic and engaged environment.

KEY TAKEAWAYS

- **Community builds brand loyalty and advocacy:** A strong community fosters deep relationships, turning members into advocates who naturally promote the brand.

- **Purpose, belonging, and emotional connection drive engagement:** When members feel a shared purpose and emotional connection, they stay engaged, identify with the brand, and remain loyal.

- **Communities fill the gap of "third places":** Digital spaces provide opportunities for connection, support, and shared experiences.

- **Scalable relationships through digital platforms:** Online communities enable brands to grow engagement in a sustainable way.

- **User-generated content and recognition strengthen bonds:** Encouraging members to contribute content and recognizing their efforts deepens their investment and motivation.

- **Events and shared experiences increase participation:** Hosting interactive activities fosters stronger connections and keeps engagement high.

- **Feedback loops and adaptability foster trust:** Listening to members, making changes, and evolving the community based on feedback ensures long-term relevance.

- **Successful brands show community's power:** Examples like LEGO and Sephora prove that strong communities drive innovation, engagement, and loyalty.

- **Define and attract the right members:** Identifying your ideal community member profile ensures you build a space that meets their needs and interests.

- **Encourage both passive and active engagement:** Design low-pressure participation options for casual members while offering deeper involvement for engaged contributors.

- **Shape and reward desired behaviors:** Establish clear guidelines, promote collaboration, and recognize contributions with rewards, badges, or exclusive perks.

- **Create a positive, inclusive culture:** Clear guidelines, respect, and conflict resolution processes ensure a welcoming environment.

- **Leverage habit and growth loops:** Design triggers and incentives that encourage consistent participation and long-term engagement.

- **Foster knowledge sharing and leadership:** Offer forums, webinars, and mentorship opportunities while ensuring community leaders actively set the tone.

- **Monitor, adapt, and plan for growth:** Use data and insights to refine strategies, scale the community, and maintain alignment with members' evolving needs.

- **Community building is an ongoing process:** Get comfortable with flexibility and be open to evolution.

Note: Adapt each subsection based on your unique community goals, audience, and niche. Feel free to add additional sections or modify existing ones to suit your specific needs.

Notes

1 A. Quizon-Colquitt. Third places: What are they and why are they important to American culture? University of Chicago, November 1, 2023. esl.uchicago. edu/2023/11/01/third-places-what-are-they-and-why-are-they-important-to-american-culture/ (archived at perma.cc/5UYL-73LE)

2 A. Patov. How LEGO engages customers through creative customer experience (CX) strategies, *Renascence Journal*, 2024. www.renascence.io/journal/how-lego-engages-customers-through-creative-customer-experience-cx-strategies (archived at perma.cc/7VVB-9SSK)

11

Designing, Onboarding, and Measuring Success

The Full Community Journey

Building a successful community is more than just creating a space for interaction—it's about designing an intuitive and welcoming journey for members. From designing a community that resonates with members to onboarding to long-term engagement, every step should be intentionally structured to encourage participation and retention. A strong onboarding process ensures members understand the community's purpose, connect with others, and feel motivated to engage. However, onboarding is just the beginning. To create a sustainable and thriving community, leaders must also develop engagement strategies, measure key metrics, and continuously refine their approach.

This chapter will explore the essential components of branding, onboarding, personalization, engagement, and measurement, followed by selecting the right technology and structuring a realistic community building timeline to guide long-term success.

Designing the Community Identity

A strong brand identity differentiates the community from competitors and strengthens member loyalty. Clearly defining the community's mission, values, and unique selling proposition (USP) ensures that interactions remain aligned with long-term goals.

Consistency in branding and messaging across communication channels reinforces the community's identity. From tone of voice to visual design elements such as logos, colors, and typography, maintaining brand cohesion fosters recognition and trust.

Training community leaders and managers on branding guidelines ensures a consistent experience for all members. Encouraging user-generated content further deepens member investment by making them feel like active contributors to the community's identity.

Creating a strong brand identity for your community helps establish its purpose, values, and overall presence. A well-defined brand guides how your community is perceived, how members interact, and how the community stands out. Below is a breakdown of key considerations and questions to help you develop and implement effective branding guidelines.

Brand Identity

Start by defining the purpose and values. What is the primary goal or mission of your community? Understanding this helps you articulate the core values the community aims to uphold. Identifying these values ensures that all community activities and interactions align with the overarching mission. Your community's USP is what sets it apart. Ask yourself what makes the community unique and valuable to members. Knowing this not only attracts your ideal audience but keeps them engaged and invested.

Next, consider the brand personality. How do you want the community to be perceived? Determine what brand personality will resonate with your ideal community member profile. This personality should be reflected in the way the community is presented, how it engages with members, and the culture it fosters. What kind of culture do you want? Consider how members should interact with one another and how this culture supports the community's mission and values.

Tone of Voice

Your communication style is crucial to brand identity. Decide what tone should be used in community communications. Whether it's formal, informal, or conversational, the tone should align with the desired brand personality and remain consistent. Messaging guidelines are vital to maintaining clarity and consistency in communication. Define the key messages you want to convey and be clear about the language and terminology that should be used or avoided. This ensures that all interactions reflect the brand ethos.

Visual Guidelines

In terms of logo and design elements, identify symbols that represent the community and specify the colors, fonts, or shapes to include in the logo.

These elements should resonate with the community's purpose and evoke the right emotions or feelings. For visual consistency, specify primary and secondary brand colors and describe how these colors should be used across different materials. Choose typography that reflects the brand's identity, providing usage guidelines for headings, body text, and so on. Imagery guidelines should clarify the types of images to use or avoid and specify the style of photography or illustration that aligns with the brand.

Naming Conventions

A community's name is a vital reflection of the brand's identity, purpose, and values. It establishes an emotional connection, communicates the community's mission, and fosters a sense of belonging. A strong name unifies members, aligns with the brand's goals, and resonates with the target audience.

When naming a community, ensure it reflects the brand's objectives and ethos while staying relevant to the community's purpose. The name should be memorable, meaningful, and easy to associate with the brand. For communities with sub-brands or sections, develop consistent naming guidelines to maintain alignment with the overarching identity.

Involving members in the naming process can build ownership and connection, while testing the name for cultural and linguistic nuances ensures inclusivity and avoids misinterpretation. A thoughtfully chosen name becomes the foundation for a thriving community, fostering unity and reinforcing the brand's mission.

Implementation and Guidelines

Develop a comprehensive brand guidelines document to enshrine all the elements of your brand—such as logo usage, color codes, and messaging. This document serves as a reference for everyone involved and ensures alignment with the brand identity. Training and onboarding community builders on these guidelines is vital. Consider providing resources or workshops for community members to foster understanding and adherence to the brand.

Feedback and Adaptation

Finally, establish processes for feedback and adaptation. Collect feedback regarding the brand and assess community needs. Is there a procedure in place for adapting the brand based on this feedback? Flexibility and responsiveness to community input can enhance brand effectiveness and member satisfaction, ensuring your brand evolves positively over time.

Constructing the Onboarding Process

A well-structured onboarding process sets the foundation for long-term engagement. The primary objectives should align with the community's overall goals, ensuring that new members feel a sense of belonging, understand the purpose, and are encouraged to participate. This process should be broken into structured phases that guide members from initial awareness to full integration.

Onboarding Phases

The onboarding journey begins with pre-registration, where awareness is raised through marketing efforts, referrals, and external partnerships to attract potential members. Once they decide to join, the registration process should be intuitive, allowing easy sign-ups while collecting necessary member information. Immediately after registration, a welcome message or email should reinforce their decision to join, setting expectations and introducing key resources.

The orientation phase helps new members familiarize themselves with the community's mission, values, and key activities. Providing a mix of guides, videos, and interactive elements can help them navigate the platform effectively. During this stage, new members should be encouraged to complete their profile setup, which allows them to personalize their experience, showcase their interests, and connect with others who share similar goals.

A critical part of onboarding is the community norms/guidelines agreement, where new members review and acknowledge behavioral expectations. This ensures a respectful and inclusive environment from the outset. To encourage early participation, leaders should establish connection points such as a buddy system or mentoring program, pairing new members with experienced ones. Hosting icebreaker events or community challenges also fosters engagement in a welcoming environment.

The engagement ramp-up phase should gradually introduce members to participation opportunities, recognizing their contributions early to reinforce positive behavior. Finally, ongoing support and feedback collection should be implemented to refine the onboarding process continuously. Providing orientation resources, hosting check-ins, and incorporating new feedback ensures onboarding remains effective and relevant.

Personalizing the Member Experience

A strong welcome message plays a key role in setting the tone for new members. It should include information about the community's mission, values, and expectations while being personalized based on a member's interests or referral source. This level of personalization makes new members feel valued and increases the likelihood of engagement.

During profile setup, members should be encouraged to share relevant information such as their expertise, interests, and engagement preferences. A well-developed profile enhances networking opportunities and makes it easier for members to connect with like-minded individuals.

Providing diverse orientation resources caters to different learning styles. Guides, videos, quizzes, and interactive sessions help members understand community norms and engagement opportunities. Encouraging new members to join discussion forums and Q&A sessions fosters deeper interactions and engagement.

Building early connections helps members feel a sense of belonging. Implementing a buddy system, mentorship program, or structured introduction events allows new members to integrate more quickly. Community events, social gatherings, and interest-based networking groups further strengthen these connections.

Establishing Engagement and Retention Strategies

Encouraging long-term engagement requires a combination of gradual participation, recognition, and meaningful contributions. New members should feel comfortable engaging at their own pace while being encouraged to take part in community discussions, projects, and leadership roles.

Implementing recognition programs for active members—such as milestone celebrations, badges, or public acknowledgments—motivates continuous participation. Regular feedback loops through surveys and direct conversations help leaders refine engagement strategies based on real member experiences.

Proactive reengagement strategies ensure that members who become inactive are brought back into the fold. Identifying disengaged members through analytics and outreach campaigns helps maintain community vibrancy. Personalized reengagement messages, curated content recommendations, and incentives such as exclusive events or rewards can effectively rekindle interest.

Hosting diverse events and challenges provides ongoing opportunities for participation. Whether through collaborative projects, competitions, or themed discussions, these initiatives help sustain enthusiasm and reinforce member investment in the community.

These tactics lead to metrics that leadership cares about, but you will need to translate how your work converts to leading and lagging indicators. Social media managers and community builders often joke that their work runs on vibes, and while this is certainly true it needs to be converted into the language that the C-suite understands: metrics.

Mad Libs (sentences or stories with missing words that people can use to create their own stories or silly jokes) provide an easy framework for translating vibes to metrics. Use this Mad Lib as a starting point to convert your vibes into trackable business impact:

If you make people feel this [emotion], then they are more likely to do this [behavior], which correlates to this [KPI] that is tracked here [link or dashboard].

Measuring Success and Optimizing Growth

Tracking key community metrics helps leaders assess engagement, retention, and impact. Membership growth and retention rates indicate how well the community attracts and sustains members. Monitoring active participation levels, post engagement, and event attendance provides insight into what drives interaction.

Sentiment analysis, conducted through discussions and feedback tools, helps gauge overall community morale and satisfaction. Aligning community engagement with business objectives—such as conversions, referrals, and brand advocacy—ensures that the community contributes to broader organizational goals. Using data-driven insights, leaders can refine engagement strategies for sustained success.

Depending on the life stage of your community, you'll find that you look at different levels of metrics from foundational to engagement to impact.

Foundational Metrics

MEMBERSHIP GROWTH RATE

Tracking the rate of membership growth provides insight into the community's health and appeal, helping gauge how effectively it attracts new members over time, whether quarterly or annually. By examining factors influencing growth—such as recent marketing efforts, partnerships, or changes in membership benefits—you can identify which strategies support member acquisition. For instance, a surge in new memberships might correlate with a successful social media campaign or a partnership that raised awareness, while a slowdown could indicate that recruitment efforts need adjustment or that the community's value isn't clear to potential members. Understanding these factors allows for refining recruitment strategies and implementing initiatives like targeted outreach, referral programs, or enhanced onboarding processes to encourage steady and sustained growth, ensuring the community remains vibrant and appealing to new members.

NEW MEMBERS VS. CHURN RATE

Assessing the balance between new members and those leaving provides insight into member retention and satisfaction levels, revealing whether the community maintains enough members to support ongoing growth. If departures exceed new arrivals, the turnover rate might suggest challenges in engagement, satisfaction, or alignment with member expectations. Analyzing the reasons for member departures through exit surveys or activity data can uncover common trends—such as insufficient engagement, perceived lack of value, or unmet expectations—that, if addressed, can help reduce churn. By responding to these findings with adjustments like improving member interaction, enhancing content, or refining membership benefits, you can create an environment that encourages both retention and steady new memberships. Regular monitoring and responding to these metrics can help sustain a balanced and flourishing community experience.

Engagement Metrics

ACTIVE MEMBERS

Measuring the percentage of members who are active on a daily, weekly, or monthly basis gives a view into the community's engagement levels and overall vitality. It's helpful to define what constitutes an "active" member— whether that means logging in regularly, posting content, commenting, or participating in discussions. By clearly identifying active member behaviors, you can better track engagement patterns and evaluate the success of initiatives aimed at increasing activity. Initiatives like regular content updates, member challenges, or engaging discussions can help maintain and grow member activity. Analyzing the impact of these efforts over time allows you to fine-tune engagement strategies to keep members consistently involved.

AVERAGE POSTS AND COMMENTS PER MEMBER

The average number of posts and comments per member provides insight into member participation and content interaction. Comparing this metric with community engagement goals highlights how well the community meets its intended level of interaction. High activity around specific content types or topics can reveal what resonates most with members, whether that's educational posts, social discussions, or event recaps. These insights guide content planning, allowing the community team to focus on popular themes and interaction styles, encouraging members to contribute and engage more frequently.

EVENT PARTICIPATION

Tracking the average participation rate in community events sheds light on the effectiveness of events in fostering engagement. Analyzing how event attendance aligns with overall member activity can reveal if events are driving sustained interaction within the community. Some events, such as live question-and-answer (Q&A) sessions or networking meetups, may see higher engagement than others. Understanding which event formats attract the most participation helps refine future event planning to align with members' interests and needs, ensuring events are both engaging and meaningful to the community.

Impact Metrics

USER-GENERATED CONTENT

Tracking the percentage of user-generated content in the community provides insights into member engagement and ownership of the space. Encouraging members to create their own posts, share experiences, or offer advice can strengthen their connection to the community. Strategies like content prompts, recognition programs, or featuring member posts can motivate contributions, helping cultivate an environment where members feel valued and heard. High levels of UGC tend to foster trust and loyalty, as members see the community as a place where they can contribute meaningfully, which can positively impact retention.

SENTIMENT ANALYSIS

Assessing the sentiment within community discussions—whether positive, neutral, or negative—provides a pulse on member satisfaction and morale. Tracking sentiment over time helps identify shifts in community mood, signaling areas that may need attention. Regular sentiment monitoring can reveal trends or recurring concerns, and strategies like proactive moderation, open feedback channels, or direct responses to concerns can address any negative sentiment before it impacts the wider community atmosphere. A positive sentiment overall encourages member engagement and strengthens community bonds.

CONVERSION RATE FROM COMMUNITY

Evaluating how effectively community participation contributes to business goals, such as sales or subscriptions, connects community engagement to organizational success. Identifying specific actions within the community—such as attending events, participating in discussions, or completing courses—that correlate with higher conversion rates helps refine engagement strategies. By tracking these behaviors, you can identify and enhance pathways that lead members from community involvement to business outcomes, optimizing the community's role in achieving broader business goals.

ADVOCACY AND REFERRAL RATES

Understanding what percentage of members actively refer others to the community highlights member satisfaction and loyalty. Identifying and supporting advocates who naturally promote the community can amplify its reach and attract new members. Programs that recognize advocacy, like referral rewards or ambassador opportunities, can further incentivize referrals. These initiatives not only grow the community but also strengthen member commitment, as advocates feel more invested in the community's success.

KEY INSIGHTS AND ACTIONS

Tracking and analyzing these metrics provides valuable insights into community dynamics and areas for growth. Identifying the most impactful findings—whether they relate to engagement trends, member satisfaction, or content preferences—helps shape a clear understanding of the community's strengths and areas needing attention. These insights directly inform strategic decisions, guiding adjustments in content planning, engagement initiatives, and member support to align with what members find most valuable.

Each metric informs specific actions designed to enhance both the community's health and its contribution to business goals. For example, if user-generated content is shown to boost engagement, increasing prompts for member contributions could be a priority. Similarly, if sentiment analysis reveals recurring concerns, addressing these issues with targeted support or communication may be needed to maintain a positive environment. By taking data-informed actions, the community team can make meaningful improvements that not only enrich member experience but also support overall business objectives, creating a balanced strategy for ongoing success.

Tech Requirements and Timeframe

There is a reason why you had to complete the other subsections before we even start considering tech stack. It's tempting to jump right into the different community platforms to think about where you will have your community, but this is putting your own needs before the community members.

The right community platform won't necessarily be from the most recognizable brand or logo. It won't necessarily be the one that you have used in the past either. It all comes down to which platform will make it easy for members to do what they need to do, while the community builder and business attached is able to execute their vision and track the corresponding metrics.

Platform Selection

Start with understanding the primary goals and purpose of your community. What are you trying to achieve, and what are the core functions your community needs? Once you have clarity on this, think about how your members prefer to interact—whether through forums, chat, or video conferencing. This knowledge will guide you toward the most suitable platform. Additionally, it's essential to assess the scalability of your platform choice to ensure it can grow alongside your community.

A crucial question here is, "What type of platform aligns best with our community's objectives?" You need a solution that not only offers user-friendliness across both desktop and mobile devices but also supports multimedia content, such as videos and documents. Dedicated community platforms like Discourse or Mighty Networks offer focused community features, while collaboration tools like Slack or Microsoft Teams provide flexible communication options. For more tailored needs, a custom-built solution might be necessary.

Integrations

Incorporating integrations with existing business tools can enhance community operations. Consider how well potential platforms integrate with commonly used software in your industry, as well as the automation possibilities that could streamline workflows. Important questions include which integrations are indispensable for community success and whether CRM or project management tools need to be integrated. Additionally, think about how easily members can share content from external sources.

Potential integrations might involve CRM tools, project management software like Asana or Trello, email marketing platforms, and analytics tools, which allow for seamless data flow and enhanced user interaction.

Essential Features

Identify the features that will boost member engagement and collaboration. It's crucial that the platform supports sharing multimedia content and offers event management and scheduling functionalities. Key questions to explore include what features are vital for effective communication and collaboration, the need for discussion forums, polls, or Q&A sessions, and how members can easily access and share valuable resources.

Features to consider include discussion forums, multimedia content sharing, events and webinars, member profiles with direct messaging capabilities, and tools for conducting polls and surveys, all designed to foster an engaging and collaborative community environment.

Privacy and Security Measures

Ensuring data protection and privacy is critical. Prioritize secure login/authentication methods and ensure that your platform complies with data protection regulations, such as GDPR. Questions to explore include what measures are in place to protect member data, how user authentication is handled, and whether there's an option for private, invitation-only groups or discussions.

Implement security measures like HTTPS encryption, two-factor authentication, regular security audits, and compliance with relevant regulations to safeguard your community.

Implementation Timeline

Start with research and planning to explore available platforms and integrations and define a detailed plan outlining your community's purpose and goals. For the platform setup, select and configure the chosen platform, ensuring necessary business tool integrations are in place.

As you move into feature implementation, activate and customize necessary features based on community needs, thoroughly testing functionality and user experience along the way. When implementing privacy and security measures, make sure to communicate privacy policies clearly to community members.

Provide training for community leaders and members and develop comprehensive onboarding materials and guides to ensure smooth adoption. Finally, launch the community officially, and continually monitor engagement levels. Gather feedback and adjust to enhance the community experience as necessary.

Community Building Timeline Table

The community building table will help you break down your work into various stages along with the associated timing and tasks (Table 11.1). Feel free to make this your own and edit/change based on your own community goals and tasks.

To maximize the benefits of this table, start by adjusting the timeline to align with the scale and complexity of the community. Regularly review progress, making adjustments to the plan as needed to ensure it remains effective. Throughout the process, engage key stakeholders and community leaders to foster collaboration and ensure the approach meets community needs.

TABLE 11.1 Community building timeline

Phase	Timeframe	Tasks
Ideation	1–2 months	1. Define the purpose and goals of the community.
		2. Identify the target audience and key stakeholders.
		3. Research and analyze competing communities.
		4. Develop a unique value proposition for the community.
		5. Create a preliminary content plan and community structure.
		6. Establish KPIs for measuring community success.
Planning	1–3 months	1. Select the community platform and tools.
		2. Develop a detailed project plan and timeline.
		3. Identify and establish key integrations (CRM, project management).
		4. Create a budget for community development and maintenance.
		5. Define privacy and security measures.
		6. Outline community guidelines and code of conduct.

(continued)

TABLE 11.1 (Continued)

Phase	Timeframe	Tasks
Development	2 weeks– 2 months	1. Set up the chosen community platform. 2. Configure essential features (forums, multimedia sharing, etc.). 3. Implement integrations with business tools. 4. Design and customize the community interface. 5. Develop onboarding materials and training resources. 6. Set up a system for content management.
Testing	2–4 weeks	1. Conduct beta testing with a small group of users. 2. Gather feedback and identify areas for improvement. 3. Test security measures and privacy settings. 4. Conduct usability testing for user experience. 5. Iterate and make necessary adjustments based on feedback.
Launch	1 month	1. Finalize community content and resources. 2. Develop a marketing and launch strategy. 3. Communicate launch date to target audience. 4. Conduct a pre-launch webinar or event. 5. Launch the community and open registration. 6. Monitor initial user engagement and address issues promptly.
Optimization	Ongoing	

Building a thriving community requires thoughtful design, strong branding, and data-driven decision-making. A well-crafted onboarding process, combined with personalized engagement strategies, fosters a welcoming and dynamic environment. Establishing a strong brand identity and choosing the right technology ensures a sustainable foundation for long-term success. By continually measuring and refining community strategies, leaders can create an evolving space where members feel connected, valued, and actively engaged.

KEY TAKEAWAYS

- **Define purpose and values:** Establish a clear purpose and set of values for the community, guiding all activities and interactions to align with the community's overarching mission.

- **Identify a unique selling proposition:** Determine what sets the community apart, focusing on qualities that attract and retain the ideal members.
- **Cultivate a brand personality:** Shape a personality that resonates with the target audience, influencing the community's culture, interaction style, and overall atmosphere.
- **Determine tone of voice:** Select a tone that aligns with the brand personality—whether formal, conversational, or casual—and maintain it consistently in all communications.
- **Develop messaging guidelines:** Outline the key messages, language, and terminology that represent the community's ethos, ensuring clarity and alignment in every interaction.
- **Establish visual guidelines:** Design a cohesive visual identity through logos, colors, and typography that reflect the community's purpose and evoke the desired emotional response.
- **Set imagery standards:** Define the style of photography or illustration that aligns with the brand, specifying types of imagery to use or avoid.
- **Consistent naming conventions:** Choose a community name that represents the brand identity and create guidelines for naming any sub-brands or projects to maintain consistency.
- **Create a brand guidelines document:** Compile all brand elements—logos, color codes, messaging—in a document that serves as a reference for community builders, ensuring alignment with the brand identity.
- **Train community builders:** Onboard community managers and builders on brand guidelines through training resources, ensuring consistent application across the community.
- **Implement feedback and adaptation processes:** Regularly collect feedback and be willing to adapt the brand as community needs evolve, reinforcing relevance and member satisfaction.
- **Foster community understanding:** Provide resources for members to understand the brand identity, helping them feel connected to and aligned with the community's goals and values.
- **Design with empathy and purpose:** Craft an onboarding experience that fosters belonging, aligns with community objectives, and transitions members smoothly into engagement.
- **Structure and personalize onboarding:** Guide members through clear phases, provide a warm welcome, encourage profile setup, and introduce community norms to create a strong foundation.

- **Facilitate early connections and gradual engagement:** Implement mentorship programs, buddy systems, and interactive events while allowing members to participate at their own pace.

- **Offer ongoing support and learning:** Provide accessible resources, training materials, and continuous updates to enhance engagement and community knowledge.

- **Collect and act on feedback:** Regularly gather insights through surveys and discussions, iterating on the experience to keep the community relevant and responsive.

- **Re-engage and retain members proactively:** Identify disengaged members early, use personalized outreach, and provide incentives, curated content, and engaging challenges to reignite interest.

- **Define and maintain a strong brand identity:** Establish a clear mission, values, and USP while ensuring consistent branding, messaging, and communication across all interactions.

- **Foster ownership and recognition:** Encourage user-generated content, reward contributions, and highlight members to reinforce their value within the community.

- **Measure success and align with business goals:** Track membership growth, retention, engagement, advocacy, and business impact to assess and refine strategies.

- **Choose the right platform and tools:** Prioritize user-friendly, scalable technology that supports interaction needs, ensures security, and integrates with essential business tools.

- **Plan, launch, and optimize strategically:** Beta test, onboard members effectively, engage stakeholders, and use data-driven insights for continuous community improvement.

12

Beta Testing

Even with all this preparation completed, you are building something for humans. Living, breathing beings who have lives, challenges, and other things fighting for their attention. What you have built might be great but not great enough to warrant your ideal community member profile to join and engage in your community.

You need to beta test your community and actively seek feedback. What works? What could be better? What could be added or removed for an improved experience? Beta testers will give you priceless community feedback but also serve as the initial foundation of your community. These people get to be the voice of the community early on and can gain a sense of ownership along with belonging as they become a part of how the community evolves and thrives.

Beta Test Community Group

Objectives

DEFINE OBJECTIVES

Establishing clear objectives for the beta community is essential to guide its development and success. Begin by identifying specific goals you aim to accomplish during the beta phase. These goals may include gathering insights into user preferences, testing platform functionality, identifying engagement patterns, or assessing the effectiveness of community features. Think about how these objectives align with the larger vision for the community—whether it's to create a space for meaningful interaction, provide access to exclusive resources, or build a foundation for shared learning and collaboration. By defining these objectives upfront, you set a purposeful direction for the beta phase, ensuring that feedback and outcomes directly contribute to shaping a community that meets both member needs and organizational goals. Clear objectives also provide measurable benchmarks, allowing you to assess progress and make informed adjustments as you prepare for a full-scale launch.

TARGET AUDIENCE

Choosing the right target audience for the beta community is crucial for obtaining useful insights and fostering an engaging, dynamic environment. Consider the specific demographics, interests, and characteristics you want in your beta testers. This audience might be early adopters, those with a strong interest in the community's niche, or individuals who can provide diverse perspectives that reflect the wider target member base. Defining this audience helps ensure that the feedback gathered during the beta phase will be relevant and actionable. Additionally, an engaged and invested beta group can help set the tone and culture for the community, building a foundation that attracts similar members as it grows. By carefully selecting the target audience, you're more likely to identify needs, preferences, and challenges that inform valuable enhancements and foster a supportive, vibrant community.

Platform and Tools

COMMUNITY PLATFORM

Selecting the right platform and tools for hosting the beta community is a foundational decision that impacts the entire user experience. Consider platforms that offer core features like forums, chat, collaboration tools, and content-sharing capabilities that facilitate interaction and communication. Think about the type of engagement you want to encourage—whether it's open discussions, resource sharing, or real-time collaboration—and choose a platform that supports those objectives. Additionally, evaluate the platform's scalability, ease of use, and customization options, ensuring it aligns with your long-term vision for the community. During the beta phase, you may also want to explore various tools for data analytics and user feedback, enabling you to monitor engagement patterns and gather insights. A well-chosen platform allows for seamless member interaction, enhances user satisfaction, and provides a robust environment to support the beta community's objectives.

ACCESS CONTROLS

Deciding on access controls for the beta community is vital for managing the experience and ensuring that it meets initial goals. Determine whether the beta community will be a private, invite-only group, or if it will be accessible to a broader audience. A private beta can create a focused environment, allowing you to work closely with select members who are invested in providing feedback and shaping the community. If privacy is prioritized, decide how members will be granted access, possibly through an application process, exclusive invitations, or specific criteria that match the target audience profile. This selective access helps maintain quality interactions and allows for targeted testing. In contrast, a wider access beta could generate more varied feedback and showcase the community to potential future members. Ultimately, the approach to access controls should reflect the objectives of the beta phase, balancing exclusivity with inclusivity as needed to ensure valuable, actionable insights.

Selection Criteria

Qualifications

BETA TESTER CRITERIA
Establishing clear criteria for selecting beta testers is essential to create a community that provides valuable insights and represents the audience you hope to attract long-term. Consider factors such as expertise, engagement level, and diversity in experiences and perspectives. For example, if the community centers on professional development, you may want testers with varying levels of expertise, from beginners to seasoned professionals, to ensure feedback captures a range of needs. Similarly, you might prioritize candidates with high engagement histories, as active participants will likely provide richer insights into community functionality and interaction quality. Additionally, diversity in demographics, such as age, background, and geographic location, will allow you to identify usability or accessibility issues that may only emerge in specific contexts. Thoughtfully defined criteria ensure that your beta testers represent a comprehensive cross-section of the target audience, offering feedback that supports a balanced and inclusive community experience.

APPLICATION PROCESS
Designing a streamlined, targeted application process will help identify the right individuals for your beta testing phase. This process should include questions that allow you to assess applicants' qualifications, interests, and alignment with the beta community's objectives. Ask specific questions that reveal applicants' familiarity with the community's subject matter, their motivations for participating, and any relevant experience they bring to the table. Additionally, consider incorporating questions about applicants'

engagement style, preferred communication methods, and the aspects of the community they are most interested in exploring. Depending on the nature of your community, you might also seek testers with a history of participating in similar environments or providing constructive feedback. By designing an application process that balances qualifications with enthusiasm, you can build a beta group that is not only well-suited for testing but also passionate about shaping the community's early direction.

Group Composition

SIZE OF BETA GROUP

Determining the optimal size for the beta community requires a balance between diversity and manageability. A group that is too large can be challenging to monitor and may dilute the quality of feedback, while a group that is too small may lack the diversity needed to provide comprehensive insights. Consider selecting a group size that allows for active engagement and effective management of interactions. This may vary depending on the community's focus but typically ranges from 50 to 200 participants for initial beta testing. The goal is to create a beta group that's large enough to reflect the diversity of the broader audience but small enough to maintain focused, quality interactions. A manageable group size enables deeper connections, meaningful feedback, and efficient moderation, ensuring that you capture actionable insights without overwhelming resources.

REPRESENTATION

Diversity in the beta group is crucial to avoid biases and ensure inclusivity from the outset. Strive to include members from a wide range of backgrounds, interests, and experience levels to create a well-rounded perspective on the community's strengths and areas for improvement. To avoid unintentional bias, use the application process to gather data on applicants' demographics and experiences, ensuring that no group is over- or under-represented. Consider implementing a scoring system that evaluates candidates based on different diversity factors, balancing these with other qualifications like expertise and engagement history. Regularly assess the composition of the beta group to ensure it continues to reflect the diversity you aim to achieve in the larger community. By actively prioritizing representation, you can foster a community that feels welcoming, relevant, and accessible to a broad audience from day one, setting the foundation for an inclusive community culture as it grows.

Test Period

Duration

Setting a clear and realistic duration for the beta test period is crucial to ensuring you gather meaningful feedback and implement improvements before a full launch. The duration should be long enough to allow beta testers to explore various features, establish routines within the community, and provide thoughtful, well-rounded feedback. Typically, a beta test lasts between 4 and 12 weeks, but this can vary depending on the complexity of the community's structure and the extent of features being tested. The goal is to allocate enough time for participants to experience the community authentically, encountering and reflecting on different aspects of functionality, usability, and engagement patterns. Balancing thorough testing with a manageable timeframe will ensure that feedback is timely and actionable, avoiding beta fatigue and allowing for efficient refinement.

Phases

Dividing the beta test period into phases can enhance the testing process by focusing on specific features or community aspects at each stage. A phased approach enables you to systematically test, refine, and roll out features, gathering targeted feedback and making iterative improvements as the beta progresses. For example, the first phase might focus on foundational features like registration, onboarding, and navigation, ensuring that new members can easily access and explore the community. A subsequent phase could then shift attention to engagement features, such as discussion forums, messaging tools, and content-sharing options, where testers can provide insights into interaction quality and usability.

In each phase, provide testers with clear goals, specific features to explore, and feedback guidelines to ensure relevant insights. This approach allows you to address specific issues early on and optimize each part of the community gradually, rather than attempting to fix everything at once. Additionally, a phased rollout can help identify unforeseen interactions between features, providing a holistic view of how members will experience the community in its entirety. This structured, phased strategy leads to more organized feedback, minimizes overwhelm for testers, and results in a well-rounded, user-focused community experience at launch.

Feedback Mechanisms

Feedback Platforms

Selecting the right channels for collecting feedback is essential to ensure that beta testers feel comfortable sharing their insights openly and constructively. Consider utilizing a combination of forums, surveys, and direct messages to gather diverse types of feedback. Forums or dedicated feedback threads within the community allow testers to discuss their experiences and engage with each other's ideas, creating a collaborative space where feedback is shared and refined through interaction. Surveys offer a more structured approach, enabling you to ask specific questions that can yield targeted insights, while direct messaging provides a private, one-on-one channel for more sensitive feedback that members might prefer to share confidentially. Encouraging open communication is key to this process; let testers know that all feedback—positive and critical—is valuable and will contribute directly to community improvements. Regularly expressing gratitude for their insights and demonstrating how their feedback is being used can foster a trusting, open feedback culture.

Regular Check-Ins

Scheduling regular check-ins with beta testers keeps them engaged and allows you to gauge progress in real-time. These check-ins can take various forms, from weekly or bi-weekly group updates to individual progress surveys or live Q&A sessions. Frequent updates can serve to remind testers of ongoing objectives and encourage ongoing participation, ensuring that feedback is continuous rather than concentrated at the end of the beta period. Consider holding live virtual check-ins, such as monthly video calls, where testers can share feedback directly and interact with the team behind the community, allowing for real-time responses to their questions or concerns. Alternatively, weekly update emails or progress surveys can provide a more structured approach, focusing on specific aspects of the community experience each time. This regular communication fosters a sense of inclusion and accountability, demonstrating to beta testers that their contributions are actively shaping the community and providing them with the support needed to engage fully in the beta process.

Iterative Improvements

Feedback Analysis

Establishing a structured process for analyzing feedback is necessary to draw actionable insights and make targeted improvements. Begin by outlining a system to categorize feedback into meaningful categories, such as usability, engagement, functionality, and feature requests. This categorization helps identify recurring themes and issues, making it easier to spot patterns that may affect the overall user experience. Additionally, consider assigning priority levels to each piece of feedback based on its potential impact on the community. For instance, feedback related to core functionalities, such as navigation issues or login difficulties, should be addressed promptly, while suggestions for aesthetic improvements or optional features might be categorized for later consideration. Regularly reviewing these categories and priorities with the community team ensures alignment and focus on the most critical areas. This organized approach to feedback analysis is necessary for creating a prioritized roadmap that guides improvements and enhances the community experience efficiently.

Implementation Plan

With a clear understanding of feedback priorities, develop a structured plan for implementing improvements throughout the beta period. Decide on a timeline for rolling out updates, which could range from weekly to monthly releases depending on the complexity of the changes and the urgency of the feedback received. Consider implementing an agile approach, where updates are released in small, manageable increments, allowing the community team to respond to feedback quickly and enabling beta testers to see that their input is actively shaping the platform. Regular updates not only improve the user experience but also help maintain engagement by demonstrating the team's commitment to refining the community based on real-time input.

During each update phase, communicate changes to beta testers, outlining what has been addressed and any areas still under review. This transparency reassures testers that their feedback is valued and keeps them informed of ongoing improvements. Providing release notes or brief summaries of the updates ensures that testers are aware of new or enhanced features to test, creating a continuous cycle of feedback and improvement. By adhering to a well-defined implementation plan, the team can efficiently refine the community in response to user insights, paving the way for a polished, user-centered platform at launch.

Acknowledgments

Recognition

Creating a structured plan for acknowledging and recognizing beta testers' contributions is key to building loyalty and appreciation within the community. Recognizing their efforts not only motivates testers to remain engaged but also signals to them that their input directly shapes the community's development. Consider offering rewards or exclusive badges that symbolize their role in the beta phase, such as a "Beta Pioneer" badge that early testers can display in their profiles. This badge serves as a visible mark of their contributions, offering a sense of accomplishment and identity within the community. Other forms of recognition might include access to special features, exclusive content, or personalized thank-you notes, each adding a level of personal appreciation. By implementing thoughtful and meaningful recognition strategies, you reinforce the testers' value to the community, increasing their likelihood of staying active and contributing in the long term.

Feedback Acknowledgment

Acknowledging individual feedback is a powerful way to show beta testers that their perspectives are valued and directly impact the community's development. Establishing a feedback acknowledgment process helps ensure that testers feel heard and appreciated, motivating them to continue sharing their insights. This could include automated messages upon submission that thank them for their input, as well as more personalized follow-ups for significant suggestions. In cases where feedback leads to visible changes or improvements, consider notifying the specific tester or even highlighting their contribution in a community update. This approach communicates that feedback is an ongoing, impactful process, and it builds a culture of transparency and trust within the community.

Example Acknowledgments

Recognizing beta testers can be both symbolic and public, providing them with lasting acknowledgment of their role in shaping the community. One effective example is awarding a unique "Beta Pioneer" badge (discussed above) to early testers, symbolizing their foundational contributions. In addition, publicly acknowledging testers in community updates or newsletters allows everyone to see their contributions, reinforcing a collective sense of progress. Mentioning specific testers or groups who provided feedback that led to positive changes fosters a collaborative atmosphere, and highlights the community's commitment to growth shaped by its members. By thoughtfully combining private and public acknowledgments, the community can build a foundation of trust, loyalty, and mutual respect among its early contributors.

Questions for Community Builders

Refinement of Objectives

As initial findings from the beta community come in, revisiting and refining the objectives becomes a dynamic process to better align with both tester experiences and the overarching goals of the community. Early feedback may highlight areas of interest or interaction that were previously unanticipated, suggesting opportunities for new features or shifts in focus. For example, if beta testers demonstrate a high level of engagement with discussion-based activities over content consumption, objectives could pivot to emphasize user-generated content and active participation. Adjustments based on these insights allow the community to evolve in ways that resonate with member expectations and strengthen engagement. Regularly revisiting and fine-tuning objectives in response to these findings keeps the beta phase responsive and sets a solid foundation for a successful community launch.

Flexibility in Criteria

Flexibility in beta tester criteria is vital for adapting to unforeseen dynamics and ensuring an inclusive, engaged group that accurately reflects the future community. Early experiences may reveal that certain criteria, such as specific experience levels or topic familiarity, aren't yielding the expected diversity or interaction quality. This insight can prompt adjustments to the criteria, inviting members who represent different backgrounds or engagement styles. For instance, if high-expertise members dominate feedback, refining criteria to bring in more beginner or intermediate users can provide a balanced perspective that is essential for building an accessible community. As the beta phase progresses, continuous evaluation of criteria flexibility can reveal which aspects foster a positive, productive environment, helping to shape a community that attracts a wide range of members and encourages varied contributions.

Community-Building Strategy

The beta phase offers a unique lens into shaping a broader community-building strategy, providing lessons that extend well beyond initial testing. Observing how beta testers engage, share, and respond to community features can provide a wealth of insights into the types of activities, content, and interactions that resonate most. These insights can directly inform the strategy for full-scale community development, guiding decisions on content strategy, engagement techniques, and feature prioritization. For example, if the beta reveals that live Q&A sessions are especially popular, incorporating similar events in the broader community could be a valuable tactic for long-term engagement. Lessons learned from the beta phase, from communication preferences to interaction styles, serve as a foundation for a thoughtful community-building approach that's grounded in real member behavior and needs.

Feedback Loop Closure

Closing the feedback loop with beta testers is an essential step for fostering a collaborative environment and demonstrating that their insights have real impact. Communicating the outcomes of feedback, along with the specific changes or decisions made as a result, helps build a culture of transparency and appreciation. Consider implementing a regular update process, such as monthly newsletters or platform announcements, to highlight how feedback has been acted upon and its effect on the community's development. Where feasible, mention specific feedback contributions to show individual testers that their voices are valued. This mechanism of closing the feedback loop not only encourages continued input but also strengthens the relationship between testers and community managers, laying the groundwork for a launch where members feel they are active participants in the community's success.

KEY TAKEAWAYS

- **Human-focused approach:** Recognize that community members have unique needs and competing priorities; design engagement accordingly.

- **Clear beta objectives:** Define specific beta goals to ensure feedback shapes a community that meets both user and organizational needs.

- **Right beta audience:** Select early adopters who align with the community's purpose and offer diverse perspectives, creating a strong foundation.

- **Purposeful platform choice:** Choose a platform that supports interaction, scalability, and analytics to monitor engagement and improvements.

- **Controlled access:** Decide between private or open beta access based on feedback needs, balancing quality and broad input.

- **Balanced selection criteria:** Define criteria to include diverse levels of experience and engagement, ensuring inclusive feedback.

- **Optimal group size:** Choose a manageable beta size (typically 50–200) that enables quality interactions without overwhelming resources.

- **Inclusive diversity:** Build a diverse beta group to avoid bias and capture comprehensive insights for improvement.

- **Defined timeline and phased testing:** Set a realistic timeline, with phased testing to focus on key features, allowing for organized feedback.

- **Robust feedback mechanisms:** Use forums, surveys, and direct messaging to gather open feedback, reinforcing its value.

- **Regular check-ins:** Maintain engagement with scheduled updates, emails, or Q&As to show testers that their input is valued.

- **Organized feedback analysis:** Categorize and prioritize feedback by impact to direct improvements that elevate the user experience.

- **Incremental updates:** Roll out updates regularly, keeping the community responsive to real-time feedback and showing progress.

- **Meaningful recognition:** Acknowledge testers with badges or public mentions to build loyalty and show appreciation.

- **Close feedback loop:** Communicate changes based on feedback, strengthening trust, and a collaborative community culture.

- **Adaptive objectives:** Refine beta objectives based on feedback to keep the community relevant and engaging.

- **Flexible criteria:** Adjust selection criteria as needed to ensure a balanced mix of members and enhance inclusivity.

- **Strategic insights for growth:** Use beta learnings to inform long-term community-building strategies, fostering sustainable engagement.

13

Community Launch, Communications, and Promotion

We have a strategy, tech stack, metrics, and beta testing feedback and now it's time to launch. Community builders need to see this like other campaigns, but with a focus on how human and empathetic it needs to be.

Depending on how you like to project manage and execute your work, you might create a Gantt chart with clear timeframes for tasks, and may even have a run of show spreadsheet for all the individual moving pieces of the launch. No matter what path you choose, you want to ensure you identify each individual task in the launch and create a punch list so you mitigate risk during the launch and can also ensure that each task has a purpose for ensuring launch success.

Choosing the right partners to help build a community hinges on the principle of creating network effects. By collaborating with individuals or entities that already have a strong connection with your desired community member audience, you can leverage their existing networks to amplify your reach and engagement. These partners, whether they are influencers, brand ambassadors, or niche community leaders, bring authenticity and credibility to your efforts, making it easier to foster trust and interest within your target audience. Their established relationships and influence can catalyze awareness and prompt action, encouraging more people to join and actively participate in your community. This strategic partnership not only broadens your community's base but also enriches it through the diverse connections and insights these partners bring, ultimately leading to a more vibrant and engaged member network.

Launch Plan

Launch Objectives

Begin by clearly defining the objectives for the community launch. Identify the primary goals, considering what the launch aims to accomplish both in the short term and long term. These goals might include increasing community engagement, fostering connections among community members, or encouraging user participation in specific activities or discussions. Additionally, clarify the key outcomes that will indicate a successful launch, such as membership growth, content generation, or activity rates within the community. Setting these objectives will guide every phase of the launch plan, helping to ensure alignment across all activities and keeping efforts focused on what matters most for the community's initial and sustained impact.

Launch Date and Timeline

LAUNCH DATE

Select a specific date for the launch, ensuring it aligns with the broader strategy and readiness of the community. Be mindful of any external events, holidays, or industry occurrences that might impact user availability or engagement, adjusting as necessary to maximize launch visibility and participation. The chosen date should also allow sufficient time for testing, feedback collection, and any final preparations, ensuring that the community is ready to provide an optimal user experience from day one.

TIMELINE

Develop a comprehensive timeline that outlines all key steps leading up to the launch. This timeline should include significant milestones, tasks, and deadlines, ideally presented through a punch list or a Gantt chart with clear task markers for each preparatory activity. Some of these milestones might include initial design phases, content creation, stakeholder reviews, beta testing, and promotional planning. Each milestone should have a deadline to ensure the process remains on track and allows for timely adjustments if unexpected challenges arise.

Pre-Launch Teasers

Teaser Content

Begin the teaser campaign by creating a variety of compelling teaser content designed to generate excitement and curiosity about the upcoming community launch. This content should offer just enough detail to intrigue the target audience without fully revealing the community's offerings, building anticipation and sparking interest. Consider using a mix of media types—

such as short videos, engaging images, and mysterious or thought-provoking posts—to appeal to different segments of your audience. Videos can offer a dynamic glimpse into the community, showcasing snippets of features, potential activities, or testimonials, while images and posts can provide snapshots or hints about the community's value. Each piece of teaser content should have a cohesive visual and thematic style that resonates with your brand, reinforcing a sense of identity and attracting the target audience's attention.

Countdown Mechanism

To amplify anticipation, implement a countdown mechanism that actively builds excitement as the launch date approaches. This countdown can be displayed on social media platforms, embedded in a dedicated launch page on your website, or included in email newsletters. Countdowns provide a visual reminder of the upcoming launch, creating a sense of urgency that encourages the audience to stay engaged and look forward to the launch day. To make this countdown even more engaging, consider using interactive elements—such as daily reveals of specific features or benefits, sneak peeks into community events, or limited-time pre-launch offers. Additionally, encourage audience participation by inviting them to share the countdown or tag friends to join in, helping to expand awareness and increase anticipation across social circles.

Launch Event

Event Format

The launch event's format will set the tone for how the community engages with its members from the start, so selecting the right approach is essential. Begin by deciding whether the event will be virtual, in-person, or live-streamed, considering the geographical reach and preferences of your audience. A virtual event can allow for a broader, more inclusive experience, attracting participants regardless of location, whereas an in-person gathering can offer more direct engagement and foster a sense of exclusivity. A live-streamed event may serve as a hybrid, providing accessibility while preserving the energy of real-time interaction. Establish a structured agenda or schedule for the event, ensuring it includes specific segments—such as introductory remarks, key presentations, and breakout sessions if applicable. This structure will keep the event organized and help guide attendees through each aspect of the launch, maintaining engagement and enthusiasm throughout.

Guests and Speakers

To elevate the impact of the launch, invite key guests, influencers, or community leaders whose presence aligns with the community's values and mission. Their participation can not only attract more attendees but also lend credibility and spark greater interest in the community. Carefully select individuals who have established followings or expertise relevant to your audience and the community's focus. Consider including these guests in roles such as keynote speakers, panelists, or live discussion leaders, as their insights can add depth and drive engagement among attendees. Promote their involvement ahead of time through social media or email marketing, highlighting their participation to increase anticipation and encourage broader attendance. Leveraging these guests' reach and influence will also extend the launch's visibility beyond current members, potentially attracting new participants and building a stronger foundation for future growth.

Activities

To keep the launch event lively and interactive, plan a series of engaging activities that involve attendees directly. Activities could include live Q&A sessions, where participants can ask questions and receive real-time responses, or a virtual scavenger hunt that familiarizes new members with the community's features. Consider scheduling exclusive announcements, such as unveiling new features, benefits, or upcoming community events, to captivate and inspire excitement among attendees. Encourage community members to participate actively, perhaps by sharing their experiences, stories, or feedback during the event, which fosters a sense of belonging and involvement from day one. Such interactive elements will make the launch event memorable, allowing members to feel like they're an integral part of the community from the outset and helping to solidify their long-term commitment.

Initial Content Plan

Content Themes

An effective content strategy begins with defining content themes that resonate with the community's mission and goals. These themes should be thoughtfully chosen to reflect the interests and needs of community members, setting the foundation for engagement from the outset. Start by identifying key topics that will be the focus of early content, ensuring they align closely with the goals of fostering interaction, sharing knowledge, or providing inspiration. For instance, if the community is centered on professional development, initial themes might include skill-building, industry trends, and personal growth stories. To maintain interest and appeal to various user preferences, plan for a diverse mix of content types, including text-based articles, informative infographics, eye-catching images, and dynamic videos. By offering variety, you can cater to different learning styles and engagement preferences, thereby enhancing the content's impact and encouraging more members to participate and contribute.

Content Calendar

A structured content calendar is essential to provide consistency and sustain momentum in the weeks and months following the launch. Create a comprehensive calendar that outlines content topics, formats, and publishing dates, ensuring a regular cadence that keeps the community active and engaged. Decide on the frequency of new content based on community needs and available resources—whether that means daily posts, multiple times per week, or weekly. This schedule should allow for a steady flow of information without overwhelming members, striking a balance between consistency and quality. Include placeholders for time-sensitive topics or trending themes that may arise, allowing for flexibility in the calendar. This initial content strategy, supported by a reliable calendar, will provide the foundation needed to build momentum in the community and ensure that members remain interested, engaged, and connected as they explore and contribute to the growing content library.

Community Incentives

Launch Promotions

To encourage early engagement and participation, consider offering exclusive promotions or incentives for members who join the community at launch. These incentives serve as an appealing introduction, adding immediate value to the community experience and motivating potential members to take action. Early-bird rewards could range from discounted membership fees, access to premium features, or limited-edition merchandise that showcases community affiliation. Additionally, exclusive content or early access to certain features can be particularly enticing, as they provide members with a sense of privilege and inside access. Carefully choose rewards and benefits that not only attract initial members but also foster long-term loyalty. Promotions that emphasize the community's unique value—such as networking opportunities, access to expert insights, or valuable resources—will enhance the appeal, making it more likely that members will remain active beyond the launch period.

Recognition Programs

Acknowledging and celebrating active contributions from the outset helps to foster a vibrant and engaged community atmosphere. Establish recognition programs, such as badges or titles, that reward members who actively participate and contribute to the community during its early stages. These badges can signify various forms of engagement, from creating popular content and participating in discussions to offering helpful advice or providing feedback. In addition to digital badges, consider implementing leaderboards or highlighting top contributors in community newsletters, creating multiple avenues for recognition that make members feel valued. These forms of acknowledgment not only encourage continued participation but also create a positive feedback loop, where recognized members inspire others to contribute. Rewarding early contributors with recognition and even potential perks, such as exclusive event invites or access to advanced features, will establish a supportive and enthusiastic community culture that endures as the community grows.

Outreach Strategy

Social Media Campaign

Launching a targeted social media campaign is critical to generating visibility and excitement around the community's debut. Start by identifying which platforms are most relevant for reaching your target audience; for example, LinkedIn might be ideal for a professional network, while Instagram and TikTok may appeal to younger or more visually driven audiences. Tailor each platform's content to fit its unique format and user expectations, whether through short, dynamic video teasers, engaging stories, or informative posts that highlight the community's value. Develop a cohesive campaign theme and schedule, with content that builds up in anticipation over several weeks leading to the launch. Consider using hashtags, countdowns, and interactive elements—such as polls or Q&A sessions—that encourage potential members to engage with the content and spread the word to their networks. By aligning content with each platform's strengths, the campaign can reach a wider audience, create buzz, and drive traffic to the community at launch.

Email Marketing

Email marketing remains a powerful tool for connecting directly with an audience, making it an ideal channel for notifying potential members about the launch. Begin by segmenting your email list based on criteria such as prior engagement, interests, or demographics, allowing for more personalized messaging that resonates with each group. For instance, existing subscribers who have already shown interest in the community's topics might receive an early access invitation, while new subscribers could be offered an introductory overview with highlighted benefits. In each email, emphasize what makes the community unique, such as networking opportunities, exclusive content, or early member benefits. Personalization can go a long way in making each recipient feel valued, and incorporating dynamic elements—like countdown timers or personalized invitations—can enhance excitement. By carefully timing and sequencing emails, you can maintain interest throughout the launch period, reinforcing the community's value and making the transition from awareness to action as seamless as possible.

Collaborations and Partnerships

Strategic collaborations and partnerships can significantly amplify the community's launch by expanding its reach beyond existing audiences. Identify influencers, organizations, or brands with values that align with your community's mission, as these partnerships will lend credibility and attract relevant, engaged users. For example, a community focused on health and wellness might collaborate with fitness influencers, while a business community could partner with entrepreneurial groups or industry associations. Work with these partners to design mutually beneficial promotions, such as co-hosted events, guest posts, or shoutouts on social media, that can introduce their audience to the community in an authentic and impactful way. Consider offering them a preview or exclusive content that they can share with their followers, creating a sense of curiosity and anticipation. By establishing these partnerships early on, you can generate broader awareness and draw in new members, many of whom will likely find long-term value in the community.

Post-Launch Evaluation

Analytics and Metrics

Effective post-launch monitoring begins with defining clear, relevant KPIs that align with the community's goals and growth objectives. Start by selecting metrics that provide meaningful insight into the community's health and engagement, such as membership growth rate, engagement per post, active users, retention rates, and user-generated content contributions. These KPIs should be consistently tracked and analyzed to understand how the community is evolving, whether members are finding value, and where potential gaps in engagement might exist. Utilize analytics tools tailored to the community platform—whether built-in analytics or third-party tools—to gather comprehensive data. Regularly reviewing these metrics will allow you to assess progress against the launch objectives and make informed decisions on how to enhance community interactions, foster retention, and sustain growth.

Feedback Mechanisms

Establishing feedback channels is essential for capturing the experiences and perspectives of community members, who are ultimately the best source for understanding what is working and where improvements are needed. Create various avenues for members to share feedback, including surveys, polls, and suggestion forms within the community platform. Additionally, consider implementing live feedback options, such as focus groups or periodic Q&A sessions, where members can openly discuss their experiences and suggest changes. Gathering both quantitative and qualitative feedback provides a more complete view of member satisfaction and challenges. By actively encouraging feedback and making it simple for members to share, you can create a culture of transparency and inclusivity. Analyzing this feedback at regular intervals will help identify patterns and priorities, guiding adjustments that reflect members' needs, and enhance their community experience.

Iterative Improvements

Continuous improvement is fundamental to maintaining an engaged and thriving community, and this requires a structured approach to assessing and implementing changes over time. Plan for regular intervals—such as monthly or quarterly check-ins—where you review analytics and member feedback to determine areas for enhancement. These iterative improvements could involve adjusting content themes, modifying engagement strategies, or introducing new features based on evolving needs. Establish a flexible road-map that allows for incremental updates, whether technical tweaks, content additions, or community guidelines enhancements. By treating the community as an evolving ecosystem, you can ensure that it remains responsive to member needs, maximizing long-term value and loyalty. This proactive approach to refinement demonstrates commitment to delivering a high-quality experience and fosters an environment where members feel heard and appreciated.

Community Communications and Promotion

Building a community and having a solid launch plan in place is only the beginning. The next crucial step is to communicate effectively and promote the community so people know it exists and understand why they should join. Simply creating the community doesn't guarantee that members will come; they need to be aware of its existence and see its value clearly articulated. The way you communicate and promote the community will set the tone for how members perceive it, influencing their decision to join and shaping how they feel about being part of it.

While you might be deeply passionate about the community and fully understand the value it provides, your audience may not yet see things the same way. They're constantly facing demands on their time, attention, energy, and financial resources, so capturing their interest requires a messaging strategy that resonates and makes the community feel worth the investment. The competition isn't other communities or even other brands; it's everything else vying for their time. Crafting a message that conveys the unique benefits and experiences of the community will help to make it stand out and feel indispensable.

Messaging

CORE MESSAGE
A powerful core message is essential for conveying the community's purpose and appeal. This message should distill the heart of the community—why it exists, who it's for, and the benefits it offers to members. Consider what values, experiences, or resources will matter most to your target audience

and shape the core message around these aspects. Whether the community provides exclusive insights, networking opportunities, or support on specific topics, the message should clearly highlight how members will benefit from joining. A well-crafted core message will resonate across promotional materials and serve as the foundation for all subsequent communication, helping prospective members see the community as a meaningful addition to their lives.

CONSISTENT BRANDING

Consistency in branding is critical for establishing a recognizable and cohesive community identity. Ensure that all promotional materials, from social media posts to email newsletters and website updates, follow the same visual and verbal language. Use specific color schemes, logos, taglines, and visual elements that reflect the community's tone and mission. Whether the brand feels welcoming, professional, innovative, or supportive, the visual and written style should be consistent across channels. This reinforces the community's unique identity, helping it stand out and making it memorable to those who encounter it. Every piece of content should reinforce this brand, creating a sense of familiarity and trust.

Communication Channels

COMMUNITY PLATFORM

Leverage the community platform as a primary channel for communication, especially for members who are already part of your network or have expressed interest. Use features such as forums, announcement boards, or direct messaging to share news about the launch and provide updates. Consider using pinned posts, event reminders, and message notifications to ensure that important launch information is visible and accessible. Regular updates within the platform not only promote the community program but also create an engaging, in-the-moment experience for members, encouraging them to explore and engage right from the start.

OFFICIAL WEBSITE

The official website should serve as a central hub for all community program details. Update the website with a dedicated page for the community program, providing an overview, benefits, and instructions on how to join. Highlight this information on the homepage and consider adding a call-to-action banner to maximize visibility. Incorporating visuals, testimonials, or an introductory video can also help to illustrate the program's unique value. This centralized, comprehensive resource makes it easy for visitors to understand the community's purpose and join, giving prospective members all they need in one convenient location.

Content Calendar

Pre-Launch Content

TEASERS AND COUNTDOWNS

Build anticipation with teaser content that hints at the community's upcoming launch. Countdown posts, sneak-peek visuals, and short videos can create excitement and curiosity. Each teaser should give a taste of what members can expect—whether it's exclusive access to resources, an exciting new feature, or a spotlight on the community's mission. The aim is to create a sense of urgency and anticipation, encouraging potential members to mark their calendars and look forward to the launch.

EDUCATIONAL CONTENT

Pre-launching educational content can help familiarize your audience with the community's offerings and unique advantages. Share informational posts, FAQs, or "What to Expect" guides to help potential members understand how the community operates and what benefits it provides. Videos, blog posts, or even email series can be effective formats for introducing the program's value. This content will help the audience see how the community aligns with their interests, increasing the likelihood of a strong turnout at launch.

Post-Launch Content

WELCOME CONTENT

Prepare a series of welcoming posts and resources to make new members feel immediately engaged and valued. Welcome messages, introductory guides, and member spotlights can help them feel connected from the beginning. Consider creating a "Getting Started" guide, onboarding emails, or even a virtual meet-and-greet to introduce members to each other and the community's features. This approach not only fosters a sense of belonging but also encourages members to explore the community actively.

REGULAR UPDATES

An ongoing content calendar will ensure consistent updates, keeping members engaged long after the initial launch excitement. Schedule regular posts to share new features, upcoming events, and major community milestones, as well as to spotlight members' achievements or contributions. Consider monthly or weekly content updates to keep the community fresh and dynamic. This steady flow of information reinforces the community's value, showing members that it's evolving and responsive to their interests. Regular communication helps sustain engagement, ensuring that the community remains a valuable and relevant space for members over time.

Building a Communication Plan

You can check out the template to build out your comms plan in Table 13.1. Start building out your communications plan with the following steps.

Step 1: Define Your Objectives

Begin by clarifying the goals of your communication plan. Ask yourself what the primary purpose is—are you trying to raise awareness about the program, drive participation, or educate the community? Clearly defined objectives will serve as the foundation for the entire plan. Once your goals are established, set measurable metrics to track success. Examples might include attendance rates at events, social media engagement levels, or feedback from stakeholders. These metrics will help evaluate the effectiveness of your communications.

Step 2: Identify Stakeholders

Next, identify the groups or individuals who need to be engaged through your communications. These could include community members, program participants, partners, sponsors, local government officials, and internal teams. Once you have listed your stakeholders, consider their specific needs. Determine what information each group requires and how they prefer to receive it. Tailoring your approach to each stakeholder ensures your communications are relevant and impactful.

TABLE 13.1 Communication plan template

COMPLETED	STAKEHOLDERS	DELIVERABLE	FREQUENCY	PRIORITY	DIRECTLY RESPONSIBLE INDIVIDUAL (DRI)	PREFERRED DELIVERY METHOD	COMMENTS
☐							
☐							
☐							
☐							
☐							
☐							

Step 3: Develop Key Messages

With your objectives and stakeholders in mind, craft the core messages you want to convey. These messages should be clear, concise, and aligned with the program's goals. Adapt your language and tone to suit each stakeholder group while maintaining a consistent brand voice. For instance, community members might respond well to conversational messaging, while sponsors may prefer data-driven communication. Personalizing your messages will help strengthen engagement.

Step 4: Plan Deliverables and Channels

Identify the materials you'll need to support your communication plan. This could include emails, newsletters, social media posts, flyers, meeting agendas, or video updates. For each stakeholder group, select the most effective communication channels. Some may prefer emails or newsletters, while others might respond better to in-person meetings or social media updates. Aligning deliverables and channels ensures that your message reaches the right audience in the best possible way.

Step 5: Assign Responsibilities

To ensure smooth execution, designate directly responsible individuals (DRIs) for each communication task. These individuals will oversee creating, approving, and distributing specific deliverables. Once responsibilities are assigned, set clear deadlines to keep the plan on track. Accountability and time management are critical to ensuring a successful communication rollout.

Step 6: Establish a Schedule

Create a schedule that outlines the frequency of communications for each stakeholder group. Determine whether messages need to be sent weekly, monthly, or at key program milestones. Additionally, map out a timeline for when communications should occur relative to program events. A well-organized schedule will help ensure that stakeholders remain informed and engaged throughout the program.

Step 7: Monitor and Adjust

Finally, establish mechanisms to monitor the effectiveness of your communication plan. Use feedback loops to gather insights from stakeholders about the quality and relevance of the information they receive. Evaluate engagement metrics, such as response rates or attendance, to identify what's working and what isn't. Based on this feedback, refine your communication strategy as needed to ensure continuous improvement and sustained success.

Social Media Strategy

Platform Selection

TARGETED PLATFORMS

Selecting the right social media platforms is essential for reaching and engaging the community's target audience effectively. Begin by researching the platforms where your potential members are most active and where they're likely to connect with the community's themes and interests. For instance, LinkedIn might be ideal for a professional-focused community, while Instagram or TikTok may be better suited for visually driven or lifestyle-based communities. By focusing on platforms popular with your audience, you'll ensure that your efforts are directed where they'll have the most impact, creating an immediate sense of relevance and familiarity. Tailoring your content approach to fit each chosen platform is equally important— what works on Instagram may differ greatly from LinkedIn or Facebook. This approach will help each platform feel native, maximizing the effectiveness of your outreach and engagement efforts.

ENGAGEMENT STRATEGY

Once the platforms are chosen, developing a clear engagement strategy is key to building an active and connected community. To foster interaction, plan posts that encourage members to engage through likes, shares, and comments. Craft questions, polls, or discussions that invite opinions or experiences, sparking conversation among followers. For visual platforms, consider using eye-catching images, behind-the-scenes content, or short videos that offer a sneak peek into the community's unique experiences. Each post should ideally include a call-to-action, prompting followers to engage in ways that feel authentic. Engaging directly with comments and shares also helps to strengthen the community vibe, showing members that their voices are valued. Regular interaction, paired with diverse content, will help establish a rhythm that keeps the audience interested and invested over time.

Campaigns and Challenges

HASHTAG CAMPAIGN

Creating a unique hashtag for the community program launch can foster a sense of unity and make it easier to track engagement. This hashtag should be easy to remember, clearly associated with the community's mission, and branded to reflect its unique identity. Launch a campaign that encourages members to use the hashtag in their own posts, whether they're sharing their reasons for joining, expressing excitement, or showcasing their engagement. To boost participation, consider running a contest or challenge tied to the hashtag, where participants can earn recognition or small rewards. By encouraging members to use and promote the hashtag, you amplify the reach of your launch, creating a ripple effect that brings in new members organically and builds awareness beyond immediate followers.

PHOTO/VIDEO CHALLENGES

Interactive photo or video challenges are a powerful way to encourage members to actively share their experiences with the community program. These challenges could invite members to post photos or videos related to specific themes, such as sharing their goals, celebrating milestones, or showcasing how they benefit from the community. Adding incentives like feature highlights, exclusive content access, or small prizes can make these challenges even more appealing. Clear instructions and examples will help members feel comfortable participating, and regular encouragement to post submissions will keep the momentum going. These challenges not only engage existing members but also demonstrate the community's value to potential members, giving a glimpse into the unique experiences and camaraderie that await them.

Email Campaigns

Targeted Segments

An effective email strategy begins with audience segmentation, ensuring that each message is relevant to its recipient. By dividing your email list based on specific criteria—such as member interests, past engagement levels, or demographic information—you can tailor communication to resonate with each segment's unique needs and motivations. For instance, individuals who have shown consistent interest in similar topics may receive content that highlights how the new community aligns with those interests, while new subscribers or less active members might benefit from introductory content that provides a welcoming overview. By acknowledging these differences and adjusting messaging accordingly, segmented emails help each recipient feel that the message was crafted with their specific needs in mind. This targeted approach not only increases the likelihood of engagement but also nurtures stronger connections with members by consistently delivering value-aligned content.

Launch Announcements

To build excitement and keep potential members informed, plan a structured series of email announcements leading up to and following the community launch. Begin with early teasers that hint at the community's purpose and the benefits of joining, sparking curiosity without fully revealing what's in store. As the launch date approaches, gradually share more information—such as unique features, testimonials, or a countdown—to maintain interest and create anticipation. Include clear calls-to-action in each email, encouraging recipients to sign up, reserve a spot, or spread the word.

After the launch, follow up with a series of welcome messages designed to guide new members through the community's offerings and help them get started. These emails can include links to popular content, tips for navigating the platform, or introductions to community leaders. Additionally, send periodic updates that celebrate community milestones or introduce new features, ensuring that members remain engaged and aware of the community's evolving value. By keeping the lines of communication open and focusing on meaningful content, you can turn these announcements into a long-term strategy for nurturing engagement and loyalty.

Collaborations and Partnerships

Identify Partners

Identifying the right external partners or influencers can be instrumental in amplifying the visibility and impact of a program launch. Start by researching potential collaborators whose values, missions, or audiences align with those of your community. Consider influencers, thought leaders, or organizations within your industry who have established credibility and a following that overlaps with your target audience. Selecting partners with genuine interest in the community's purpose ensures that collaboration feels authentic and enhances the program's appeal. These partners can play a key role in introducing the community to a broader audience, leveraging their established trust and engagement to lend credibility and excitement to the launch. Collaborators can provide valuable insights into audience preferences and trends, allowing you to tailor the launch approach to better resonate with potential members. The right partners can extend the program's reach exponentially by sharing content, creating joint promotional materials, or directly endorsing the community to their followers.

Joint Events or Campaigns

Planning joint events or campaigns with collaborators is a powerful way to generate buzz and encourage active participation in the program's early days. Consider hosting webinars, live Q&A sessions, or virtual panel discussions that feature both community representatives and essential partners. These events provide an engaging platform for potential members to learn about the community's benefits, interact with influencers they already trust, and ask questions in real time. Alternatively, collaborative campaigns—such as a co-branded social media series, blog exchanges, or contests—can sustain interest and keep the community visible across different platforms. For example, you could launch a challenge on social media where both your audience and the collaborator's followers participate using a unique hashtag, fostering a sense of community and shared excitement.

Joint initiatives also enable you to tap into the partner's audience base, creating an introduction to your community that feels like a natural extension of their existing interests. Throughout these events and campaigns, maintaining a cohesive message that reflects both brands is essential for building a lasting impression and drawing new members to the community. By leveraging partners' reach and credibility through engaging, interactive events, you can create a strong initial impact that drives membership growth and establishes the community as a trusted, valuable resource.

KEY TAKEAWAYS

- **Launch strategy:** Plan the community launch with precision and purpose, treating it as a structured campaign. Define clear objectives, including short- and long-term goals like member engagement, content creation, and user participation, to align all activities with impactful outcomes.

- **Timeline and task management:** Use tools like Gantt charts or punch lists to break down each task in the launch process, ensuring accountability and reducing the risk of oversights. Effective task management supports a smooth launch and guarantees that each step contributes to overall success.

- **Network effect through partnerships:** Leverage partnerships with influencers, ambassadors, or leaders to extend reach and credibility. Strategic collaborators who share values with your target audience can build trust, enhance authenticity, and attract engaged members to the community.

- **Teaser and countdown campaigns:** Generate excitement with teaser content and countdowns across social media or email to build anticipation. Curate content that offers a glimpse into the community's unique value, creating a sense of urgency and anticipation leading up to the launch.

- **Launch event design:** Choose an event format (virtual, in-person, livestreamed) that aligns with your audience's preferences. Structure the event to include influential speakers and interactive activities like Q&As to enhance engagement and establish the community's tone.

- **Engaging content strategy:** Develop an initial content plan focused on themes that reflect community goals and encourage participation. Use a content calendar to maintain consistency, balancing different content types to sustain interest and engagement in the community's early stages.

- **Member incentives and recognition:** Attract members with launch promotions and early incentives, such as discounts or exclusive content, to enhance value. Implement recognition programs for active members, reinforcing loyalty and encouraging a supportive, engaged environment.

- **Outreach and communication channels:** Use social media campaigns and segmented email marketing to reach potential members effectively. Tailor content to each platform, and ensure consistent branding to build familiarity, trust, and alignment with the community's identity.

- **Collaborative events and campaigns:** Plan joint campaigns or events with partners to broaden the community's reach. Webinars, Q&As, or social media challenges can introduce the community to a new audience while creating an engaging experience that attracts and retains members.

- **Continuous post-launch monitoring:** Track KPIs such as growth rate, engagement, and retention to evaluate community health and progress. Regularly gather and analyze member feedback to make iterative improvements, creating a responsive, member-focused community environment that sustains long-term engagement.

- **Feedback, feedback, feedback:** There are a lot of mentions of feedback in this chapter and this book, because it is the lifeblood of customer-brand relationships.

14

The Role of Online Platforms and Social Media

Online platforms and social media play a pivotal role in building and maintaining customer communities. These digital spaces have become transformative tools for businesses seeking to fortify and deepen customer relationships. They act as dynamic environments where brands can communicate, engage, and grow their customer base. By leveraging these platforms strategically, brands can move beyond mere communication and create genuine connections that foster loyalty and trust. This chapter explores how social media can be used to share content, provide customer support, and engage communities while delving into the influence of behavioral psychology, long-term community building, and adapting to the ever-changing demands of tech and human need.

Social Media as the New Third Place:
A Digital Space for Connection

Third places—those social environments beyond home and work—have traditionally been cafés, libraries, bars, and community centers. These were places where people gathered, formed relationships, and engaged in meaningful conversations. Earlier in this book, we explored the significance of third places and their role in fostering connection. Now, social media and online platforms have become a makeshift third place, offering a space where people can interact, build relationships, and connect not just with each other but also with brands.

People no longer rely solely on physical locations for social engagement. Instead, they seek community and conversation online, where they can find others with shared interests, participate in discussions, and engage with content that resonates. Social media serves as a hub for both casual interactions and deeper conversations, replacing traditional gathering spaces with digital alternatives that are accessible at any time. Platforms such as Reddit, Discord, LinkedIn, and Twitter/X bring people together around common interests, allowing them to take part in brand-led conversations, cultural moments, and shared experiences.

A true third place is not just a platform—it is a space where people form real emotional connections. Consumers do not visit these digital spaces just to consume content; they come to share, contribute, and belong. The brands that succeed in making this shift focus on storytelling that creates emotional resonance, personal interactions that make people feel seen, and opportunities for participation that allow customers to help shape the brand experience. When people feel that they are active participants rather than passive consumers, their connection to a brand becomes much stronger.

Behavioral Psychology in Social Media Interactions

Understanding customer behavior is essential for crafting effective social media strategies. Behavioral psychology offers key insights into why customers engage, trust, and remain loyal to brands in digital spaces. By applying these principles, businesses can design interactions that resonate deeply with their audience.

One foundational principle is reciprocity; customers are more likely to engage with a brand when they feel the brand is genuinely engaging with them in return. When businesses respond thoughtfully to comments, messages, or mentions, it creates a relationship rooted in mutual respect and responsiveness. This sense of reciprocity builds a positive cycle: as customers receive attention and validation, they are motivated to contribute to ongoing interactions, fostering both loyalty and engagement over time.

Social proof is another powerful psychological concept. Customers are influenced by the behavior of their peers, so when brands share user-generated content, reviews, or testimonials, they provide visible social proof that reinforces trust and credibility. Potential customers who see others sharing positive experiences or showcasing products are encouraged to explore the brand themselves. This ripple effect makes user-generated content a valuable tool, not just for validation but for creating an authentic presence that resonates with audiences.

The principles of commitment and consistency also play a significant role in driving engagement. When customers post about a product, share their experiences, or interact with branded content, they make a public commitment. This public expression makes them more likely to remain consistent with their stated preferences, fostering long-term loyalty. Brands can encourage this by inviting customers to share photos, stories, or reviews, creating opportunities for public declarations that deepen their connection to the brand.

Finally, the principle of authority underscores the importance of positioning the brand as a knowledgeable and trustworthy voice. By sharing insightful content, addressing industry trends, and responding to questions with valuable information, brands establish credibility and attract customers seeking guidance. An authoritative presence reassures customers in their decision-making process, strengthening their trust in the brand.

By leveraging these behavioral psychology insights, brands can create meaningful connections that transform everyday digital interactions into long-lasting customer relationships.

The Importance of Social Media

Social media is a dynamic environment where brands can cultivate meaningful, enduring connections with their audiences. Both B2B and B2C brands can harness the unique capabilities of social platforms to foster relationships, amplify voices, and drive business outcomes.

Social media is more than just something to be updated. As Director of Social Strategy at Massachusetts Institute of Technology, Jenny Li Fowler, shares, "Long gone are the days when social media was about changing the song on your home page or updating your relationship status. Social media has become more sophisticated and more integrated into our personal lives beyond scrolling. Online is the primary place where people congregate. It's where we find people who share our passions without physical limitations. We join communities and build communities. A lot of what happens online now shapes real life, and how people experience your brand online is fundamental to how people perceive your brand."[1]

For B2B brands, social media serves as a stage to demonstrate expertise, build credibility, and engage professionally. Platforms like LinkedIn allow brands to share insights, thought leadership, and client success stories that establish them as trusted advisors. By focusing on value-added content—such as white papers, industry analysis, or product innovations—B2B brands can build a loyal audience of professionals who view the brand as an essential partner in their growth.

In the B2C space, social media is an opportunity to humanize the brand and foster direct engagement with customers.[2] Platforms like Instagram, TikTok, and Twitter/X allow brands to showcase their personality, share behind-the-scenes content, and connect with audiences on a personal level. For example, a fashion retailer can use Instagram Stories to seek feedback on new designs, while a home goods brand might share TikTok videos demonstrating creative ways to use their products. These interactions build trust and strengthen emotional connections between customers and the brand.

Krystal Wu, lead marketing program manager at CommonRoom, captures the distinction between various platforms beautifully: "Online platforms and social media play completely different roles in the community-building toolkit. Platforms like Slack, Discord, and forums feel intimate, like a living room where people can have meaningful, real-time conversations. Social media, on the other hand, is more like a bustling town square. It's loud, fast, and designed for discovery and amplification, not deep connection. Both are powerful, but they're designed for entirely different kinds of engagement."

Slack and Discord, as Wu suggests, bring people together with intention. They aren't built for mindless scrolling; instead, they focus on meaningful interactions, knowledge-sharing, and fostering a sense of belonging within groups with shared interests. Forums add another dimension, offering structure and searchability for ongoing discussions and collaborative problem-solving. These platforms are ideal for creating deep, purposeful connections centered around specific goals or passions.

Social media, by contrast, acts as a bridge for sparking curiosity and discovery. It's the space where you share highlights, engage with a wide audience, and invite them to take the next step—whether that's joining a forum, participating in an event, or exploring a more intentional community space. As Wu explains, "Social media is a bridge, not the destination." For instance, a LinkedIn Live session might start as a broad public discussion but ultimately funnel participants into a more focused Slack group or webinar where the real, meaningful conversations take place.

Through this thoughtful approach, brands can utilize both social media and other platforms in tandem to create a holistic, connected experience that nurtures both broad discovery and deep engagement.

Holistic Management of Customer Interactions

Successfully managing customer interactions on social media requires a balanced approach to handling both negative and positive feedback. Each type of interaction offers unique opportunities to demonstrate attentiveness, strengthen relationships, and reinforce trust.

Addressing negative feedback promptly and empathetically is crucial. Customers who voice concerns on social media expect acknowledgment and resolution. Brands can show their commitment to customer satisfaction by responding quickly and publicly while moving the conversation to a private channel to discuss specifics. This approach demonstrates transparency and professionalism, helping to diffuse tensions while building goodwill. Proactive social listening is also critical—monitoring mentions and reviews, even those not directly tagged, enables brands to address issues before they escalate.

Community Engagement

Equally important is the recognition and celebration of positive feedback. When customers share praise or loyalty, brands have an opportunity to amplify those sentiments and strengthen the relationship. Featuring customer success stories, sharing user-generated content, or publicly thanking loyal followers are powerful ways to build a culture of recognition. For instance, a fitness brand could highlight a customer's transformation journey, or a tech company might showcase a user's innovative application of their product. These acts of acknowledgment not only deepen individual connections but also inspire others to engage.

Build a culture of recognition where positive interactions are highlighted across your platforms. This could be through "customer of the month" features, sharing success stories, or public thank-you posts.

Remember: Put Out the Fires, But Don't Forget to Water the Flowers

As Christina Le, Plot's Head of Marketing, explains, "An easy way to look at it is, treat engagement like building friendships: put in effort, be real, and show genuine interest. If you're replying to someone, make it meaningful." This mindset ensures that every interaction feels personal and valued, fostering stronger relationships across the board.

Recognition can also be formalized through structured programs, such as loyalty rewards, exclusive access, or public thank-you posts. By balancing the effort to address challenges with the intentional act of celebrating positive moments, brands create an environment where their customers feel supported and appreciated.

Long-Term Community Building

Building a community is not a one-time achievement—it's an ongoing process that requires nurturing, innovation, and adaptability. While short-term campaigns and initiatives can generate spikes in engagement, sustained effort is essential to foster long-term loyalty and a thriving, active community.

One of the most effective strategies for long-term community building is creating spaces where customers can interact not just with the brand but also with each other. Peer-to-peer interaction fosters a deeper sense of belonging and reduces reliance on the brand to drive every conversation. Platforms like Facebook Groups, Discord servers, or branded forums provide ideal environments for these interactions. For example, a fitness company might create a private community where members share progress photos, exchange workout tips, and celebrate milestones. This approach builds camaraderie and keeps members engaged for the long haul.

Consistency is another key element in long-term community building. Regularly showing up with valuable content, interactions, and incentives ensures that the community feels supported and valued. Brands can create rhythms of engagement through recurring initiatives, such as weekly challenges, monthly Q&A sessions, or annual events. These consistent touchpoints create rituals that members come to expect and look forward to, strengthening their bond with the community.

Another powerful tactic is empowering community members to take on leadership roles. Community ambassadors or moderators can act as champions of the brand, helping to foster a positive atmosphere while also lightening the workload for the brand's team. These leaders—who are often loyal customers or superfans—help ensure the community thrives, even during periods when the brand is less active.

Lastly, long-term community success depends on listening and responding to your members' needs. Actively gathering feedback, whether through surveys, direct conversations, or social listening tools, enables brands to adapt their approach as the community evolves. For instance, if members express interest in new features, events, or content formats, incorporating those suggestions not only meets their expectations but also demonstrates that the brand values their input. This continuous feedback loop fosters trust and keeps the community vibrant and aligned with members' interests.

Adapting to Changing Platforms and Trends

Social media is an ever-changing experience, with platforms rising and falling in popularity, algorithms shifting constantly, and audience behaviors evolving. For community builders, staying adaptable is not just an advantage—it's a necessity. The ability to pivot in response to change while staying aligned with your community's needs is critical for maintaining relevance.

To adapt effectively, community builders must first remain deeply connected to their audience. By fostering direct relationships with customers and consistently monitoring feedback, brands can stay attuned to shifts in preferences, habits, and expectations. Conducting regular sentiment analysis or engaging in one-on-one conversations with community members can provide valuable insights into what resonates and what's falling flat. For example, if a core audience begins favoring short-form video over static posts, the brand can pivot its content strategy to meet that demand.

Experimentation is another vital tool for navigating changing platforms and trends. Brands should adopt a test-and-learn mindset, trying new content types, formats, or features as platforms evolve. For example, when a new platform like TikTok gains popularity, brands can start with small-scale campaigns or pilot programs to gauge audience response. This low-risk experimentation allows the brand to stay relevant without overcommitting resources to unproven trends.

Similarly, staying informed about platform updates and algorithm changes is essential for maintaining visibility. For instance, as platforms like Instagram prioritize video content or LinkedIn introduces new tools like newsletters, community builders who embrace these changes early gain a competitive advantage. Following thought leaders in social media, attending webinars, and engaging in industry discussions are practical ways to stay ahead of the curve.

Finally, maintaining a strong brand identity across platforms ensures continuity even as trends change. While the tactics or formats may shift, the core values and tone of the brand should remain consistent. This consistency builds trust and helps the brand weather platform-specific fluctuations.

As Christina Le, Plot's Head of Marketing, suggests, "Social media is far more nuanced now, and that means you need to tie your metrics and strategies directly to your business objectives." This advice also applies to adapting to change by grounding social media efforts in clear goals and customer insights. Chasing trends and virality doesn't guarantee that brands are truly connecting with their audience and customers. By building a strategy based on goals and customer-centricity, brands can ensure their focus remains effective, regardless of how technology, culture, and humanity evolve.

Staying Close to Your Audience

At the heart of both long-term community building and adapting to change is staying close to your audience. The bridge from audience member to community member is connectivity. Community builders who prioritize relationships and maintain open lines of communication are better positioned to navigate shifts in platforms, trends, or customer expectations.

One approach is to embed customer feedback into your community management practices. Beyond surveys and polls, actively monitoring comments, direct messages, and social mentions can reveal emerging preferences or areas for improvement. Social listening tools can help community builders track conversations about their brand, competitors, or industry trends, offering a comprehensive view of the audience's sentiment.

Creating opportunities for dialogue is another important tactic. Hosting live events, such as Q&A sessions or town hall meetings, allows brands to hear directly from their community members. These events also give customers a chance to voice their concerns, share ideas, and feel heard—key factors in building trust and loyalty.

Finally, staying close to your audience requires a willingness to evolve alongside them, so you both can grow and transform. Communities are dynamic; what resonates today may not work tomorrow. By maintaining a growth mindset and embracing change, community builders can ensure their strategies remain aligned with their audience's evolving needs. Whether it's adopting a new platform, refreshing a content approach, or revisiting the structure of a loyalty program, being adaptable is the key to staying relevant in a fast-paced digital world.

KEY TAKEAWAYS

- **Behavioral psychology drives social media engagement:** Principles like reciprocity, social proof, commitment, consistency, and authority help brands design interactions that foster trust, loyalty, and meaningful connections.

- **Social media is more than a marketing tool:** It serves as a dynamic environment for both B2B and B2C brands to humanize their presence, amplify voices, and create lasting relationships with their audience.

- **Different platforms have unique purposes:** Platforms like Slack, Discord, and forums foster deep, intentional connections, while social media platforms act as a bridge for discovery and amplification.

- **Celebrate positive feedback to foster loyalty:** Build a culture of recognition through initiatives like "customer of the month" features, success story highlights, and public thank-you posts.

- **"Put out the fires, but don't forget to water the flowers":** Address negative feedback with empathy and transparency but also focus on nurturing positive interactions to strengthen relationships.

- **Long-term community building requires consistency:** Regular engagement, peer-to-peer interaction spaces, and empowering community ambassadors are critical for sustaining active and thriving communities.

- **Stay adaptable to platform changes and trends:** Monitor evolving audience behaviors, experiment with new features or formats, and embrace platform updates to remain relevant in a shifting social landscape.

- **Listen to your audience to stay connected:** Use feedback, live interactions, and social listening tools to understand your audience's needs and adapt strategies as their preferences evolve.

- **Tie metrics to business objectives:** Move beyond vanity metrics like follower count and focus on meaningful KPIs such as engagement rates, conversion metrics, and audience sentiment to measure social media success.

- **Social media is a bridge, not the destination:** Use it to spark curiosity, guide your audience to deeper connections, and create holistic, connected experiences that extend beyond the platform.

Notes

1 C. Alves. The rise of micro-communities: What this means for social media marketers, *Search Engine Journal*, December 4, 2024. www.searchenginejournal.com/the-rise-of-micro-communities/532677/ (archived at perma.cc/9AEM-UKTX)

2 A. C. Das, M. Gomes, I. L. Patidar, and R. Thomas. Social media as a service differentiator: How to win, McKinsey & Company, April 27, 2022. www.mckinsey.com/capabilities/operations/our-insights/social-media-as-a-service-differentiator-how-to-win (archived at perma.cc/X7SW-SMHT)

PART THREE

Overcoming Challenges

15

When Affinity Falters

Bad things happen. When it comes to customers, brands will inevitably encounter challenges that test their strength and resilience. When customer affinity falters, it is crucial for brands to take proactive measures to regain trust and rebuild their connections.

What can brands do when this happens and what can they prepare in advance to minimize their risk? This chapter explores the common reasons behind the loss of customer affinity, strategies to address these issues, and real-world examples of brands that have successfully navigated crises to restore their customer relationships.

Common Reasons for Faltering Customer Affinity

To maintain and grow customer affinity, brands must understand and proactively manage factors that can erode loyalty and trust. Here's an expanded analysis of common pitfalls that affect brand affinity, including indicators (red flags) to watch for and strategies for risk mitigation.

Poor Customer Service

Customer service is often the most direct interaction customers have with a brand, making it a key factor in shaping perception and loyalty. Poor service—whether slow responses, inadequate support, or unhelpful interactions—can turn minor issues into major frustrations, driving customers to competitors.

Red flags include a surge in complaints, long wait times, and high staff turnover, all of which signal deeper operational problems. To improve service quality, businesses should invest in comprehensive training, adopt AI-driven chatbots and CRM systems for efficiency, and create a feedback loop to drive company-wide improvements. Proactively addressing these issues enhances customer satisfaction, strengthens loyalty, and prevents recurring problems.

Negative Publicity

Scandals, controversies, or negative media coverage can severely damage a brand's public perception, sometimes irreversibly. Negative publicity can quickly decrease customer trust and loyalty, particularly if not managed well.

According to John Long, SVP of Creative at Digitas North America, with "social media, where everyone has a voice, a brand trust problem can go from 0 to 100 practically overnight. And the longer it goes unattended, the worse the damage gets—and eventually the damage becomes irreparable."

RED FLAGS

Recognizing early warning signs helps prevent crises from escalating. A sudden rise in negative media coverage signals potential trouble, requiring swift assessment and response to limit further damage. Likewise, critical discussions on social media can quickly amplify, affecting public perception. Addressing these concerns openly and professionally is crucial, especially when influencers join the conversation, as their influence can accelerate reputational harm.

RISK MITIGATION STRATEGIES

Effective crisis management requires a proactive, well-structured approach. A strong crisis plan should define clear roles, response templates, and communication protocols to address issues before they escalate. Prompt acknowledgment and transparent updates help manage expectations and prevent external narratives from taking control.

Continuous media and social monitoring allow companies to detect shifts in sentiment early, using tools like social listening and sentiment analysis to anticipate potential challenges. During a crisis, open and professional engagement reassures stakeholders and reinforces trust. Transparent communication demonstrates accountability and commitment to resolution, helping to de-escalate situations before they worsen.

By identifying risks early and maintaining clear, proactive communication, companies can safeguard their reputation and navigate crises with confidence.

Failure to Meet Expectations

Meeting customer expectations is essential to maintaining trust and loyalty. Customers form perceptions based on marketing promises, and if those expectations are not met, disappointment can lead to reputational damage and customer loss.

Warning signs include negative feedback, high return rates, and public complaints on review sites and social media. To prevent these issues, brands must align marketing with reality through clear communication between marketing and product teams, regular quality checks, and transparent messaging that avoids exaggeration.

Proactively addressing concerns through customer feedback, marketing audits, and active engagement on public platforms helps brands stay connected to customer sentiment, protect their reputation, and foster long-term loyalty.

REAL-WORLD EXAMPLE
KFC UK[1]

John Long loves how KFC turned a problem into a brand win. "When KFC ran out of chicken in the UK as a result of their decision to change shipping companies, the backlash was fierce—and deservedly so. Their response was to create an ad of apology featuring the letters 'FCK' on their iconic bucket. They took responsibility for the issue and explained how they were going to fix it. Pitch perfect."

KFC apologized, addressed the issue in a cheeky way, while owning the issue. Customers love when brands take accountability. That plus the brand being open to being playful means you turn anger into laughter, and thus laughter into a deeper connection with the brand.

CX professional Eli Weiss sees the power of transparency and treating customers like partners. "Early in my career, I worked at a Kickstarter-backed luggage brand that was in deep trouble. They had spent all their funds on R&D, leaving customers waiting for over a year without a product, which led to a wave of refund requests and unhappy backers. Despite having no experience, I saw an opportunity: these customers weren't just buyers—they felt like co-founders who wanted to be part of the journey.

"We decided to embrace radical transparency. We did a Facebook Live and a Kickstarter update with the CEO, explaining in grave detail exactly what went wrong, apologizing for misleading updates, and asking for patience as we worked to deliver the product. That honest communication struck a chord. Not only did most of the backers stick with us, but when we launched a new version of the product based on their feedback, 93 percent of those original backers supported the new campaign.

"The key action? Treating customers as partners and being genuinely transparent about our situation. This approach turned a potential disaster into a success story, and many of those initially dissatisfied customers became our biggest advocates. It taught me that when you handle a crisis with honesty and humility, and involve customers in the solution, you can build deeper loyalty than you had before."

The Importance of Transparency and Timely Communication for Restoring Confidence

Transparency and timely communication play crucial roles in restoring customer confidence during a crisis. Customers appreciate brands that are honest about their mistakes and proactive in addressing them. By keeping customers informed and involved, brands can mitigate negative perceptions and begin rebuilding trust. However, the benefits extend beyond merely managing reputational damage—they also provide psychological safety for customers, an often-overlooked but vital aspect of customer experience.

Entrepreneur and strategist Adrienne Sheares emphasizes that one simple message on social media can't magically fix a bad situation. "Taking too long to address a crisis can have a snowball effect and can make the situation worse. The last thing you want people wondering about during a crisis is what you're covering up. Especially in the age of social media, misinformation can spread like wildfires."

Having a crisis plan in place before an issue arises is essential—every business will face challenges, and being unprepared can worsen the situation. While public statements matter, actions speak louder than words. A brand must not only acknowledge the problem but also take responsibility and work toward a solution.

How a company responds in the first moments of a crisis sets the tone for recovery. Honest acknowledgment and clear communication reassure customers, reducing uncertainty and reinforcing trust. Frequent updates across multiple channels—social media, email, and company websites— keep customers informed and engaged, ensuring they feel heard and valued.

Transparency prevents misinformation and helps brands control the narrative. When customers know a brand is addressing the issue openly and proactively, they are less likely to lose trust. Timely updates and visible corrective actions rebuild credibility, showing that the brand's commitment to customer well-being goes beyond words.

Working to improve internal and external communication can strengthen the brand, developer and engineering community builder and consultant Tristan Lombard shares. "Effective communication drives higher internal and external performance, with increased productivity (72 percent) and customer satisfaction (63 percent) topping leaders' list of outcomes. Of those reporting higher customer satisfaction, 69 percent say that the increase is 10 percent or more. Yet most leaders (68 percent) lost at least $10,000 or more in business in the past year due to poor communication—13 percent even report $50,000+ lost. One in five also say it eroded their brand credibility or reputation."

We will discuss how to improve internal and external communication in this chapter.

Elements of an Effective Crisis Communication Strategy

A crisis can escalate rapidly, affecting a brand's reputation almost instantaneously. A robust crisis communication strategy is essential, serving as a lifeline that helps a brand navigate through storms of customer distrust and public scrutiny. Such a strategy is not just about damage control but is also a proactive cornerstone in safeguarding a brand's image and maintaining its customer base in the long run.

Why a Proactive Crisis Communication Strategy is Essential

A proactive crisis communication strategy helps companies manage unexpected challenges, preserving their reputation and mitigating damage. With a well-prepared plan, organizations can address crises effectively, maintaining control and preventing issues from spiraling into major problems.

PREVENTS ESCALATION

The primary advantage of a crisis communication strategy is its ability to contain issues before they grow out of proportion. Having communication tools and clear protocols in place allows companies to respond promptly, keeping the narrative focused on solutions rather than problems. Swift action helps prevent negative information from spreading widely, limiting its impact. By addressing crises head-on, companies can protect their brand image and ensure public perception remains as positive as possible under the circumstances.

BUILDS TRUST THROUGH TRANSPARENCY

Transparency during a crisis fosters trust. When a company openly shares information about a challenging situation and communicates with honesty, it reassures customers that the brand values their trust and loyalty. This openness shows accountability and reinforces the company's commitment to integrity. By being transparent, a brand can transform difficult situations into opportunities to strengthen relationships with customers and other stakeholders, creating long-term loyalty even after the crisis is resolved.

PROTECTS MARKET POSITION

In competitive industries, the ability to handle crises effectively can set a company apart. A well-managed response to a crisis helps a company maintain its service quality and customer loyalty, preserving its market position. Companies that address challenges promptly and efficiently are more likely to retain customer confidence, as they demonstrate reliability and resilience. This approach keeps the company's value proposition intact, helping it stand out against competitors that may struggle to manage similar issues.

ENSURES REGULATORY COMPLIANCE

For industries with strict regulations, such as finance, healthcare, or technology, mishandling crises can result in serious legal consequences. Data breaches, product recalls, or service disruptions that are poorly communicated may lead to fines, lawsuits, and compliance violations. A predefined crisis communication plan ensures that all communications meet regulatory standards, reducing legal risks. By adhering to these guidelines, companies not only avoid immediate penalties but also strengthen their reputation for accountability with both regulatory bodies and customers who prioritize compliance.

SUPPORTS QUICK RECOVERY

The speed at which a company recovers from a crisis often depends on its level of preparedness. A proactive communication strategy helps streamline responses, reducing confusion and limiting disruptions for both internal teams and external stakeholders. A clear, organized communication plan allows companies to reassure customers, employees, and partners quickly, enabling a smoother and faster return to normal operations. By maintaining stability and providing timely information, companies can restore order, preserve confidence, and focus on recovery efforts with minimal setbacks.

A proactive crisis communication strategy equips companies to respond effectively and protect their reputation in challenging times. By fostering transparency, ensuring compliance, and managing issues before they escalate, companies can turn difficult situations into opportunities to reinforce trust, preserve market position, and maintain the loyalty of their stakeholders.

Integrating Game Theory into Crisis Planning

Game theory, a theoretical framework for understanding interactions among competing players, offers valuable insights for businesses navigating complex social situations, particularly in times of crisis. In the business context, game theory can be instrumental in predicting the range of responses from various stakeholders—including competitors, customers, and regulators—based on their individual interests and strategies. By applying game theory, companies can better anticipate scenarios that may unfold during a crisis and develop strategies that consider the likely actions of others, providing a structured approach to decision-making when tensions are high, and timing is critical.

APPLICATION IN CRISIS COMMUNICATION

As we have talked about before, game theory unlocks all the possible scenarios that a customer can experience during their relationship with a brand. It also helps when you look at risk and crisis mitigation. Game theory enhances crisis communication by helping brands anticipate stakeholder reactions and develop contingency plans. By predicting customer and regulator responses, companies can craft empathetic, transparent messaging that prevents missteps and strengthens trust.

Beyond immediate response, game theory shapes strategic communication by guiding brands to influence the narrative and foster positive stakeholder perceptions. It also aids decision-making if there is uncertainty, offering a structured approach to balancing short-term crisis management with long-term brand resilience.

Incorporating game theory into crisis planning ensures brands are prepared for various outcomes, equipping them with calculated response strategies. This proactive approach reinforces reliability, reassures stake-holders, and positions the brand as a trusted, adaptable entity in times of uncertainty.

Crisis Communication Plan

Let's build out your plan.

STEP 1: DEVELOP A PROACTIVE CRISIS IDENTIFICATION SYSTEM

To protect your brand effectively, crisis management should go beyond reaction—it should focus on anticipation. Developing a proactive crisis identification system allows companies to spot potential issues before they escalate, minimizing the impact and enabling a more strategic response. This begins with implementing robust monitoring tools that offer real-time insights into brand mentions, customer sentiment, and media coverage. Social listening tools, for instance, can detect sudden increases in negative sentiment on social media, while media monitoring services can alert teams to emerging adverse news coverage. By catching these early signals, companies can assess the severity of potential issues and take timely action to manage them.

Technology is just one part of an effective crisis identification system; employee training and awareness are equally important. Employees across all departments should be trained to recognize early warning signs and understand the procedures for reporting them. With regular training sessions, employees become equipped to handle such scenarios with confidence and report them promptly, creating a culture of vigilance that benefits the entire organization.

Integrating these proactive measures into your crisis communication strategy not only shields your brand from potential fallout but also reinforces customer trust and loyalty. When a brand demonstrates its commitment to handling issues responsibly—even before they become full-fledged crises—customers are more likely to view it as reliable and transparent. This level of preparedness not only safeguards reputation but also fosters long-term affinity, strengthening the bond between brand and customer in good times and bad.

STEP 2: ESTABLISH A CRISIS COMMUNICATION TEAM

A foundational step in crisis preparedness is building a dedicated crisis communication team that represents key areas across the organization. This cross-functional team should bring together representatives from PR, legal, customer service, and senior management, ensuring that every aspect of the company's response is covered by individuals with the necessary expertise. Each member of this team should have a clearly defined role and set of responsibilities, allowing them to act swiftly and decisively when a crisis arises. By assigning these roles in advance, the team is positioned to operate smoothly, with each member understanding exactly how they contribute to a coordinated response.

Alongside role clarity, maintaining accurate and up-to-date internal and external contact lists is essential for fast communication. These lists ensure that the team can quickly reach key stakeholders, from employees and partners to customers and media, with reliable and timely information. Regularly updating contact information, and designating backup contacts, enables the team to respond rapidly and keeps communication consistent during critical moments.

This dedicated and cohesive team serves as the foundation of an effective crisis response. By preparing well in advance and ensuring each team member's readiness, the organization can navigate challenging situations with a steady and unified voice. A well-prepared team not only helps manage the immediate situation but also reinforces trust and credibility, showing stakeholders that the brand is organized, reliable, and transparent, even in difficult times.

STEP 3: CREATE COMMUNICATION PROTOCOLS AND TEMPLATES

After establishing a crisis communication team, the next step is to ensure they have the tools to respond swiftly and effectively under pressure. Step 3 focuses on creating communication protocols and response templates that empower the team to act quickly and consistently in any situation. Templates—whether for press releases, social media updates, or customer service emails—serve as a reliable foundation that can be customized as needed. Having these templates pre-drafted allows the team to maintain a steady, clear brand voice, even in high-stakes situations where time is of the essence.

An equally important component is implementing a streamlined approval process for all crisis-related communications. By defining clear approval steps in advance, the team can ensure that every message is carefully vetted for accuracy, appropriateness, and alignment with brand values before it reaches the public. This process strikes a necessary balance between speed and oversight, allowing the team to release timely updates while preserving brand credibility.

These prepared protocols and processes enhance the team's readiness, ensuring that the response to any crisis is both swift and considered. In turbulent times, this structured approach not only protects the brand's reputation but also reassures stakeholders that the company is responsive, transparent, and dependable.

STEP 4: EMPHASIZE TRANSPARENCY AND TIMELY COMMUNICATION

Transparency and timely communication are essential components of effective crisis management, helping to maintain trust and control the narrative. In the initial phase of a crisis, it's important to publicly acknowledge the issue within the first 24 hours, even if not all details are yet available. This early acknowledgment helps curb misinformation and speculation, showing that the brand is aware of the situation and actively addressing it. A prompt response conveys responsibility and sets the tone for open, honest communication throughout the crisis.

After the initial acknowledgment, the focus should shift to providing regular updates as more information becomes available. These updates should be shared across multiple channels—social media, email, and the company website—to ensure that all stakeholders are kept informed. By maintaining frequent and transparent communication, the brand demonstrates accountability and commitment to addressing the issue, allowing customers and stakeholders to follow the steps being taken.

This ongoing communication not only manages expectations but also builds a sense of reliability and responsiveness. By staying open and transparent, brands foster trust, assure stakeholders that they are acting, and position themselves as accountable and proactive throughout the crisis.

STEP 5: PRACTICE EMPATHY[2]

Empathy plays a vital role in restoring trust during and after a crisis. When reaching out to customers, it's important to communicate from their perspective, showing a sincere understanding of how the situation affects them. Craft messages that acknowledge their concerns, using language that reflects genuine care and empathy. This approach reassures customers that the brand recognizes the impact on their lives and is committed to addressing their needs. By acknowledging their discomfort and offering a compassionate response, brands can turn a potentially negative experience into an opportunity to demonstrate dedication to customer well-being.

In addition to empathetic messaging, it's equally important to create accessible feedback channels where customers can share their concerns or seek clarification. Dedicated avenues, such as a crisis-specific email address, active social media channels, or a responsive customer service hotline, ensure that customers feel heard and valued throughout the situation. This two-way communication enables brands to address individual concerns promptly while reinforcing a commitment to open, empathetic dialogue.

By prioritizing empathy and creating accessible feedback mechanisms, brands foster a sense of support and understanding. This approach not only helps address customer concerns but also strengthens long-term relationships, demonstrating that the brand genuinely cares about its customers and their experiences.

STEP 6: OUTLINE AND COMMUNICATE THE ACTION PLAN

A clear action plan is fundamental in managing a crisis effectively, outlining the specific steps the company will take to resolve the issue and mitigate its impact. This plan acts as a roadmap, guiding internal teams and informing external stakeholders, so all parties understand the approach and timeline for managing the situation. By presenting a well-defined plan with actionable steps and realistic timelines, the company demonstrates its commitment to resolving the issue and minimizing the chances of recurrence. This transparency not only reduces uncertainty but also provides a sense of stability and reassurance for customers, employees, and partners.

A practical action plan is not only thorough but also executable. It should specify who is responsible for each step and ensure there is clarity on the cadence of follow-up actions. If follow-up communications are required, the frequency and format should be clearly defined and shared with customers, helping them understand when they can expect updates. This proactive approach to follow-up reinforces the company's dedication to keeping stakeholders informed, while showing accountability for each stage of the crisis resolution.

Communicating these steps with precise timelines and maintaining regular progress updates fosters a strong sense of trust and accountability. By consistently sharing what actions have been taken and what remains in progress, companies create an open line of communication that strengthens relationships and reassures stakeholders that the situation is under control and steadily improving.

STEP 7: REVIEW AND LEARN

Once a crisis has been resolved, the next step is to conduct an in-depth analysis of the entire response process, examining what aspects worked well and identifying areas where improvements could be made. This post-crisis analysis is not merely a retrospective exercise; it's an opportunity to gain valuable insights into the effectiveness of each phase of the crisis management strategy. By reviewing actions taken, timing, communication effectiveness, and stakeholder reactions, the team can build a comprehensive understanding of the strengths and weaknesses in the response.

Gathering input from all involved departments, such as PR, legal, customer service, and senior management, allows for a well-rounded view of how each function contributed to managing the crisis. Additionally, collecting feedback from employees, customers, and partners about their experiences and perceptions can uncover blind spots or unanticipated issues. Analyzing this feedback enables the team to understand both internal operations and external stakeholder reactions, providing a full spectrum of insights that can guide future improvements.

Following the analysis, it is important to channel these insights into continuous improvement of the crisis communication plan. Each lesson learned becomes a stepping stone for refining processes, updating protocols, and preparing more effectively for future challenges. This refinement might include updating response templates, adjusting timelines, enhancing training programs, or improving coordination among departments. By treating each crisis as a learning opportunity, the company builds resilience, improving its capacity to manage any future challenges with increased confidence and precision.

Regularly incorporating these findings into the organization's crisis preparedness framework demonstrates a commitment to growth and responsiveness. Not only does this proactive approach strengthen the crisis response over time, it also reassures stakeholders that the company values accountability and is continually working to enhance its capacity for effective crisis management.

Integration with Red Flags and Risk Mitigation

This crisis communication strategy directly addresses the red flags identified in risk mitigation—such as high volumes of customer complaints or negative media coverage—ensuring a swift and organized response. Linking these strategic elements with ongoing monitoring and training ensures that the company is not only prepared to handle crises as they arise but also positioned to prevent many potential issues before they escalate.

By meticulously planning and implementing these steps, a brand can effectively navigate the complexities of a crisis, preserving and potentially even enhancing customer trust and loyalty through proficient and thoughtful communication.

Long-Term Strategies for Rebuilding Customer Relationships

Rebuilding and strengthening customer relationships after trust has been compromised requires sustained efforts and long-term strategies. A one-time apology or a brief spike in communication is not enough to mend fractured relationships. Instead, brands need to deploy a multifaceted approach that demonstrates their commitment to quality, engagement, and responsibility over time.

Here are some key strategies you can use.

Provide Consistent Quality Improvement

One of the most effective ways to rebuild trust is through consistent quality improvement. Customers need tangible evidence that the brand has addressed the root cause of the issue and made significant improvements. This could include refining product designs, enhancing service protocols, or implementing new technologies to ensure higher standards. Brands should communicate these improvements transparently, highlighting how these changes directly address the previous shortcomings. Over time, delivering consistently high-quality products or services can help restore confidence and reassure customers that the brand is reliable and committed to excellence.

Actively Engage With Customers

Active customer engagement is another crucial component of rebuilding relationships. Brands should utilize surveys, feedback forms, and community interactions to gather insights into customer needs and preferences. This not only shows that the brand values its customers' opinions but also provides actionable data to further improve products and services. Engaging in open dialogues on social media platforms or community forums can also foster a sense of belonging and involvement.

In the end, you must care and show it. For CX professional Alison Bukowski, saying you're customer-centric isn't enough. You must live it. "When a customer has a negative experience, own it and take accountability. If someone comes to my dinner party, breaks a glass, and then hides the shards in the cupboard, I'm not likely to invite them over again. If, however, someone breaks a glass, apologizes and notifies me, I can accept appreciate their situation and accept their apology. If that guest also offers to help me clean up the mess, then we've taken a negative and we're actually turning it into a positive. Asking a customer directly, 'How can we make this right?' goes a long way to neutralizing that negative experience."

Reward Customers for Their Loyalty

Implementing or enhancing loyalty programs can be an effective strategy for incentivizing customers to return and rebuild their connection with the brand. These programs can include special discounts, reward points, exclusive offers, and members-only events. By recognizing and rewarding customer loyalty, brands can create a sense of appreciation and encouragement for customers to engage more deeply.

Showcase Corporate Social Responsibility

Demonstrating a commitment to social and environmental causes through robust corporate social responsibility (CSR) initiatives can significantly enhance brand reputation and positively influence customer perceptions. Customers are increasingly conscious of the ethical practices of the brands they support. Engaging in meaningful CSR activities such as sustainable sourcing, community development projects, or charitable partnerships can help rebuild trust. These initiatives showcase the brand's dedication to making a positive impact beyond its immediate business interests, fostering a deeper emotional connection with socially conscious customers.

Successfully navigating a crisis isn't just about damage control—it's about reinforcing trust, demonstrating accountability, and emerging stronger. By prioritizing transparency, proactive planning, and thoughtful communication, brands can turn challenges into opportunities to deepen customer loyalty and solidify their reputation for resilience and integrity.

KEY TAKEAWAYS

- **Anticipate and monitor potential crises:** Implement social listening tools to catch early signs of trouble. Regularly train employees to identify and report potential issues.

- **Establish consistency across all touchpoints:** Develop clear, standardized procedures to ensure consistency in product quality, customer service, and overall user experience. Train employees regularly and use customer feedback to resolve inconsistencies.

- **Deliver exceptional customer service:** Invest in quality training programs and advanced customer service technologies. Establish feedback loops to make tangible improvements based on customer service insights.

- **Manage negative publicity effectively:** Develop a robust crisis management plan that includes proactive communication. Monitor media and social channels regularly; engage openly and transparently with stakeholders during crises.

- **Align marketing with customer expectations:** Ensure marketing messages align closely with actual customer experiences. Conduct regular quality checks and foster honest marketing practices to set realistic expectations.

- **Assemble a crisis communication team:** Create a cross-functional team with clear roles and responsibilities, including members from PR, legal, customer service, and senior management. Maintain up-to-date internal and external contact lists for rapid communication.

- **Create and use communication protocols and templates:** Develop response templates for press releases, social media posts, and customer emails that can be swiftly adapted in a crisis. Implement a streamlined approval process to ensure all communications are accurate and appropriate.

- **Emphasize transparency and timeliness:** Publicly acknowledge issues within the first 24 hours to prevent misinformation. Provide regular updates through various channels to keep stakeholders informed and build trust.

- **Practice empathy:** Communicate with customers from their perspective, illustrating genuine understanding and concern for how they are impacted by the crisis. Use empathetic language to rebuild trust and demonstrate accountability.

- **Review and learn from each crisis:** Conduct a post-crisis analysis to identify what worked well and what didn't. Use insights gained to refine the crisis communication plan and prepare more effectively for future challenges.

Notes

1 A. Brownsell. KFC: FCKing clever campaign, Campaign Live, 2018. www.campaignlive.co.uk/article/kfc-fcking-clever-campaign/1498912 (archived at https://perma.cc/AFE4-GENJ)

2 CSG. How empathy-driven customer experiences accelerate business results, CSG Insights, March 28, 2023. www.csgi.com/insights/how-empathy-driven-customer-experiences-accelerate-business-results/ (archived at perma.cc/3E53-RZRE)

16

Navigating Change

The Psychology of Consumer Trust: How Change Affects Emotional Bonds With Consumers

Change, whether anticipated or abrupt, triggers complex psychological responses in consumers. At the core of brand affinity lies trust, which is built over time through consistent and reliable experiences. When a brand introduces significant change—be it a product redesign, policy adjustment, or a merger—it can disrupt the consumer's perception of stability and reliability. This disruption can lead to feelings of uncertainty and skepticism, ultimately challenging the emotional bonds that have been established.

Research in consumer psychology suggests that trust acts as a stabilizer in brand-consumer relationships. A study by Edelman's Trust Barometer highlights that 63 percent of consumers will purchase from a brand they trust, even if it's more expensive.[1] When trust is shaken due to unforeseen changes, customers may feel disconnected, making them more inclined to explore alternative brands that appear more predictable and aligned with their expectations.

Identifying Triggers: Types of Changes That Most Commonly Disrupt Brand Affinity

Brands must understand that certain types of changes can significantly impact the loyalty and perception of their customer base. These changes, when not managed with care and insight, can fracture the emotional bonds that are essential for maintaining brand affinity. Below, we delve deeper into how these specific changes can disrupt the consumer relationship and why they matter.

Mergers and Acquisitions

Mergers and acquisitions are transformative events that can shift a brand's identity, operational culture, and overall service quality. When two companies join forces, consumers may be left uncertain about what the combined brand will represent and whether their expectations will continue to be met. For loyal customers of a smaller, more niche brand acquired by a larger entity, this change can feel like the loss of a valued community or culture. The fear that the distinct qualities and values that initially attracted them will be overshadowed or diluted by the larger brand often leads to mistrust. If not addressed through proactive and empathetic communication, this perception can drive customers to seek alternatives that still resonate with their values and experiences.

A merger's success in maintaining brand affinity hinges on transparent, continuous dialogue that reassures customers that their relationship with the brand remains a priority. Highlighting what will remain the same and what improvements can be expected can mitigate the unease that comes with such transitions.

Rebranding Initiatives

Rebranding can be a double-edged sword. On one hand, it can revitalize a brand's image and attract new demographics; on the other, it risks alienating existing customers who have developed a deep connection to the original identity. Rebranding often entails changes to visual elements such as logos, packaging, and taglines, but these symbols carry emotional weight for consumers. If a rebranding initiative is perceived as too drastic or dissonant from the brand's established ethos, customers may feel that the brand no longer aligns with their identity or expectations.

In 2009, Tropicana's packaging redesign, which aimed to appear modern and minimalist, resulted in a 20 percent drop in sales within two months.[2] The new look failed to resonate with consumers who were accustomed to the familiar design and emotional cues of the original packaging. This misstep highlights that, while visual refreshes are sometimes necessary to stay relevant, they must be executed with a deep understanding of what visual and emotional elements are non-negotiable to loyal customers.

Policy Shifts

Changes in policies—such as adjustments to return policies, pricing strategies, or data privacy practices—can have a profound impact on how a brand is perceived. Customers often interpret these shifts as indicators of a brand's priorities and values. For instance, a sudden tightening of a return policy may be seen as prioritizing profit over customer satisfaction, eroding trust that took years to build. Similarly, pricing changes without clear justification can lead to accusations of greed or disregard for customer loyalty.

Privacy practices are another critical area. In today's digital age, transparency around data collection and use is paramount. Any perceived deviation from previously stated commitments can lead to significant consumer backlash. Policy changes must be introduced thoughtfully, with open communication that emphasizes the reasons behind the shift, how it benefits the consumer, and the continued dedication to the brand's core values.

Leadership Changes

Leadership transitions can be highly visible and often signal potential strategic shifts. When a brand announces a new CEO or major leadership overhaul, consumers may read between the lines, questioning whether this change will align with their expectations or if it foreshadows a departure from what they have come to trust. For example, a leader known for aggressive cost-cutting measures may instill fear that product quality or customer service will suffer.

The departure of a well-liked leader who has been the face of the brand—often a person consumers associate with its values and vision—can create apprehension. The incoming leader must work not just on establishing their credibility but also on maintaining the brand's emotional connection with its audience. Transparent introductions, inclusive brand storytelling, and a focus on continuity can help ease consumers into accepting the change.

The Need for Clear and Consistent Communication

Each of these triggers—whether a merger, rebranding, policy change, or leadership transition—underscores the delicate nature of customer relationships. The common thread across all types of change is the potential to disrupt trust and create uncertainty. To navigate these periods effectively, brands must prioritize clear, transparent, and consistent communication. Proactively engaging with consumers, reiterating the brand's values, and addressing potential concerns head-on can turn challenging transitions into opportunities for reinforcing loyalty and connection.

Maintaining an open dialogue not only alleviates consumer anxiety but also demonstrates that the brand values its relationship with its audience.

This can transform moments of potential disruption into ones of strengthened affinity, showcasing the brand's resilience and commitment to its core community.

Evaluating the Potential Impact of
Changes on Audience Loyalty and Perception

To navigate change effectively, brands must prioritize assessing the potential risks associated with shifts in strategy or operations. Understanding how these adjustments may impact customer loyalty and perception is vital to maintaining brand affinity. This begins with leveraging tools and strategies that provide a clear picture of consumer sentiment and potential challenges.

One powerful approach is customer sentiment analysis, which utilizes social listening. As we discussed in the previous chapter on social listening, this approach is a vital tool for evaluating customer sentiment, especially during periods of change. Leveraging social listening allows us to review real-time feedback and identify shifts in audience perception. By applying these principles, we can track how conversations evolve and uncover whether customers respond with excitement, hesitation, or concern regarding proposed changes.

This evaluation goes beyond simply monitoring what is said; it involves interpreting the underlying emotions and broader themes present in these discussions. Analyzing this sentiment helps pinpoint whether consumers view the change as consistent with the brand's values or as a potential misalignment. By understanding these nuances, brands can proactively address concerns, adjust their messaging to reassure their audience, and foster trust before issues grow into larger challenges.

Feedback surveys and focus groups offer another layer of insight, tapping directly into the voices of loyal customers to understand their perspectives on upcoming changes. These methods create an open channel for feedback, revealing pain points and opportunities that may not be apparent from a distance. The candid responses gathered from these sessions can guide brands in refining their approach, ensuring that potential risks are addressed before a wider rollout. This customer-first approach demonstrates that the brand values its audience's input, fostering a sense of partnership and trust.

A/B testing for strategic messaging serves as an experimental safeguard before fully committing to a new communication strategy. By presenting different messages to small segments of the target audience, brands can assess which version best resonates and instills confidence. This method not only refines the wording and tone of key announcements but also helps identify the most effective ways to reinforce trust during periods of change. Brands that employ A/B testing can confidently scale the preferred approach to broader audiences, knowing that it has been validated through direct interaction.

Another indispensable tool in assessing risk is a structured evaluation framework that examines strengths, weaknesses, opportunities, and threats—a SWOT analysis. This analysis enables brands to map out potential internal and external challenges, aligning their strategic plans with realistic assessments of their capabilities and market conditions. By identifying potential pitfalls and aligning them with actionable strategies, brands can ensure that their decisions are not only ambitious but also informed and balanced.

Proactive Change Management

Proactive change management refers to the strategic process of anticipating, planning, and addressing the effects of change to maintain stability and trust within an organization's audience. It involves a coordinated approach that ensures stakeholders are informed, reassured, and engaged throughout the transition. By addressing the needs and concerns of the audience through strategic planning and communication, companies can navigate change in a way that preserves trust and strengthens relationships. This involves thoughtful stakeholder mapping, transparent communication, and setting realistic expectations—all of which contribute to a smoother transition that respects the emotional connection consumers have with the brand.

Stakeholder mapping involves identifying and understanding the different groups within the audience who will be impacted by the change. This step is crucial because not all customers share the same priorities or concerns. For instance, loyal long-term customers may worry about losing the consistency they've come to value, while newer customers might be more open to innovation but need reassurance that the brand will continue to deliver on its promises. By mapping out these key segments—such as high-value customers, casual users, and industry partners—companies can tailor their communication strategies to address the specific needs of each group. Effective stakeholder mapping ensures that the brand's message resonates with diverse audience perspectives, minimizing confusion and fostering a sense of inclusion.

Transparency as a strategy is fundamental in guiding customers through change. Early, open, and honest communication reinforces the trust that forms the bedrock of brand affinity. When a brand is transparent about what is changing and why, it signals respect for its customers and their loyalty. This type of communication should focus not just on the logistics of the change, but also on the brand's commitment to maintaining its core values and the benefits that the transition will bring to the consumer. Sharing the story behind the change—what prompted it and how it aligns with the brand's vision—can transform an uncertain period into an opportunity for strengthening emotional connections. Transparency also invites dialogue, enabling customers to express their concerns and providing the brand with a chance to respond thoughtfully, reinforcing trust and credibility.

Setting realistic expectations is another crucial aspect of proactive change management. It is natural for brands to want to project optimism and excitement about new directions, but overpromising can lead to disappointment and erode trust when expectations aren't met. Preparing the audience for change involves clear, measured communication that sets achievable goals. Companies should articulate what will change, how it will affect the customer experience, and what might remain the same. By being candid about the potential challenges or limitations during the transition, brands show that they are grounded in reality and dedicated to serving their audience with integrity.

When these proactive measures are combined, they create a framework that allows brands to navigate significant changes while preserving the emotional bonds that underpin customer loyalty. Stakeholder mapping ensures that communication is relevant and targeted, transparency builds trust and invites engagement, and setting realistic expectations manages customer perceptions effectively. By prioritizing these strategies, companies can not only process changes more smoothly but also demonstrate a commitment to customer-centric values that resonate long after the transition is complete.

Messaging During Transition

Crafting effective messaging during times of transition is a delicate art that requires understanding the audience's emotions and maintaining a coherent brand presence. The way a brand communicates during significant change can either strengthen the emotional bond with customers or create confusion and distance. Central to this is an emphasis on empathy, consistency, and the reinforcement of core values.

Empathy and relatability should be the cornerstones of any communication during periods of change. When consumers face the uncertainty that accompanies shifts in a brand's strategy or identity, they often experience anxiety or skepticism. Brands need to acknowledge these emotions and respond in a way that shows genuine understanding and concern. Crafting empathetic messaging means putting oneself in the customer's shoes, considering their potential questions and worries, and addressing them in a human, conversational tone. For instance, using phrases that validate customer feelings ("We know this change may feel unexpected, and we want to explain why we believe it's best for you") can bridge the emotional gap between the brand and its audience. Empathy helps humanize the brand, fostering trust and encouraging consumers to remain engaged even through uncertainties.

Maintaining a unified voice across channels is another vital aspect of effective messaging during transitions. Consumers interact with brands through multiple touchpoints, including social media, email, websites, and in-person experiences. Ensuring that these channels convey a consistent voice and message is crucial for reinforcing trust. Discrepancies in tone or content across different platforms can create confusion and dilute the impact of the communication. For example, if social media posts sound upbeat while email communications take a formal, detached tone, consumers may feel disconnected from the overall message. A unified voice provides a sense of stability and reliability, reassuring the audience that, despite changes, the brand remains cohesive and dependable.

Reinforcing core values throughout the communication process is essential for maintaining the emotional bond between the brand and its customers. Change can often prompt consumers to question whether a brand is still aligned with their values or has strayed from its original mission. By emphasizing and reiterating the brand's core beliefs, businesses can remind audiences of the fundamental principles that remain intact despite the shifts. For example, if a brand that prides itself on sustainability announces operational changes, its messaging should highlight how these changes continue to support, or even enhance, their commitment to environmental responsibility. Phrases that evoke the brand's long-standing values ("Our dedication to sustainability is stronger than ever, and this change allows us to pursue our mission even more effectively") can reassure customers that the brand's essence remains unchanged.

Preserving Consistency Amid Change

When brands undergo significant changes—whether it be a shift in visual identity, product offerings, or strategic direction—their audience often experiences uncertainty and may question whether the brand they once trusted will continue to meet their expectations. To navigate this, brands must prioritize stability by anchoring in familiarity, implementing gradual transitions, and clearly highlighting continuity. Each of these strategies reinforces the sense of reliability that customers seek when confronted with change. Think of it as holding your customers' hands as you make the transition as smooth as possible.

Anchoring in familiarity involves retaining key elements of the brand that consumers associate with its identity and values. These elements can include visual components such as logos, color schemes, or the tone of communication, as well as flagship products that define the brand's legacy. When a brand preserves these familiar touchpoints, it provides customers with a sense of stability. For example, if a well-known brand known for its classic packaging decides to modernize its look, it can do so by keeping signature colors or core design elements intact while updating fonts or secondary graphics. This balance between old and new ensures that the brand remains recognizable and maintains its emotional connection with its audience.

To implement this, brands should start by conducting a thorough audit of their most recognized and valued brand elements. This may include surveys or focus groups to determine what consumers associate most strongly with the brand's identity. From there, marketers can create a roadmap that highlights which elements will remain unchanged and which can be adapted or modernized without risking the emotional ties customers have developed.

Gradual transitions are another effective technique to help customers acclimate to change. Unlike abrupt shifts that can feel jarring or unsettling, phased rollouts provide consumers with time to adapt and adjust to new brand elements. For instance, if a company plans to update its product design, it can start by releasing limited versions with the new look while maintaining the original in other product lines. This approach allows consumers to become familiar with the new design over time without feeling that their trusted brand has suddenly become unrecognizable.

To successfully execute gradual transitions, brands should plan their rollout strategy with clear stages and checkpoints. For instance, the initial phase may involve introducing a new element through digital platforms or promotional materials before integrating it into physical products or large-scale marketing campaigns. Brands should also maintain open communication throughout this process, explaining why changes are occurring and what customers can expect in future stages. This step-by-step method fosters a sense of involvement and helps customers feel prepared rather than surprised.

Highlighting continuity is vital for reassuring customers that the brand's core essence remains unchanged, even as it evolves. Change often prompts consumers to question whether the brand values or characteristics they trust will continue to guide its future direction. To address this, brands should be transparent about which aspects of their identity are evolving and which remain steadfast. For example, a company known for its commitment to sustainability can emphasize that, despite visual or operational updates, its environmental mission is stronger than ever. Messages like "Our new look reflects our growth, but our commitment to sustainability stays the same" can provide the reassurance customers need to maintain their loyalty.

Clear action items for highlighting continuity include developing consistent messaging across all communication channels that reiterates the brand's core values and mission. Brands can utilize newsletters, social media posts, and website updates to share stories or case studies that link new developments to their longstanding principles. Additionally, integrating familiar slogans or images in new campaigns helps bridge the gap between the past and the present.

Brand Values Through Action

It is one thing to state values in mission statements or marketing materials, but it is quite another to show those values through purposeful actions and decisions. When brands align their changes with deeper missions or social responsibility goals, share authentic examples of their commitment, and practice transparency about challenges they face, they reinforce their integrity and strengthen customer loyalty.

Purpose-driven adjustments involve making strategic changes that are not only beneficial to the company but also reflect its deeper mission and dedication to social or environmental causes. For instance, a brand that has built its identity around sustainability can incorporate eco-friendly practices into new initiatives, product launches, or operational adjustments. This alignment between change and mission helps reassure customers that the brand's evolution is an extension of its core values rather than a departure from them. Purpose-driven adjustments should be strategic and genuine, ensuring that any new policies or product developments are consistent with the brand's proclaimed values.

For brands to implement purpose-driven adjustments, it is crucial to identify key areas where the brand's values and the proposed changes intersect. This could involve auditing current practices to find opportunities for sustainable improvements or developing new partnerships with organizations that align with the brand's goals. Once these opportunities are identified, brands should communicate their intentions clearly, explaining not only the changes themselves but also how they contribute to the broader mission. This proactive approach shows that change is part of a thoughtful evolution, instead of just a response to market pressures.

Case studies of authenticity provide powerful examples of how brands can successfully manage change while staying true to their values.

REAL-WORLD EXAMPLE
Patagonia

One notable case is Patagonia, a brand that has consistently aligned its business strategies with its environmental mission.[3] When Patagonia decided to shift to more sustainable materials and commit a portion of its profits to environmental causes, it faced potential operational and financial challenges. However, by demonstrating that these changes were rooted in its core mission, the brand not only maintained customer trust but also strengthened its standing as an industry leader in corporate responsibility. This commitment reinforced the authenticity of its purpose, showing that the brand's words were backed by concrete actions.

REAL-WORLD EXAMPLE
Ben & Jerry's

Another example is Ben & Jerry's, known for its social activism.[4] When the company launched new policies and product lines focused on fair trade and environmental impact, it emphasized that these changes were aligned with its founding values of justice and community. The brand openly shared stories, data, and the rationale behind these initiatives, showcasing a commitment that resonated deeply with its audience. Brands looking to emulate this level of authenticity should prioritize consistent actions that reflect their stated values and actively communicate the why and how behind their strategic decisions.

Transparency in challenges is equally critical for brands looking to navigate change without compromising customer trust. Every significant change comes with its hurdles and acknowledging them rather than glossing over or avoiding the subject can create a deeper connection with customers. When brands are transparent about the difficulties they encounter—whether these involve supply chain issues, regulatory barriers, or unanticipated consumer reactions—they demonstrate honesty and resilience. Customers appreciate being treated as informed stakeholders and are more likely to continue their support when they see that a brand is upfront about its journey, including the obstacles along the way.

For instance, if a company focused on sustainability needs to temporarily use less environmentally friendly materials due to supply chain disruptions, it should communicate this openly. Statements such as "We are facing challenges sourcing sustainable materials, but here is what we are doing to overcome this" can resonate with consumers as sincere and accountable. Sharing updates on progress, setbacks, and solutions further reinforces that the brand's commitment to its values is unwavering, even when circumstances make it difficult.

To maintain trust through transparency, brands should leverage various communication channels, such as detailed blog posts, press releases, and social media updates. This allows customers to stay informed and engaged, fostering a sense of partnership as the brand navigates change. Clear and consistent messaging ensures that customers view the brand as authentic and committed, even in challenging times.

Rebuilding Trust Post-Change

Addressing negative feedback is an essential aspect of building trust and credibility for any brand. When faced with criticism or public concern, brands should prioritize responding constructively and transparently. Acknowledge the feedback promptly, demonstrating that you value customer input and take their concerns seriously. Avoid being defensive or dismissive; instead, focus on finding solutions and communicating any steps being taken to address the issue. Publicly addressing negative feedback in a thoughtful and empathetic manner not only diffuses tension but also showcases your brand's commitment to improvement and customer satisfaction.

Demonstrating adaptability is another critical element in managing relationships with your audience. By using consumer insights and real-time feedback, brands can make informed decisions to adjust their strategies or offerings. Whether it's tweaking a product, rethinking a campaign, or refining customer service processes, showing that you are willing to evolve based on what your audience needs builds trust. Adaptability signals to your customers that their voices matter and that you are proactive in meeting their expectations, even when it means pivoting from your original approach.

Consistent follow-up engagement after making changes is just as important as the initial response. Once you've implemented adjustments or addressed concerns, maintain open lines of communication with your audience to reinforce your commitment to them. This could involve sharing updates on social media, sending personalized emails to affected customers, or hosting Q&A sessions to discuss the changes. Following up demonstrates accountability and shows your customers that you're not just reactive but invested in building a long-term relationship based on mutual respect and collaboration.

By addressing negative feedback constructively, adapting to consumer insights, and maintaining follow-up engagement, brands can turn challenges into opportunities to strengthen their connection with customers. This approach not only helps to repair trust in difficult situations but also builds a foundation for deeper loyalty and advocacy in the long run.

KEY TAKEAWAYS

- **Trust during change:** Disruptions can weaken emotional bonds and push customers toward alternatives, making trust essential to maintain loyalty.

- **Mergers and acquisitions:** These events create uncertainty, but proactive and transparent communication can help reassure customers and preserve confidence.

- **Rebranding initiatives:** Changes to a brand's identity risk alienating loyal customers if they don't align with established values and expectations.

- **Policy shifts:** Adjustments to return policies, pricing, or other customer-facing practices can erode trust if perceived as prioritizing profits over customers; clear, customer-focused explanations are critical.

- **Leadership changes:** These transitions may cause apprehension, but emphasizing continuity of core brand values can help reassure and retain customer trust.

- **Effective communication:** Using empathy, consistency, and transparency during transitions addresses concerns and reinforces trust with customers.

- **Risk evaluation:** Tools like sentiment analysis, surveys, and A/B testing help brands understand customer perceptions and refine strategies to navigate changes effectively.

- **Proactive change management:** Thoughtful planning, stakeholder mapping, and setting realistic expectations are crucial for smoothly managing transitions.

- **Preserving familiarity:** Retaining recognizable brand elements and introducing changes gradually helps customers adapt without feeling disconnected.

- **Demonstrating brand values:** Aligning actions with stated values and maintaining transparency strengthens authenticity and customer loyalty, even during challenging times.

- **Rebuilding trust:** Addressing feedback constructively, showing adaptability, and maintaining follow-up engagement are key to regaining and reinforcing customer trust after changes.

Notes

1 Edelman. Trust barometer: Special report—brand, Edelman Trust Barometer, 2024. www.edelman.com/trust/2024/trust-barometer/special-report-brand (archived at perma.cc/9NCA-K847)

2 M. Andrivet. What to learn from Tropicana's packaging redesign failure, *The Branding Journal*, May 2015. www.thebrandingjournal.com/2015/05/what-to-learn-from-tropicanas-packaging-redesign-failure/ (archived at perma.cc/73NL-XG5K)

3 K. Stroh. Patagonia to source alternative packaging materials, Fashion Dive, 2024. www.fashiondive.com/news/patagonia-canopy-pack4good-alternative-packaging-materials/726455/ (archived at perma.cc/5R54-MJ85)

4 Ben & Jerry's. Fairtrade, 2024. www.benjerry.com/values/issues-we-care-about/fairtrade (archived at perma.cc/Z2TW-G4RH)

Conclusion

The Future of Customer Experience and Brand Affinity

Looking ahead, the world of customer relationships and brand loyalty is shifting fast—but the lessons in this book give us a solid playbook for keeping up. From tuning into customer voices and harnessing the power of social media to building vibrant communities and tackling inevitable challenges, one thing is clear: brands that stay human, show emotional intelligence, and bring empathy to every interaction will thrive.

The Journey to Emotional Connection

At the heart of it all, we've learned that strong customer relationships aren't about making a sale; they're about creating real, emotional connections. Part One walked us through how social listening, personalized engagement, and compelling storytelling lay the groundwork for customer affinity. People are drawn to brands that not only meet their needs but also reflect their values and dreams. It's not enough to just satisfy customers anymore—the goal is to inspire loyalty and advocacy.

But here's the thing: all the tools in the world won't work if the intent isn't genuine. Personalization, for instance, can't just be about crunching data—it has to feel personal. Customers want to feel seen, heard, and valued. Moving forward, brands need to double down on these emotional ties, using every touchpoint as a chance to build trust and a sense of belonging.

Metrics will keep evolving, but the ones that matter most will be those that measure emotional connection—think customer sentiment, engagement, and advocacy. And let's not forget the power of good customer service. Quick, empathetic, and effective responses to customer concerns will separate the good from the great. Brands that invest in training their teams to deliver these standout experiences will see that loyalty translate into long-term success.

Community as the Heart of Brand Relationships

In Part Two, we zeroed in on the power of community. In today's digital world, the brands that win are the ones creating spaces where customers feel like they truly belong. These aren't just consumers—they're advocates, creators, and co-authors of the brand's story.

As we broke down the steps to building and maintaining communities, one truth stood out: people crave connection. Brands that foster these connections—whether through shared values, mutual interests, or authentic interactions—become indispensable. The future of brand loyalty hinges on how well companies can build ecosystems of trust and collaboration, making customers feel like they're part of something bigger.

But building a community isn't just about having the right tech. It's about knowing who your community is for and meeting their needs. Thoughtful branding, smooth onboarding, and keeping people engaged over time are key to keeping communities lively and meaningful. Metrics like participation rates, user-generated content, and direct feedback will help brands fine-tune their approach.

Social media and online platforms will continue to open new doors for connection and collaboration, but authenticity will be the name of the game. Genuine interactions resonate far more than any polished marketing campaign. Plus, creating inclusive, diverse communities where everyone feels welcome will be essential. Brands that cultivate safe spaces for all voices won't just deepen loyalty—they'll tap into a richer, more engaged audience. The true measure of a community's success isn't its size, but the strength of the relationships within it.

Overcoming Challenges with Empathy

In Part Three, we faced the tough stuff—the bumps in the road that come with maintaining customer relationships, like when affinity starts to waver or big changes shake things up. Change is a given, and it'll always test the strength of customer trust. The brands that come out on top are the ones that tackle these challenges with empathy and honesty.

When things go wrong, brands can't hide behind a curtain. They need to face issues head-on, communicate openly, listen actively, and show they're willing to adapt. Whether it's shifting market trends, internal shake-ups, or unexpected crises, staying customer-focused is key to weathering the storm.

And as AI, automation, and data become bigger parts of the picture, staying "unapologetically human" will matter more than ever. Sure, tech can make things faster and more efficient, but it can't replace the emotional intelligence that makes customers feel valued. When hiccups happen, customers aren't looking for perfection—they want understanding, a quick response, and a promise to improve. Brands that put human connection first will stand out from the crowd.

Plus, with all this tech integration, customers will expect brands to be upfront about how their data is being used and where human oversight still matters. Transparency here isn't just a nice-to-have—it's essential for building deeper trust and keeping those relationships strong.

The Future of Customer Experience: We Have to Talk About AI

Looking forward, the future of customer experience will be all about balancing tech with a human touch. AI will play a huge role in streamlining interactions, offering personalized recommendations, and boosting efficiency. But here's the kicker—what will really set brands apart is their ability to humanize those experiences. Being clear about how AI is used, designing thoughtful, empathetic touchpoints, and making sure real people step in when it counts—that's where the magic happens.

AI tools such as chatbots and virtual assistants have dramatically improved customer service efficiency.[1] They provide 24/7 availability, enabling customers to access support at any time. This is particularly useful for addressing straightforward queries, such as order tracking or account information, which can be resolved quickly without human intervention. This reduces wait times and improves customer satisfaction by providing instant solutions.

How Brands Can Leverage This Benefit

Brands can enhance their customer service strategies by integrating AI to manage routine inquiries while reserving human agents for more complex or sensitive situations. This approach improves efficiency and ensures that customers receive appropriate support based on the nature of their needs.

To maximize the benefits of AI, companies should routinely assess chatbot performance to maintain accurate, relevant, and helpful responses. It's equally important to provide clear options for customers to escalate their concerns to a human representative, ensuring a smooth transition when personal interaction is required. Balancing automation with human touch-points prevents frustration and builds customer trust.

As they adopt AI-driven solutions, businesses must reflect on whether their efforts are simplifying the customer journey or inadvertently creating additional challenges. They should also ensure that customers can easily connect with a human agent when necessary. These considerations are vital for using AI to enhance the customer experience effectively.

Personalization at Scale

As we discussed earlier in the book, personalization is a core way to form deeper connections with customers. AI has transformed how brands approach personalization, enabling tailored customer experiences at an unprecedented scale. By analyzing vast amounts of data, AI can recommend products based on past purchases or craft marketing messages that align with individual preferences. This technology makes interactions feel uniquely relevant, fostering stronger customer engagement.[2] Additionally, predictive analytics allows businesses to anticipate needs, enabling proactive outreach that adds value to the customer journey.

To leverage AI-driven personalization effectively, brands should implement tools that analyze customer behavior to deliver tailored content and product recommendations. Machine learning can uncover patterns in customer interactions, providing insights to guide future campaigns or product development. However, it's important to approach personalization thoughtfully. Overuse or overly targeted strategies can feel intrusive, so transparency about how data is collected and used is essential to maintain trust.

When designing personalization strategies, brands should ask critical questions to ensure they align with customer expectations. Are they respecting privacy while using data to enhance experiences? And does the personalization genuinely add value, or is it simply a gimmick? Addressing these concerns ensures that AI-driven personalization serves both the customer's needs and the brand's goals, creating meaningful connections that drive loyalty.

AI offers businesses a powerful tool for proactive problem-solving by monitoring customer interactions and identifying emerging patterns. For instance, a spike in complaints about a particular product can be detected by AI tools and flagged for immediate attention. This allows brands to address issues quickly, demonstrating attentiveness and a commitment to resolving customer concerns before they escalate.

To effectively harness this benefit, brands can deploy AI systems to monitor social media platforms and customer feedback in real time, spotting trends that demand swift action. It's equally important to train teams to act promptly on AI-generated insights, ensuring that issues are resolved before they affect customer satisfaction. While AI provides valuable data, combining these insights with human judgment is essential to maintain a nuanced understanding of customer concerns and avoid one-size-fits-all solutions.

Businesses should also consider whether they are using AI insights to drive meaningful improvements in the customer experience. Another critical factor is how quickly teams can act on the issues flagged by AI systems. By addressing these questions, brands can integrate AI seamlessly into their customer service strategy, creating a more responsive and customer-focused experience.

AI Challenges in Customer Relationships

A common criticism of AI in customer service is its lack of human connection. While AI excels in efficiency and speed, it often fails to deliver the empathy and understanding that many customers value in interactions. For issues that require a personal touch, AI's limitations can make the experience feel impersonal, potentially eroding trust and loyalty. Many customers still prefer speaking to a human who can grasp the emotional nuances of their concerns and respond with genuine care.

To address this challenge, brands can adopt a hybrid approach, blending AI tools with human interactions to create a balanced customer experience. AI should handle routine inquiries efficiently, while human agents step in for more complex or emotionally sensitive issues. Let customers decide which type of service they want to receive so they can pick their own adventure and feel empowered when and where AI is a part of their experience.

Additionally, designing AI interactions to reflect the brand's tone and values can make the experience feel more personal. Conversational elements, such as friendly language and thoughtful prompts, can help AI systems feel less robotic. Transparency is also crucial—clearly communicating when customers are interacting with a bot versus a real person sets appropriate expectations and avoids confusion.

Brands should continually assess whether their AI systems align with the company's voice and tone and whether customers feel heard and understood in their interactions. Striking the right balance between automation and humanity is essential to building trust and fostering lasting relationships with customers.

Mismanagement of Customer Data

The effective use of AI depends on access to large amounts of customer data, but mishandling that data can have serious consequences, including privacy violations and a loss of trust. With customers increasingly aware of how their information is collected and used, they expect brands to act transparently and responsibly. Failing to meet these expectations can not only damage a brand's reputation but also jeopardize customer loyalty.

To address these concerns, brands must prioritize robust data protection measures to ensure customer information remains secure. Transparency is equally important. Customers should be informed about how their data is collected, stored, and used. Providing clear opt-out options for those who prefer not to share their information fosters trust and demonstrates respect for individual preferences. Regularly auditing AI systems for compliance with privacy regulations is another critical step in maintaining accountability and reinforcing consumer confidence.

As they integrate AI into their operations, brands should continually evaluate whether they are being transparent about their data practices and whether customers feel confident in how their information is managed. Striking the right balance between leveraging data for innovation and safeguarding customer privacy is essential for building lasting trust and delivering meaningful, responsible AI-driven experiences.

Over-Automation

While AI has the potential to streamline customer service, over-automation can lead to significant frustration when systems fail to address customer needs effectively. Rigid chatbot scripts and limited AI functionality can leave customers feeling trapped in interactions that don't resolve their issues. When AI systems misunderstand queries or lack flexibility, the customer experience suffers, ultimately eroding trust and satisfaction.

To mitigate these challenges, brands should regularly test their AI systems to identify and address functionality gaps. Ensuring that the technology meets customer expectations is critical to maintaining a positive experience. Equally important is providing customers with clear and accessible options to bypass automated systems and connect with a human agent when needed. Human interaction remains essential for resolving complex or sensitive issues that AI may not be equipped to handle. Incorporating customer feedback into ongoing system improvements can also help refine AI tools over time, making them more intuitive and effective.

Brands must continuously evaluate whether their automation strategies are enhancing or hindering the customer experience. Offering seamless options for customers who prefer human assistance ensures that automation complements, rather than replaces, the personal touch that is vital for building trust and loyalty.

Dead Internet Theory

The "Dead Internet Theory," which suggests that much of the internet's content is generated by bots rather than humans, raises important questions about the role of AI in shaping online experiences.[3] Whether or not this theory fully reflects reality, it highlights genuine concerns about the increasing automation of social media and other digital spaces. As AI takes on a larger role in generating and curating content, the implications for community, human connection, and brand engagement are profound.

AI-driven algorithms and automated content creation tools are transforming online platforms. While these technologies can enhance efficiency and scale engagement, they risk making the digital world feel less authentic. Social media platforms, in particular, may prioritize algorithmic content over genuine human interactions, raising concerns about the erosion of meaningful online communities. If users perceive that much of what they encounter online is generated by AI rather than real people, it could undermine trust and the sense of shared experience that fosters strong communities.

The broader adoption of AI in online spaces also raises concerns about transparency and trust. If users feel they are primarily interacting with algorithms rather than humans, they may become skeptical of the authenticity of their experiences. For brands, this means that balancing the benefits of AI with the need for genuine engagement is critical. Transparency about how AI is used and ensuring that human connection remains a priority can help mitigate these risks.

The rise of AI in digital spaces challenges brands and platforms to rethink how they use technology. Rather than replacing human interaction, AI should be employed to enhance and empower it. By leveraging AI to streamline processes and provide insights while maintaining opportunities for real human connection, brands can strike a balance that fosters trust and enriches customer relationships. In a digital world increasingly shaped by automation, ensuring that technology supports authentic interactions will be key to building strong communities and meaningful brand loyalty.

Ensuring AI Helps Instead of Hurts

To ensure AI strengthens customer relationships rather than undermines them, brands must approach its implementation thoughtfully and deliberately. Success hinges on actively incorporating customer feedback to refine AI systems and processes over time. Regular feedback loops allow companies to understand how customers experience AI interactions, ensuring that the technology evolves to better meet their needs.

As customer experience expert and author Dan Gingiss states, "Human interaction is critical and I believe it's not going away anytime soon. So as you start to talk about things like AI and technology, I'll argue all day long that the best use case for AI in a call center is help the agent, not the customer. And you help the agent by servicing information faster, by helping them solve problems, by identifying emotions that are going on, on the call, and reacting to that.

"But you then allow the agent to be what they do best, which is be human. My prediction is that we are at least a decade away from consumers being willing to interact exclusively with robots. If the consumers don't want it, then bringing it to them too fast is not going to work.

"And that's why we see so much backlash against chatbots, which launched really fast, were terrible, and people realized they didn't really solve any problem at all, let alone problem they're having."

Balancing efficiency with empathy is critical. While AI excels at streamlining routine tasks, it's essential to preserve opportunities for human interaction in situations that require nuance and understanding. Offering customers the ability to "choose their own adventure"—opting for AI when convenience is the priority and human support when empathy and complexity are needed—creates a more flexible and inclusive experience.

Transparency is equally important. Customers should understand how AI is used and feel confident that their privacy and data security are protected. Clear communication about these practices builds trust and reassures users. Additionally, continuous monitoring of AI performance is necessary to identify potential issues early and ensure that the technology aligns with customer expectations and brand values.

By prioritizing customer needs and asking the right questions, brands can leverage AI to enhance efficiency, personalization, and problem-solving without losing the human connection that drives loyalty. A balanced approach allows AI to serve as a powerful tool for improving the customer experience while preserving the trust and relationships that define successful brands.

At the heart of this future is emotional intelligence. Brands need to dive deeper into understanding their customers—not just what they're buying, but why they're buying, how they're feeling, and what they're striving for. It's about shifting from treating customers as mere consumers to seeing them as partners on a shared journey.

Success metrics will evolve beyond just sales figures to include measures of emotional engagement and community health. Brands that can read these signals and respond thoughtfully will be in a prime position to build lasting loyalty.

Immersive technologies like virtual and augmented reality will also open exciting new ways to engage customers, creating memorable, interactive experiences that deepen emotional bonds. But here's the catch—these innovations need to align with the brand's core values and genuinely serve the needs of their customers to truly make an impact.

Unapologetically Human

As tech keeps evolving, the brands that shine will be the ones that stay true to their humanity. They'll embrace vulnerability, listen with intent, and respond with care. Whether it's a heartfelt reply on social media, a thoughtfully planned community event, or owning up to mistakes and learning from them, brands need to show they're more than just businesses—they're people who genuinely care.

As Creative Executive and former LEGO Creative Director James Gregson shares, "The optimist in me wants to believe in the power of human-generated creativity. The realist acknowledges we're facing fundamental shifts in how creative work comes to life. I hope this might push us to focus more intensely on what machines can't replicate: genuine human insight and emotional intelligence."

In this future, empathy isn't just a buzzword—it's a competitive edge. The brands that lead the way will be the ones creating experiences grounded in understanding and connection. By staying unapologetically human, they won't just build loyalty—they'll inspire lifelong advocates who truly love their brand.

The future of customer–brand relationships looks bright for those ready to invest in emotional connections, community building, and empathetic leadership. By blending cutting-edge technology with timeless values like trust, authenticity, and human connection, brands can build relationships that last.

In the end, the brands that succeed will be those that see their customers not just as buyers, but as vital parts of a shared story. By prioritizing authenticity, transparency, and emotional engagement, they'll forge bonds that go beyond traditional loyalty, creating communities of passionate advocates deeply connected to the brand's mission and values. This is the future of customer–brand relationships—a future where technology supports, but humanity leads.

KEY TAKEAWAYS

- **AI and customer engagement:** AI has transformed customer engagement by offering efficiency and personalization, but careful implementation is necessary to ensure it strengthens rather than harms customer relationships.

- **Enhanced efficiency:** AI tools like chatbots provide 24/7 availability and streamline routine customer service inquiries, reducing wait times and improving satisfaction.

- **Personalization at scale:** By analyzing customer data, AI delivers tailored recommendations and marketing messages, fostering stronger connections and helping brands anticipate customer needs.

- **Proactive problem-solving:** AI monitors feedback and identifies patterns, enabling brands to address issues quickly, improve customer experiences, and demonstrate attentiveness.

- **Human connection challenges:** While AI excels in efficiency, it lacks empathy and nuance, making some interactions feel impersonal; blending AI with human touchpoints ensures a more balanced experience.

- **Data management risks:** Mishandling customer data can erode trust, making robust security measures, transparency, and compliance with privacy regulations essential to maintaining credibility.

- **Over-automation pitfalls:** Excessive reliance on AI can frustrate customers when systems fail to address their needs; providing clear pathways to human support and regularly testing AI systems is crucial.

- **AI and authenticity:** The rise of AI-generated content raises concerns about authenticity and human connection; brands must ensure AI complements rather than replaces genuine engagement.
- **Strengthening relationships with AI:** Incorporating customer feedback, balancing efficiency with human interaction, and maintaining transparency about AI use and data practices are critical for fostering trust.
- **Thoughtful implementation:** A deliberate and balanced approach to AI integration enhances customer experiences, preserves trust, and builds meaningful, long-term relationships.

Notes

1   R. Watkin. Machine learning meets customer experience: How AI is reshaping CX, Forbes Technology Council, February 13, 2024. www.forbes.com/councils/forbestechcouncil/2024/02/13/machine-learning-meets-customer-experience-how-ai-is-reshaping-cx/ (archived at perma.cc/5B8B-MSQF)

2   A. Jindal. Two years of generative AI: How has customer experience delivery changed? CMSWire, February 13, 2025. www.cmswire.com/customer-experience/two-years-of-generative-ai-how-has-customer-experience-delivery-changed/ (archived at perma.cc/EF5S-7JUG)

3   D. DiPlacido. The Dead Internet Theory explained, *Forbes*, January 16, 2024. www.forbes.com/sites/danidiplacido/2024/01/16/the-dead-internet-theory-explained/ (archived at perma.cc/7UDG-46MY)

APPENDIX: RECOMMENDED READING

This book has explored many topics related to customer experience, marketing, and behavioral insights. If you'd like to dive deeper into these areas or broaden your understanding with related concepts, consider these exceptional books.

Baer, J. (2016) *Hug Your Haters: How to embrace complaints and keep your customers*, Portfolio, New York

Berne, E. (2016) *Games People Play: The Psychology of human relationships*, Penguin Life, New York

Clinehens, J. (2020) *Choice Hacking: How to use psychology and behavioral science to create an experience that sings*, independently published

Collins, M. (2024) *For the Culture: The power behind what we buy, what we do, and who we want to be*, Public Affairs, New York

Fowler, J. L. (2023) *Organic Social Media: How to build flourishing online communities*, Kogan Page, London

Gingiss, D. (2021) *The Experience Maker: How to create remarkable experiences that your customers can't wait to share*, Morgan James Publishing, New York

Goleman, D. (2005) *Emotional Intelligence: Why it can matter more than IQ*, Bantam Books, New York

Harhut, N. (2022) *Using Behavioral Science in Marketing: Drive Customer action and loyalty by prompting instinctive responses*, Kogan Page, London

Harrison, T. (2024) *Entrepreneurial Creativity: Repeatable creative success*, independently published

Scott, D. M. and Scott, R. (2020) *Fanocracy: Turning fans into customers and customers into fans*, Portfolio, New York

Sutherland, R. (2021) *Alchemy: The dark art and curious science of creating magic in brands, business, and life*, Mariner Books, Boston

INDEX

The main index is filed in alphabetical, word-by-word order. Acronyms and 'Mc' are filed as presented; numbers are filed as spelt out. Locators in italics denote information within figures and tables.

Looking for another book?

Explore our award-winning
books from global business
experts in Marketing and Sales

Scan the code to browse

www.koganpage.com/marketing

More from Kogan Page

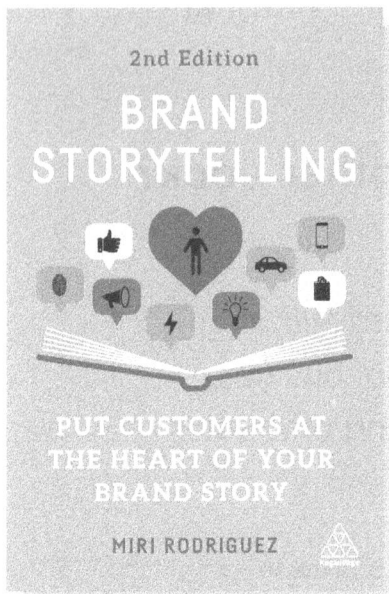

2nd Edition

BRAND STORYTELLING

PUT CUSTOMERS AT THE HEART OF YOUR BRAND STORY

MIRI RODRIGUEZ

ISBN: 9781398610088

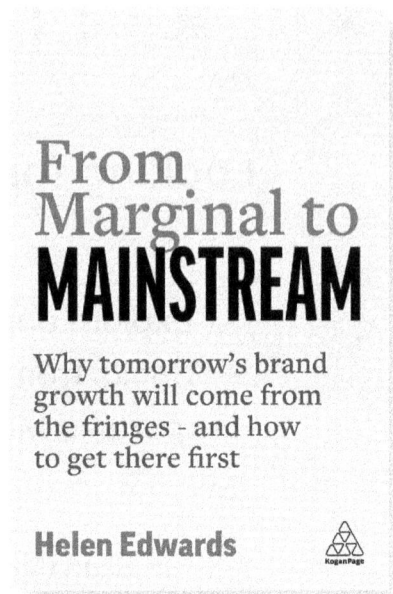

From Marginal to **MAINSTREAM**

Why tomorrow's brand growth will come from the fringes - and how to get there first

Helen Edwards

ISBN: 9781398604315

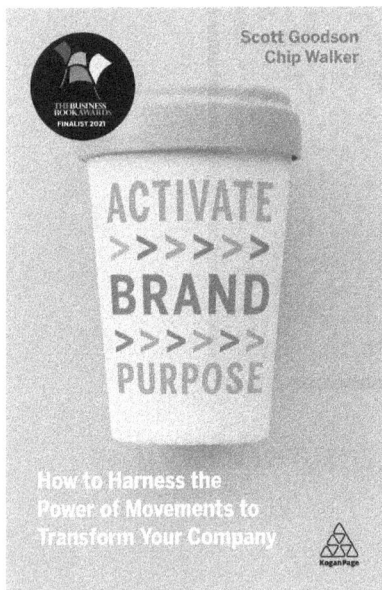

Scott Goodson
Chip Walker

THE BUSINESS BOOK AWARDS FINALIST 2021

ACTIVATE >>>>>> BRAND >>>>>> PURPOSE

How to Harness the Power of Movements to Transform Your Company

ISBN: 9781789668247

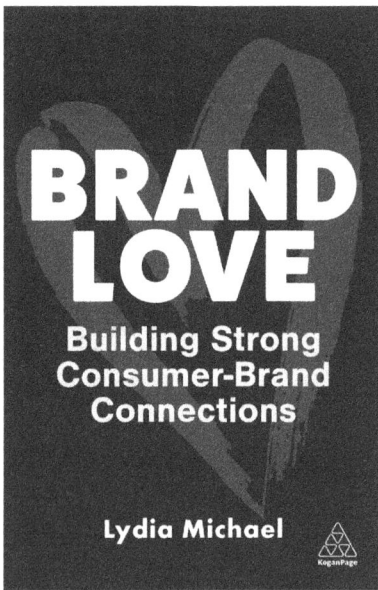

BRAND LOVE

Building Strong Consumer-Brand Connections

Lydia Michael

ISBN: 9781398611276

www.koganpage.com

KoganPage

From 4 December 2025 the EU Responsible Person (GPSR) is:
eucomply oÜ, Pärnu mnt. 139b – 14, 11317 Tallinn, Estonia
www.eucompliancepartner.com

www.ingramcontent.com/pod-product-compliance
Lightning Source LLC
Chambersburg PA
CBHW071546210326
41597CB00019B/3134